The Author

J. R. Stephenson is an author, businessman and broadcaster.

He has written several books on crime and corruption, including the banking sector and writes thriller novels based on real incidents experienced during his business career.

His broadcasting ranges from his weekly, 2-hour radio programme on current affairs to guest spots on the BBC and LBC. He also regularly comments on economics and business affairs on Aljazeera Television's global English network.

On being approached by ShieldCrest Publishing and investigating Martin Foran's story and studying copious documents, he was convinced there had been a serious miscarriage of justice which went to the very heart of the British justice system. It exposed fraud and corruption to the very top of a police force, incredulous decisions and mis-directions by the judiciary and inhuman treatment while in the care of HM prison service.

It also uncovered the extent to which senior politicians and successive Home Secretaries turned a blind eye to what was happening and refused to become involved and reopen his case.

He hopes by exposing the details this book might prevent the same treatment being meted out to others.

His other crime books include:

Crooked Justice
(ISBN978-1-910176-39-9)

D1454575

Since leaving prison there have been two legal experts who believed in his innocence and have stood by him to fight his case for over five years.

Tracy Gibbon is a lawyer with Olliers Solicitors in Manchester who specialise in criminal law. She has helped with the preparation of his case files and has worked closely with Foran throughout. She said;

"Attempting to quash Martin Foran's convictions was always going to be a somewhat daunting task. After thirty years he'd tried everything he could to clear his name.

He arrived at my office with boxes of papers he'd amassed over the course of some thirty years. The contents made me incredibly angry, and upset, at what he had gone through during the course of his trials and his subsequent terms of imprisonment and made me determined that I would do what I could to help him fight to prove his innocence.

The tirelessly hard-working Elizabeth Nichols agreed to take Martin's case and has acted for him on both successful appeals. We were also lucky to fall into the hands of the very wise Andrew Timney at the Criminal Cases Review Commission; without his work we would still be fighting."

Elizabeth Nicholls is a barrister and has represented Foran at each of his appeals. She is a member of the Lincoln House Chambers in Manchester with a successful defence and prosecution practice in General Crime.

She was called to the Bar in 1984 and has prosecuted a number of significant and difficult cases. She is a Category A prosecutor on the Attorney Generals Consolidate List.

Martin Foran

The Forgotten Man

The British prison nightmare of an innocent man
who is still awaiting justice after 40 years.

The corruption and cover-ups throughout the
criminal justice system and the lies and
corruption that was endemic within the West
Midlands Serious Crime Squad
is laid bare.

Authorised biography written and compiled by

J. R. Stephenson

Following extensive interviews and researching
documents provided by Martin Foran

Shield Crest

ISBN: 978-1-910176-15-3

(Also available as an eBook ISBN 978-1-910176-41-2)

A CIP catalogue record for this book
is available from the British Library

MMXVI

Published by
ShieldCrest Publishing Ltd.
11a Main Street, Aylesbury, Buckinghamshire,
HP22 5RR   England
+44 (0)333 8000 890
www.shieldcrest.co.uk

How can I thank my wife, Valerie, enough for her courage, fortitude, commitment, support and unwavering belief in my innocence and, in the midst of it all, bringing up all our children on her own?

I shall never be able to repay you.

Martin

Contents

Appendices

AUTHOR COMMENT

On examining his record, you could be forgiven for thinking Martin Foran is a career criminal. He has spent the last 40 years protesting his innocence but after so many convictions and with numerous appeals refused, surely the police, lawyers, judiciary, jury and Home Secretary cannot all be wrong and he must be guilty of the crimes for which he spent almost 20 years in prison?

He is the only person in British legal history to suffer a double miscarriage of justice and his story strikes at the very heart of the British justice system and shows how they were indeed all wrong. It deals with two fraudulent convictions for a total of eight trumped up charges by the notorious West Midlands Crime Squad, none of which he committed but which, nevertheless, led to his incarceration for a total of almost 20 years.

The first was a conviction in 1978 for which he was sentenced to 10 years imprisonment on four charges and released in 1984 and the second was a conviction on 10th May, 1985 where he was framed on two charges for which he was sentenced to 8 years, extended to 14 years and released in August 1996.

After fighting for almost 40 years since entering prison for the first time, his second conviction was eventually overturned and both charges quashed on 16th April 2013. He continued his fight to have his first conviction overturned.

In January 2014, the Criminal Cases Review Commission referred the first conviction to the Court of Appeal on the grounds of new evidence which they said materially affected the verdict. They made a recommendation that this too should be overturned and that he should be acquitted.

On the 3rd October that year the Court of Appeal heard the case and on 17th October 2014 agreed to quash all four charges brought against Foran for his first conviction.

In both cases compensation has been refused for his wrongful imprisonment and for which he is still fighting. However, his fight has been made much more difficult due to a controversial new law which was passed in 2013 by the coalition government. More details of this new legislation is given in chapter 25 which deals with his compensation claims.

Knowing he does not have long to live, he is determined to clear his name and that of his family before he dies and to ensure they receive compensation for the many years of torture and torment they also have endured.

He wanted to write about his experiences for all to know about the treatment he received and to act as a record but, faced with an overwhelming number of files relating to his treatment, medical records, summonses and appeals together with copious newspaper cuttings and radio & TV recordings, the task became too daunting. When the publishers asked me to assist, it became clear during my initial conversations with Foran and his wife Valerie and from the mountain of evidence he showed me that he was innocent.

Here is a man who, for nearly 40 years, has been protesting his innocence without anyone willing to listen. Lesser men would have accepted the deals he was offered to give up his fight and it is a credit to his determination that he managed to survive countless beatings and attempts to silence him while in prison. However his persistence paid off when he eventually gained his acquittals.

This determination and refusal to bend to any suggestion of his guilt was because of his certain knowledge that he had been framed by senior police officers and was innocent of the crimes they were trying to pin on him. However, his would be a lone battle while serving his terms of imprisonment and throughout the years following his release. Simply no one would listen to his pleas for justice.

Because of the deep traumas he suffered following the horrific events described in this book, his experiences are permanently seared into his mind. Together with his visible wounds they have caused serious deterioration in his health resulting in a terminal condition.

During our many conversations he was able to recall in minute detail each of the encounters with prison officers, lawyers, magistrates and police. I also discovered after examining hundreds of documents that whenever previously hidden evidence surfaced, it was found that in each case, Foran's accounts of the events were true and those of the police were seriously flawed. It showed they had lied substantively and falsified written evidence both to gain the convictions and to cover up their actions. The fact they were wrecking a man's life to suit their purposes never seemed to enter their heads.

I agreed to write his story providing the claims being made could be substantiated and from the copious amount of information I sifted through and the many discussions I had with Foran, it became clear that he was innocent of the crimes for which he was convicted. I have no doubt, therefore, that in the case of Martin Patrick Foran there has been a serious miscarriage of justice and it is my privilege to have been able to write his story.

The treatment he received from the prison service was beyond imagination and the doctors within the service were also culpable for their negligence in refusing the necessary medical treatment, medications and surgery to help with his life-threatening condition.

If it wasn't for the files he was able to smuggle out of the prison service, we would not have had the evidence of this mal-treatment. Foran knew he would not be believed once he was released and was certain any incriminating evidence would be destroyed if there were to be an inquiry, so he had to get hold of his files which contained the necessary records. How he was able to do this is another story that he prefers not to disclose at this time but, suffice to say, it was ingenious.

The files were considered sufficiently important for the Governor of the prison where he was being held at the time to arrange a visit to his wife by senior prison officers and the police accusing her of being involved in their disappearance.

They also staged a series of raids on the Foran home to try and locate them. They even offered to move him to any prison of his choice to facilitate Valerie's visits if the documents were handed back but the files remained hidden until now. These records have enabled Foran's claims to be substantiated and have been reproduced in this book.

Suffering from cancer and Type1diabetes, his doctors believe he has little time left to live. He has been deprived of the most important years of his life and prevented from being a husband and father to his children, something the rest of us take for granted. He had to watch helplessly as his wife struggled to bring up their four children alone. But his story will demonstrate that Martin Foran is nothing if not determined to get justice and I shall be delighted if this book helps to clear his name and highlight how, in the face of apparently overwhelming evidence to the contrary, a man can indeed be innocent of the crimes for which he was convicted.

After reading the book, I hope the reader will gain an insight into the character of Martin Foran and better understand the injustices he and his family have endured.

Most importantly, I hope it also serves as a reminder to those whose duty it is to ensure that justice is dispensed by our courts to question the veracity of evidence provided by those whose integrity is assumed to be unimpeachable.

Finally, I hope the justice system will grant Foran the compensation he deserves and which is due to him and his family to ensure the hardships they have endured for the last 40 years comes to an end very soon.

All royalties from the sale of this book are being donated to Martin Foran and his family.

PROLOGUE
By Martin Foran

How do I begin to explain the endless years of pain and sorrow the West Midlands police had planned for me, for it must have been planned, with the result that my life has been a living hell for over forty years? How did it happen? How did it all start? I was no one special, I hurt no one, and, looking back, I now feel my only 'crime' was the land of my birth, for I am an Irishman.

In the 1970's and 1980's it was a nightmare in the West Midlands, because of the IRA bombings. The sound of your voice branded you IRA, and it didn't matter how long you'd lived in Birmingham, or that you were married there or even that your children were born there. If you were Irish, you became an easy target for the Serious Crime Squad to fit you up. Nor did the IRA give a damn about the suffering they caused innocent people, for they ignored the fact that the bombings hurt Irish people too. So, I had two evils to contend with, the IRA and the ruthlessly dishonest Serious Crime Squad.

After the IRA bombings, who was going to hear the voice of a lone Irishman crying "I'm innocent"? Even worse, who would hear the voice of an Irishman saying; "Oh no, they've framed me again!" Nobody heard my cries for help and nobody cared. My only voice and my only hope, was my wife Val. Hers was the greatest pain of all, left with two children and another on the way. Not only did the Serious Crime Squad take away her husband, they even stole the money we had just taken out as a loan from The Provident for a pram.

Her suffering and sorrow was immense due to the endless days of walking around begging for someone to hear her cries; "Please help my husband, he is innocent," while dragging our children from prison to prison, through hail, rain and snow and at the same time knowing police were telling her husband to plead guilty or they would put our children into care. This all became too much for my pregnant wife and caused our child Valerie to be born deaf. But so great was her love for me, nobody could stop her protesting for endless years and visiting the many prisons I occupied. Never has any woman stood by her man as steadfastly as she stood by me.

How could a police force get so rotten? You will ponder this as you read the endless news cuttings and the protests outside prisons and police stations. Such was the power of the Serious Crime Squad; it seemed to be greater than the courts. Even the Home Office and Appeal Courts must have been involved for them to get away with so much before they were eventually rumbled and disbanded.

You will see that everything recounted in this book has been vindicated and the conviction quashed but they still refuse any compensation to redress the hell suffered by me and my family.

I am grateful to John Stephenson for agreeing to write my story and for the many hours we have spent discussing my arrests, convictions, prison experience and subsequent appeals. This has enabled me to explain and record my 40 year fight to clear my name and seek ultimate justice for the wrongs which I and my family have suffered.

CHAPTER 1

HIS EARLY YEARS

Martin Patrick Foran was born on the 27th February 1944 in Limerick, Republic of Ireland, the second son of Martin and Bridie. The family had early problems and his mother was absent from home for long periods while his father was working in England.

At a critical time, there was a move to have the youngest children taken into care and being the second oldest of the eight children, he took it upon himself to look after his siblings and did everything he could to prevent this happening. He would take them into the hills when Social Services were due to visit and stay with neighbours for periods to prevent his brothers and sisters being taken into care.

In his efforts to escape the authorities with his siblings, he became branded a 'bad boy' and was deported to England, which was common for those who were considered to be a nuisance. In 1968 he arrived in Birmingham by sea from Ireland on the 'cattle bus' as the deportation vehicle for 'undesirables' was known.

One of his greatest regrets was getting involved in petty thefts in his attempts to scrape together some money. After being caught breaking into a cafe in 1974, he was convicted on three counts of robbery and burglary during the period from 1971 to 1974 and was sentenced to 3 years imprisonment in 1975. These are crimes that he regrets and for which he pleaded guilty and he has never denied involvement.

While in prison, he married Valerie in 1975 and vowed to start a new life with his new wife on his release and they looked forward to the years ahead.

However, there were others who had different plans and 1977, the year of his release, became significant for very different reasons and those plans would rob him of his entire future.

It was the height of the IRA bombings which became a regular occurrence on the UK mainland at that time. The West Midlands Serious Crime Squad (SCS) was set up specifically to try and identify IRA members who might be living in the city, so all Irishmen became suspects.

Foran's misdemeanours and confinement would bring him to the attention of the SCS and no one could have foreseen the impact they would have on his future.

During his imprisonment he came under considerable pressure from the police and SCS to become an informer for the activities of the IRA. This was an organisation with which he had never had any association and therefore he did not succumb to the pressures.

Foran has always maintained the IRA caused as many problems for the Irish wishing to live peacefully and lawfully in the UK as they did for British families. All Irishmen became targets for abuse from the police and the public and the Irish clubs, which he frequently visited, were raided regularly and in some cases suffered arson attacks.

Being Irish with a criminal record and having shown his unwillingness to cooperate with the West Midlands Serious Crime Squad but knowing what they were up to, made him a target for the SCS

.

Young Martin aged 8

One of few pictures of Foran as a young man of 20 before his prison days.

Above and below, Martin & Valerie starting their life together.

Right: On their wedding day.

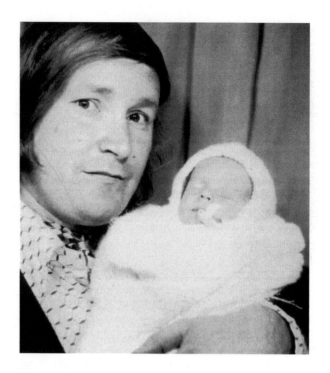

Martin and Valerie after the birth of their son, Martin.

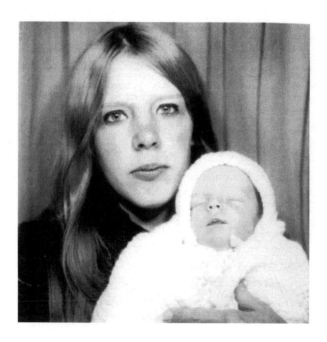

CHAPTER 2

1977 - THE NIGHTMARE YEAR

On his release from prison they were broke and were looking for ways they could raise some money until Foran was able to get work.

Valerie had two rings given to her by her grandmother, one of which was platinum, and on the 12th April, 1977, they visited a jeweller to have the rings valued. Although the last thing she wanted was to sell the rings, they needed to know how much they would raise 'just in case'. While discussing it with the jeweller two police officers entered the shop and arrested them on suspicion of selling stolen goods. It seems the jeweller suspected the rings were stolen and had pressed an emergency button which connected directly to the police station.

They were taken to the police station and interviewed on the basis that they were trying to dispose of stolen rings. However, faced with Valerie Foran's insistence they had belonged to her grandmother and the total lack of any evidence to support the police claim, they were later released.

When they asked for the return of the rings the police said they had left them with the jeweller. This seemed strange to Foran and his wife but they returned to the jeweller's shop to collect them. However, the jeweller said he had given them to the police at the time of their arrest. When they told the jeweller the police had told them they had been left with him, the jeweller became annoyed and indignant and was emphatic that the police had left with the rings and that Foran and his wife had been misinformed.

Foran and his wife were quite sure the jeweller was telling the truth and returned to the police station to insist one of them had taken the rings at the time of their arrest. However, the police then told him they had returned the goods to them before leaving the shop and that they must have disposed of them between leaving the shop and arriving at the police station. Foran then knew they were lying as they would never have returned rings believed to have been stolen, to the suspected thieves. Furthermore, why would they dispose of their own property? Valerie remains distressed that the family heirlooms were never returned.

Case 1 - 2 charges – Robbery & theft

On the 3rd May 1977, four Serious Crime Officers raided his home while he and his wife were there. They had no warrant to search his house and gave no reason for doing so. During their search they saw a clear plastic wallet on the mantelpiece which is used for holding small documents such as an insurance policy. The wallet concerned had no value and had been found by their young daughter outside her school that day, she had intended to hand it in to the school the following morning.

On seeing the plastic wallet, the officers decided it was part of stolen goods belonging to a Mr Farmer whose garage had been broken into. Among the items stolen was a wallet. Foran was arrested and taken to Digbeth police station for questioning. In their subsequent evidence to the courts, the police said they had found the wallet in Foran's house and believed it to be that of Mr Farmer, although a wallet taken from an adult was unlikely to be the same as the small plastic one his daughter had found. Foran denied having anything to do with the wallet but the police would bring the charge to court later that year.

Years later it was discovered that Mr Farmer had made no complaint and did not report his garage broken into; in fact there was no crime. This did not matter to the Squad because they had no rules and knew that if it was a case of their evidence versus the plaintiff, they would always win.

There was clearly some reason that the SCS decided to continually harass Foran. Crime was on the increase in 1977 and, as its name suggests, the Serious Crime Squad was formed to try and prevent serious crime. For four of its officers to go to so much trouble to raid his home unannounced, without a warrant and, subsequently, to use the flimsiest evidence to hound him was proof enough to Foran and his wife that they were trying to force him into co-operating with them and work for them as an informer.

During one of their attempts they threatened they would put him away for ten years if he didn't co-operate. Something they ultimately managed to accomplish.

Foran's life was turning into a living hell as the police never left him and his family alone and they became frightened each time there was a knock on the door. As a result, they made up their minds to move to Ireland and relocated to Belfast in June 1977.

After a few months Valerie missed her mother and family so much that they returned to Birmingham a short time later. This turned out to be a bad choice as he was soon arrested again. He had little or no knowledge of and had not received any information that he was due to appear in court on the 14th June for the Farmer burglary and was accused of going 'on the run' in order to avoid arrest.

He protested that far from being 'on the run' he had, in fact, been in Belfast looking for work and had not tried to disguise either his name or whereabouts. However, the police would produce their evidence to the court accusing him of dodging arrest despite him having evidence that he had been seeking work and that they had only returned due to Valerie wanting to be near her parents.

The evidence he had was a notification from the Department of Manpower in Belfast requesting he attend for interview on a specified date. There was also a letter from the manager confirming the dates Foran had been in Northern Ireland. Both these documents follow.

DEPARTMENT OF MANPOWER SERVICES

Tel. No. 35211 Ext. 252

N.I. No. 84 A   Occ. Classn. 862.1c

Employment Service Office
Gloucester House
57-63 Chichester Street
Belfast BT1 4RA

Third Floor

Mr Martin Forun
573 Crumlin Rd
BT14 7GB

Ref. EMPLOYMENT /Order No. H E   8 Aug 1977   19

Dear Sir/Madam,

A vacancy has been notified which we think is suitable for you and you are therefore recommended to call at desk   on the **Third Floor** floor of this office on   9 AUG 1977   WED 10.3 77 at 11-30 o'clock. Please bring this letter with you together with the receipt for your National Insurance card (U.B. 40) or your Employment Registration card (E.D. 24).

If you are now at work you need not call, but you should, if you have not already done so, fill up and post at once the receipt for your National Insurance Card.

Yours faithfully
H. D. McCULLOUGH
W. McD. McCARTNEY.
Manager.

NOTE—The purpose of this recommendation is to help you to find suitable employment and you are reminded that under the National Insurance Acts and regulations a person may be disqualified from receiving benefit and/or credit of National Insurance contributions if he has without good cause refused or failed to carry out any written recommendations given to him by an officer of an Employment Exchange with a view to assisting him to find suitable employment.

U.B.29
Belfast
(*Env. N.27*)

Dmd.069278 60M(4) 3/75 F.T. Gp.176 4703001

That there should be no doubt this letter confirms only
that Mr Martin P Foran was in Northern Ireland on
Friday 24 June 1977, Mondays 4, 18 and 25 July 1977 and
1 and 8 August 1977.

Yours faithfully

W R HERRON
for Manager

Case 2 – 1 charge of robbery

On the 26th September 1977, Mr Apechis, was awakened in bed by four masked men brandishing knives. During the fracas, they raised their masks and Mr Apechis later described them as being of West Indian origin. After threatening him they left with £2,800. Mr Apechis was not required to give evidence at the trial and his statement was read to the court. Foran was not linked with this crime at the time, as the descriptions of the men provided by the victim and the nature of the crime would give no reason for him to be suspected.

Case 3 – 1 charge of robbery

On 8th October, 1977 Mr Trikam and his partner were awakened by two men in their bedroom. One was described as white, aged about 25, about 5'6" tall and holding a metal bar and the other as a Jamaican, 5' tall and aged between 18 and 20. They took money out of the woman's handbag at which time the man threatened them with the metal bar and then they left. Neither Mr Trikam nor his partner was required to give evidence at the trial but their statement was read to the court.

Foran was not linked to this crime either as, once again; the descriptions and ages of the men in this case would give no reason for him to be. However, in April, 1978, the police would produce documents to show he was implicated in both these crimes

Case 4 – 2 charges of robbery

On 13th October Mr Rice was in his jewellers shop in Stratford Road, Sparkbrook, a district to the south of the city centre. Just before closing time, two men entered the shop followed by a third man brandishing a sword. The two men were described as black or West Indian and the third man as white and carrying a sword. The contents of two safes were emptied into a large bin bag along with wristwatches and cash from the till. A customer who was in the shop was also robbed of his watch and wallet.

Mr Rice described the white man as being Irish from his accent, wearing a hat and with two moles on each side of his face. He could see hair below his hat which he described as 'darkish' and of medium length. He estimated he was aged around 25 years.

The customer, a Mr Holmes, described the white assailant as being Irish, approx. five feet eight inches tall and aged approximately 40 years. He said the man had moles on his right cheek

At this time the owner's wife, Karen, and his daughter arrived and realised what was happening. In the commotion that followed, the robbers ran off dropping the bin bag on the pavement together with the sword. The evidence concerning the sword would play a major part in the trial and Foran's subsequent conviction.

On the same day Foran was driving in Birmingham when he was stopped by DC Davies who recognised his car and pulled him over. Initially, he said he wanted to question him about the Farmer robbery. However, after taking him to the police station, he said they wanted to question him about the Rice jewellery robbery. Foran was then taken to the interview room and the following are his own words describing what happened:

"I was pushed into the room where there were five officers present. These were DCI Taylor, DS Hancocks, DC Davies, PC Finch, and PC Curry. I had long hair in those days and three or four officers were standing on chairs and two held me by my hair. Two other officers grabbed me round the neck and swung me while the other beat and kicked me.

They then let me drop to the floor where they continued to savagely beat and kick me.

When I asked how they would subsequently explain away the cuts and bruises that were all over his body, he said that during the trial they told the court that after being arrested he had tried to escape and they had to forcibly restrain him.

Given the subsequent tortures to members of the Birmingham Six by the same officers, recounted later in this book, I have no reason to disbelieve his account of what happened.

Much of the evidence was given by DS Hancocks who alleged countless interviews with Foran but each was conducted when he was alone in the room with Foran so was uncorroborated. However, DI Curry, DS Hancocks and DC Davies said they had produced a joint note after the interview. Interestingly, there was neither a solicitor present nor recordings of any of these interviews.

Like me, you will possibly find it difficult to believe or understand the ways and minds of those who comprised the Serious Crime Squad. However, Foran was clearly one of their targets and would come up against them time and again. He maintains to this day these officers were amongst the biggest criminal operators in the 70's and 80's, either using others to commit the crimes (with threats of reprisals if they refused) or committing masked raids themselves in the belief they could always frame others. There is a great deal of evidence to support this view:

Firstly, the corruption within the force and their willingness to falsify information to gain wrongful convictions was subsequently proved to be true following the 'Birmingham Six' case, and led to the West Midlands Serious Crime Squad being disbanded in disgrace.

Secondly, it is known that after their dismissal from the force, members of the SCS would become major players in acquiring time share property and Foran has always wanted an enquiry into how they acquired the large sums of money involved. He rightly wonders how some of the SCS members became the biggest timeshare holders from their earnings through crime and hopes one day someone will investigate their bank statements from those years and uncover how they could get so rich on police wages.

Thirdly, there is the case of Laurence Henry Shaw, a member of the Squad who went on to commit a series of crimes for which he received jail sentences totalling over 25 years. The press cutting describing his crimes is shown.

Foran knew they feared no-one, neither the judiciary nor the law as they thought themselves above both. In his case, they gave him two choices, either work for them or get out of the West Midlands. He told me that the message was very clear. If you would not commit robbery for them, they would try and turn you into a police informer, primarily to spy on the activities of the IRA.

He maintains to this day that because of his continued dogged resistance to their attempts to get him to work for them as a robber or a police informer; they set out to destroy him. He also continues to be wary of them as certain members are still very powerful even though they were dismissed and the Squad disbanded. He was to learn in prison just how powerful and dangerous they were and this knowledge was to be the main reason for them framing him a second time. They weren't happy to just accuse him of crimes he didn't commit but they also hoped that by reporting he had provided information about the IRA, IRA prisoners would cause him serious harm or even death as they were known for 'taking care of narks'.

He is also wrathful with The Birmingham Evening Mail for contributing towards his eventual downfall as they printed whatever was passed to them by members of the Squad.

An example of what they published about Foran being an informer and the objections he raised is shown. I have seen the court notes and it does not appear that the newspaper was ever reprimanded for printing the stories fed to them by the police before the trial took place, thereby colouring the views of the jury before they heard the evidence.

The power of the SCS was also assisted by Boyars, one of the biggest law firms in the City, which naturally had inside information on all the crooks who used the firm. The woman lawyer in that practice was the girlfriend of one of the Squad, so the SCS knew all the details of Foran's defence as, unaware of the link, he had asked them to act for him.

14

26 December 2010

Life and crimes of crooked ex-West Midlands cop Larry Shaw

HE was once a high-flying detective who won a top bravery award for his crime fighting.

But disgraced ex-West Midlands officer Larry Shaw is now starting a 13-year prison sentence after being jailed for his THIRD armed robbery.

The crooked cop had worked with the force's infamous Serious Crime Squad, before it was disbanded in 1989 amid allegations that officers had fabricated confessions from suspects.

Shaw, aged 59, was even awarded the Queen's Commendation for Bravery for his work with the unit, which was ironically designed to fight armed robbers.

He retired in 1998, yet soon afterwards the decorated cop was caught up in a seedy world of vice and villains and eventually turned to crime.

Shaw was jailed for 12 years in 2001 after admitting two armed robberies in Birmingham.

He was released early in 2007 but in August this year he made another botched armed raid on a Cornwall post office.

Last week, the fallen officer was sentenced to 13 and a half years at Truro Crown Court after he admitted attempted robbery and possessing an imitation firearm.

Former undercover cop Ronnie Howard knew of Shaw's reputation during his time with the West Midlands force. He said: "Larry Shaw was nothing more than a crook with a police badge.

R. G. FRISBY & SMALL

SOLICITORS AND COMMISSIONERS FOR OATHS

5 DE MONTFORT STREET
LEICESTER LE1 7GT
(AND AT BEDWORTH AND BROUGHTON ASTLEY)

R G FRISBY
B T C SMALL M A
G C JONES

OUR REF | YOUR REF
RSW/BD | TS/KS

TELEPHONE
LEICESTER (0533)
556232 (4 LINES)

WHEN CALLING OR
TELEPHONING PLEASE ASK
FOR MR Whiting

7th February, 1980

Dear Mr. Sargant,

Thank you for your letter of 6th February. We have now received
a copy of the press cutting taken from the Birmingham Evening Mail and
enclose a copy for your information. This has been sent to us by Mr.
Whitehouse, the Probation Officer, who makes a point that, so far as he
is aware, there was no mention of the death of Robert Nairac at the trial
and it therefore seems rather strange that such a story should be printed
in the local paper. Further, it also implies that the jury may have read
information about 'Foran' in the newspaper which was not brought out at the
trial and which has no connection with the trial.

Yours truly,

T. Sargant. Esq.
'Justice'
95a Chancery Lane,
London,
WC2A 1DT

EVENING MAIL SATURDAY 17th JUNE

Police claim man was IRA informer

A 34-YEAR-OLD man gave tip-offs to the police which led to the downfall of the Birmingham public house bombers, it was said in court.

Father of two, Martin Foran, was said to have been a police informant and given leads to detectives about the IRA, it was heard at Birmingham Crown Court.

One of the tip-offs was said to be aimed at hunting down the killers of Capt. Robert Nairac, the Army officer who was murdered in Northern Ireland and whose body was never found.

Foran told the jury that he had never been a police informant and had never given them tip-offs concerning the IRA.

Limerick-born Foran, of Deelands Road, Rubery, denies five robbery charges relating to thousands of pounds worth of jewellery and money. He also denies a charge of handling.

The prosecution claimed that when Foran was arrested he tried to get the charges dropped by naming people behind a spate of robberies. Detectives were sceptical because he had fed them false information in the past.

Foran was alleged to have told them: "Well, what about what I told Mr. Banks about the IRA and the pub bombings? I helped put those lot in."

Det. Supt. Tom Banks was one of the men behind the hunt for the bombers. The court heard that Foran was then interviewed by another officer, Det. Sgt Alan Hancocks.

The officer said that during the interview, Foran told of certain "safe" IRA houses in Britain and Ireland and named two Irish brothers who could help solve the murder of Grenadier Guard Capt. Nairac.

Exact details of the interview were not read out in court, but the Serious Crime Squad officers' notes were then handed in to Judge Ross, QC.

Foran told the jury that the officers had made up the interview and that he had never given them information about the IRA. He said detectives had invented a confession to the robberies and they had beaten him up.

(Proceeding)

CHAPTER 3

FIRST TRIAL

Foran was committed for trial on December 22nd, 1977 and remanded to Winson Green prison in Birmingham where his pregnant wife was able to visit him. However, she became seriously ill with Tuberculosis and was hospitalised for three months. Meanwhile, he was moved to Leicester prison and he is convinced this was done deliberately to make it difficult for his wife to continue her visits. But it didn't deter her and she regularly made the 80 mile round trip to visit him and continue her fight for his freedom. She was also not the only one to visit.

On 3rd April, 1978, police officers DC Davies and DS Jennings from the SCS travelled to HMP Leicester to interview him. Foran refused to come out of his cell to meet with them because he knew that whatever he said would have no bearing on what would ultimately be reported. The prison officer returned and told him he must go to the interview room to tell them personally that he would not be interviewed. Reluctantly, he went to the interview room accompanied by prison officer Law. He remonstrated with the two officers when they insisted he be interviewed and tried to leave on several occasions. This account was corroborated at his trial by prison officer Law, who was standing outside the door looking in throughout.

The trial commenced on 11th June, 1978. Different officers from the SCS were called to give evidence and told the court that they had interviewed him under caution on several occasions. Mr Farmer was never called to court to give evidence or be cross-examined (of course not; remember, there was no burglary). Nevertheless, the police maintained that, in addition to his involvement in the Farmer burglary, he had confessed to being involved in the robbery of Mr Apechis in September, 1977 and that of Mr Trikam and his partner in October, 1977. These were crimes of which, until then, Foran had no knowledge.

To his relief, the jury had doubts about the Farmer case and acquitted him but he was in despair when they found him guilty of being involved in both Mr Apechis' robbery and that of Mr Trikam.

Foran's misgivings about being interviewed at Leicester prison by DC Davies and DS Jennings also proved to be justified as Jennings and Davies would tell the court that he was willing to be interviewed, had been cautioned and had confessed. The only person to throw doubt on this was prison officer Law, who had witnessed Foran's refusal to be questioned, but it was the statements of two police officers against that of Foran and Foran's account was dismissed.

'Evidence' was also provided by DS Hancocks that Foran had previously provided information to the police about the IRA pub bombings in Birmingham. Foran never had nor wanted any connection with the IRA and he knew this allegation would leave him at the mercy of the IRA and could result in his death, whether inside or outside the prison. He believes that this was precisely what the SCS wanted.

The judge referred to Hancocks' evidence during his summing up despite the fact the alleged admissions by Foran were never mentioned by any of his senior officers nor in any of the police statements produced as their evidence, these 'admissions' were only introduced during the course of Foran's defence.

Another factor Foran maintains was an attempt to ensure he was implicated with the IRA was that one of the officers had said he was seen running away from the Birmingham pub bombings. In fact Foran was in prison at the time of the pub bombings and when he told them this and appealed to the governor to verify he was in prison, they told him that it was possible for him to have broken out of the prison and then to have broken back in again the same evening!

But the worst was yet to come; the jewellery shop robbery was the focus of most of the police evidence and ultimately proved most damming.

The SCS maintained throughout that he had confessed but this was only supported by the notes of two officers with no signed papers of his admission or recordings of the interview.

There was also an identification parade during which all the men had pieces of brown paper over their faces where the moles were described as being. Three out of four witnesses, including Karen Rice, failed to identify Foran in the line-up. Mrs Rice was not called for questioning by the court but DS Whelan was allowed to read a statement, supposedly by her, where he said she had picked him out from a photo ID. It transpired much later and not until Foran's appeal that what had actually happened was that when DS Whelan had asked Karen Rice to identify the white robber, he had only shown her one photograph of a man with a mole on his face, that of Foran.

This is in clear breach of the 'Archbold Rules' which deals with the procedure to be observed during ID parades. When Whelan was questioned later about this he admitted having shown her only one picture of a man with moles on his face, namely Foran, 'because he knew he was guilty'.

Section 1(18) of the Archbold Rules for 'Identification by Recognition of a Defendant' clearly states:

"Photographs of suspects should never be shown to witnesses for the purpose of identification ..."

Rule (23) also states:

The police should inform the defence of any case where an identification is first made from photographs..." This was also not done.

Rule 4 of 'Conduct of Identification Parades' also states:

"Wherever possible the officer arranging the parade should be of not less rank than Inspector." Whelan was a sergeant.

The relevant sections of the Archbold Rules are reproduced on the next page.

It was becoming clear that Whelan had an agenda and was given the freedom to tamper with the evidence to suit his own purposes. This was further exemplified when, prior to the identification parade, Foran had objected to DS Whelan visiting him beforehand and taking a note of the clothes that he was wearing. As a result, in the parade line-up, Foran exchanged jackets with another man on the parade. Two of the witnesses subsequently picked out the man wearing Foran's jacket.

The fourth person who did pick him out was Mr Holmes, who was the customer in the Rice jewellery robbery and who Foran is convinced was shown his picture in the same way as Karen Rice as he says; "Whelan was in and out of rooms like a yoyo during the ID parade." The manipulation behind Holmes' identification would be supported later.

ARCHBOLD

PLEADING, EVIDENCE & PRACTICE
IN CRIMINAL CASES

THIRTY-NINTH EDITION

EDITOR

STEPHEN MITCHELL, M.A.(OXON.)
of the Middle Temple, Barrister

CONSULTANT EDITORS

JOHN HUXLEY BUZZARD
a Circuit Judge at the Central Criminal Court,
late open classical scholar of New College, Oxford,
a Master of the Bench of the Inner Temple and formerly
First Senior Prosecuting Counsel to the Crown at
the Central Criminal Court

AND

T. R. FITZWALTER BUTLER, M.A.(OXON.)
a Master of the Bench of the Inner Temple,
Chancellor of the Diocese of Peterborough

LONDON

SWEET & MAXWELL

1976

SECT. 1] IDENTIFICATION BY RECOGNITION OF DEFENDANT § 1852

USE OF PHOTOGRAPHS IN IDENTIFYING CRIMINALS

(18) Photographs of suspects should never be shown to witnesses for the purpose of identification if circumstances allow of a personal identification. Even where a mistaken identification does not result, the fact that a witness has been shown a photograph of the suspect before his ability to identify him has been properly tested at an identification parade will considerably detract from the value of his evidence.

(19) Any photograph used should be available for production in court if called for.

(20) If a witness makes a positive identification from photographs, other witnesses should not be shown photographs but should be asked to attend an identification parade.

(21) Where there is evidence identifying the accused with sufficient certainty to prefer a charge, a witness who has made a firm identification by photograph should not normally be taken to an identification parade. There may however be circumstances when it is desirable to ask the witness to identify the suspect from a parade. For example, identification may have been made from a poor or out-of-date photograph; the photograph identification may have been made so long previously that the present ability to identify is uncertain; the suspect's appearance may have materially altered since the photograph was taken; or the witness may think his identification is likely to be assisted by having an opportunity of hearing a suspect speaking or observing his gait. The decision whether a witness should in such circumstances be taken to an identification parade should, wherever possible, be made by an officer of not less rank than inspector.

(22) Where there is no evidence implicating the suspect save identification by photograph, the witnesses as to identification should be taken to an identification parade notwithstanding that they may already have made an identification by photograph.

(23) The police should inform the defence of any case where an identification is first made from photographs since it cannot normally be said in court that an identification was made from photographs without revealing the existence of a criminal record.

(24) Where it is necessary to show a photograph of the suspect, it should be shown among a number of other (unmarked) photographs having as close a resemblance to it as possible, and the witness should be left to make a selection without help and without opportunity of consulting other witnesses.

1352. Identification parade

Home Office Circular No. 9/1969. (1) The object of an identification parade is to make sure that the ability of the witness to recognise the suspect has been fairly and adequately tested.

(2) Identification parades should be fair, and should be seen to be fair. Every precaution should be taken to see that they are so, and, in particular, to exclude any suspicion of unfairness or risk of erroneous identification through the witnesses' attention being directed specially to the suspected person instead of equally to all the persons paraded.

CONDUCT OF IDENTIFICATION PARADES

(3) If an officer concerned with the case against the suspect is present, he should take no part in conducting the parade.

727

(4) Wherever possible the officer arranging the parade should be of not less rank than inspector.

(5) Once the identification parade has been formed, everything thereafter in respect of it should take place in the presence and hearing of the suspect, including any instruction to the witnesses attending it as to the procedure that they are to adopt.

(6) All unauthorised persons should be strictly excluded from the place where the identification parade is held.

(7) The witnesses should be prevented from seeing the suspect before he is paraded with other persons, and witnesses who have previously seen a photograph or description of the suspect should not be led into identifying the suspect by reason of their recollection of the photograph or description, as for instance by being shown the photograph or description shortly before the parade.

(8) The suspect should be placed among persons (if practicable eight or more) who are as far as possible of the same age, height, general appearance (including standard of dress and grooming) and position in life. If there are two suspects and they are of roughly similar appearance they may be paraded together with at least twelve other persons. Where, however, the two suspects are not similar in appearance, or where there are more than two suspects, separate parades should be held using different persons on each parade.

(9) Occasionally all members of a group are possible suspects. This may happen where police officers are involved (e.g. an allegation concerning a police officer which can be narrowed down to a number of officers who were on duty at the place and time in question). In such circumstances an identification parade should not include more than two of the possible suspects. For example, if there were twelve police officers on duty at the time and place in question, there should be at least six parades, each including ten officers who were not implicated and not more than two who might have been: the twelve possible suspects should not be paraded together. Two suspects of obviously dissimilar appearance should not be included on the same parade. Where police officers in uniform form an identification parade, numerals should be concealed.

1353. (10) The suspect should be allowed to select his own position in the line and should be expressly asked if he has any objection to the persons present with him or the arrangements made. He should be informed that if he so desires he may have his solicitor or a friend present at the identification parade.

(11) The witnesses should be introduced one by one and, on leaving, should not be allowed to communicate with witnesses still waiting to see the persons paraded; and the suspect should be informed that he may change his position after each witness has left.

(12) The witness should be asked whether the person he has come to identify is on the parade. He should be told that if he cannot make a positive identification he should say so.

(13) It is generally desirable that a witness should be asked to touch any person whom he purports to identify; but when the witness is nervous at the prospect of having to do this (as may occur when, for example, the witness is a woman or child who has been the victim of a sexual or violent assault or other frightening experience) and prefers not to touch the person, identification by pointing out may be permitted.

(14) If a witness indicates someone but is unable to identify him

Perhaps the strongest evidence produced by the police making their case that Foran participated in the robbery was their categorical statement that fingerprints found on the sword left at the scene had been positively identified as belonging to Foran. Foran believes this evidence probably clinched the jury's decision to find him guilty.

It would only be after Foran had spent 3 years in prison that the true facts would come out in a letter from D H. Gerty, Assistant Chief Constable of West Midlands Crime Force, who states that the fingerprints found on the sword were incontestably not those of Foran. A copy of his letter is below.

West Midlands Police

POLICE HEADQUARTERS
PO BOX 52 LLOYD HOUSE
COLMORE CIRCUS QUEENSWAY
BIRMINGHAM B4 6NQ
TELEPHONE 021 236 5000
TELEX 337321

ALL COMMUNICATIONS SHOULD BE ADDRESSED TO "THE CHIEF CONSTABLE"

Harvey Ingram
Solicitors
8 Abbey Street
Market Harborough
Leicestershire LE16 9AA

YOUR REFERENCE
RJE/JO
OUR REFERENCE
DHG/OPC   MISC 433/79
DATE
10 December 1981

Dear Sirs

PATRICK MARTIN FORAN

Thank you for your further letter of 30 November 1981 concerning Mr Foran.

I am sorry we did not make it absolutely clear in our letter to Mr John Farr MP of 26 October 1981 that Mr Foran's fingerprints were not found on the ornamental sword. The partial fingerprints that were present have not as yet been identified but I can quite categorically state that they did not originate from Mr Foran.

I hope that this now makes the position absolutely clear in regard to fingerprints and Mr Foran.

Yours faithfully

D. H Gerty

Assistant Chief Constable (Crime)

The fingerprints being incontrovertibly NOT those of Foran had been known to the SCS all along and had been suppressed by them until his case was taken up by the Leicestershire MP, John Farr.

Under normal circumstances, this would have immediately called the entire conviction of Martin Foran into question but it had no such effect. In fact things were to get yet more bizarre.

During our countless interviews, I asked Foran why he thought the SCS were targeting him as all the evidence showed it was a vendetta against him personally. His reply was forthright; he said that while he was in prison he became aware that the officers involved in his case were the same officers who were involved in the convictions of the Birmingham Six. He would emphasize this to anyone who would listen and he also stated it in one of his many appeals against his conviction. Although this was before the protests calling for the Birmingham Six to be freed, they did not want the link to be made public and were intent on silencing him.

Later, when the Birmingham Six campaign got underway he wrote to the Home Office and again repeated that the same officers who were involved in the Birmingham Six were also involved in his case. However, this fell on deaf ears and the Home Office told him that after checking, they believed there was no connection.

Of course, this would all change after the Lord Justice Leveson led appeal hearing in 2013, which demonstrated that the same officers were involved. They had previously been shown to have committed perjury and fraud, to have falsified evidence and engineered subsequent cover-ups, all of which led to the West Midland Serious Crime Squad being disbanded in disgrace in 1989.

The one thing that remains a puzzle is that, despite Foran's continued protestations that he had never been interviewed at the time of being charged or at any time when he was in prison, at no time in any of the court transcripts does anyone ask for the recordings of the interviews. These would have proved beyond doubt the police assertion that he had been interviewed and had confessed. It seems beyond reason that the judge or defence counsel would not have viewed the absence of any recordings as significant and that it strengthened Foran's statement that he had never pleaded guilty and, in fact, his assertion that no interviews ever took place.

Furthermore, there was never a single statement produced which was signed by Foran which would have corroborated the police statements nor was there ever any admission of guilt in court or out of it.

I also wanted to know more about his legal representation who appeared to have overlooked requesting the evidence of the SCS' claims of Foran's admission of guilt. He believes this is largely due to the fact he was receiving Legal Aid, and the assigned legal representatives would turn up and say they believed in his innocence and were prepared to take his case but when it came to court, they would then tell him they had obtained 'a good deal for him' and that if he pleaded guilty, they could get him a significantly reduced sentence.

This would happen repeatedly prior to his conviction and would continue while in prison, during which time he would be told a guilty plea would gain him early parole.

Foran refused each time as he knew he was innocent and said to me; *"Why would I plead guilty to crimes I had nothing to do with?"*

On 21st June, 1978, he was convicted on three counts of Robbery and committed to prison for 10 years.

CHAPTER 4

START OF HIS PRISON HELL

After he was sentenced he was taken to Winson Green prison and later moved to Leicester prison.

We can only imagine what it must have been like to be taken to a prison cell which would be one of many to become his home for the next ten years, less any parole, knowing he was innocent of all the charges brought against him.

He described his emotions as those of utter despair and anger. He was also greatly concerned for his family and, in particular, his wife, who was very poorly at this time. He said;

"It is hard to explain the heartache you feel and the weight of depression when you are locked up for something you didn't do and this leaves your family with terrible problems. I wrote to anyone who might listen, including the church, Bishops and MPs but no one did anything, no one seemed to care and no-one would listen."

Within approximately 6 months he was moved to Gartree prison, a short distance away. Gartree is a high security prison where some of the most notorious criminals have been kept. These include; Charles Bronson, Fred West, Reggie Kray and Ian Brady.

During his daily 23 hours isolation in the hospital segregation unit, he spent a long time talking to the person in the next cell to him who was Ian Brady, notorious for the Moors Murders of young children together with Myra Hindley.

Although he has no sympathy for the pair, he and Brady were both in solitary confinement and so spent many hours talking to each other. Foran managed to read Brady's file and became aware of another person who was a major player in the child murders. This was a relative of Hindley who escaped prosecution and was never charged but was implicated strongly in the crimes. He thus escaped any notoriety and lived peacefully in Ireland until he died.

It is not for this book to delve into that case so we will leave it there, except Foran recounted that Brady tried unsuccessfully to be moved from the high security prison hospital unit in Gartree to a normal prison and now simply wants to die.

One of the hardest things Foran had to contend with was the false allegation the police had made that he was an informer against the IRA. He began to receive letters from Ireland decrying him for such activities but, worse than that, it made him a marked man inside the prison. In addition to the mistreatment he was beginning to receive from the prison officers, he was also a target for other Irish inmates who viewed him as a traitor.

His biggest fear was of the prison officers, most of who were ex-military and had served in Northern Ireland. To make matters worse, he had also been falsely accused of having killed Captain Nairac, a British army officer, which increased the severity of the beatings he received from both the Irish prisoners and the prison officers. It would appear the police had deliberately set him up as a 'hate figure'.

The next two years were a living hell as he refused to stop protesting his innocence. He would receive regular beatings from the prison officers and letters written to his wife were never posted.

Foran decided he had to step up his campaign and begin protesting his innocence and wrote to anyone he thought might be in a position to help.

One such person was the Bishop of Leicester who he wrote to on the 23rd October 1980. He received a reply on the 29th October after the Bishop had made enquiries but was disappointed to learn that the Bishop had been told by the Home Office that his situation was 'under consideration'.

Foran knew precisely what that meant and that the Bishop had been fobbed off with platitudes.

BISHOP'S LODGE, 10 SPRINGFIELD ROAD, LEICESTER, LE2 3BD

LEICESTER (0533) 708985

from the Bishop of Leicester

29 October 1980

Mr Martin Foran
H.M. Prison
Gartree
MARKET HARBOROUGH
Leics

Dear Mr Foran,

Thank you for your letter of 23 October.

I am very much distressed about the intricacies of your case, and have much sympathy with your plight.

I have made such enquiries as I can and I have been assured that your situation is under consideration at the Home Office.

There does not seem to be anything that I can now do to help you further. I am not a member of the House of Lords so I do not have even that vantage point.

I expect you will have followed through Mr Baker's suggestion that you contact your MP. I am sure this would be the best thing to do.

Yours sincerely,

pp. + Richard Leicester
Dictated but not signed personally
owing to absence

:- 1 NOV 1980

His situation had become so bad that he seriously began to think about taking his own life. To this day, he says if it wasn't for his wife, Valerie's, staunch support and encouragement, he would probably have done so. She was busily fighting his case outside the prison and would plead with him not to do anything silly as his nightmare would finish when he was eventually released and they could get on with their lives.

One day, in 1979, he asked to see a representative from 'Justice', which fights cases where they believe there has been a miscarriage of justice, and he was visited by Tom Sergeant who agreed to take on his case. In March 1980, with Sergeant's help, he was successful in gaining an appeal hearing against his convictions for robbing both Mr Apechis and Mr Trikam based on the premise of mistaken identity.

At the original trial neither had been called to appear in court as they had been told Foran had pleaded guilty but at the appeal hearing for which the transcripts are available, they were both called to identify him as the robber. When the judge asked them each independently if Foran was the man who had robbed them, they each said he was definitely not and went on to say that they had told the police this on many occasions.

As the guilty verdict for these two robberies had relied only upon uncorroborated and unsupported police statements, one would have thought he would have been found not guilty and the earlier conviction overturned. However, the judge would then make a decision which, to this day, is impossible to understand. He said that because Foran had not been identified as the robber in the first place, it could not be a case of mistaken identity and returned him to Gartree prison.

Faced with this unbelievable turn of events, Foran decided to go on his first of many hunger strikes to draw attention to his case. He only stopped when advised by medical attendees that his life was in danger as his body would soon begin to close down. His thoughts of Valerie were always present and stopped him from making the decision to give up on life but, each time, as soon as he had recovered, the beatings would start again.

He was still not going to give up and, once again began to contact anyone who could possibly help him. One such person was Baroness Steadman, who had been an active member at Westminster. She decided to take up his case and wrote to the Home Secretary. She received the following reply from Lord Belstead.

HOME OFFICE
QUEEN ANNE'S GATE
LONDON SW1H 9AT

2 2 MAY 1981

The Baroness Stedman, OBE
"Green Pastures"
Grove Lane
Longthorpe
PETERBOROUGH
PE3 6ND

19 May 1981

Dear Phyllis,

Thank you for your letters of 23 April and 9 May about
Martin Foran, a prisoner at Gartree.

Mr Foran's case for parole was considered in February but,
as you know, the Parole Board did not recommend early release
on licence and, in these circumstances, the Home Secretary
has no power to grant it. Since receiving your letter I have
looked at the parole papers including the letter from Mrs Foran's
doctor and taken account of the recent petition submitted by
Mr Foran. I do, of course, understand Mr Foran's concern for
his family and I symphathise with Mrs Foran's problems while
her husband is away from home but I cannot agree that these
unfortunate circumstances present a significant new factor
as far as parole is concerned. Domestic circumstances are
important but only one of many factors which have to be taken
into account when assessing a prisoner's case, and the Board
was aware of the problems. I am afraid it is often true that
the offender's family also suffers as a result of his imprisonment but this cannot affect his suitability for parole; it is
the merits of the man's own case for early release on licence
that must be the deciding factor.

I regret I am unable to find sufficient grounds for directing
a review of Mr Foran's case earlier than the next statutory
one which is due to begin at the prison in October.

The other matter you raised bears on the rightness of two of
Mr Foran's convictions and therefore falls to be considered
in relation to the Home Secretary's power to refer a case to
the Court of Appeal or to recommend the exercise of the Royal
Prerogative of Mercy, rather than in the context of parole.
Patrick Mayhew has responsibility for matters of this kind and
he is looking into the suggestion that the police account of a
crucial interview was untrue, and that a prison officer can

confirm this. Much the same allegation was made at the
trial when the court had before it the accounts of the
two police officers, the prison officer and Mr Foran.
But, in view of the inference that there might be some
additional information that was not brought out at the
trial, we are obtaining a statement from the prison
officer concerned. This will be carefully considered
in the light of all the other relevant evidence and
Patrick Mayhew will write to you himself with the result
just as soon as he can.

Yours sincerely,

John

(BELSTEAD)

Foran and Valerie also harnessed the support of John Farr, MP for Market Harborough, where Gartree prison is located. Farr corresponded with and visited him. He was impressed by Foran's story and resolved to petition the House of Commons highlighting the judge's decision.

At 11.48 pm on Tuesday, 8th December, 1981 he presented his petition to the Deputy Speaker of the House requesting that the Secretary of State for the Home Office consider it to be a miscarriage of justice and take steps to right it. A copy of John Farr's petition is reproduced.

However, regrettably, this too fell on deaf ears and nothing was done.

Volume 14
No. 26

Wednesday
9 November 1981

HOUSE OF COMMONS
OFFICIAL REPORT

PARLIAMENTARY
DEBATES

(HANSARD)

CONTENTS
Tuesday 8 December 1981

Petition

Mr. Martin Patrick Foran

11.48 pm

Mr. John Farr (Harborough): With your permission, Mr. Deputy Speaker, and that of the House, I wish to present a petition in the name of Mr. Martin Patrick Foran, whom I have met and with whom I have corresponded, and by whose circumstances I am impressed. The petition is as follows:

To the Honourable the Commons of the United Kingdom of Great Britain and Northern Ireland in Parliament assembled.

The Humble Petition of Martin Patrick Foran showeth

That I was sentenced to 10 years in prison for crimes I did not commit, because of the way in which my trial was conducted.

That two of the main witnesses, people I was accused of robbing, were not called at my trial.

That after my trial they gave statements to my solicitor stating that I was not the person who robbed them.

That when I appealed on grounds of mistaken identity, one of these people was called as a witness to the Appeal Court and stated that I was definitely not the person who robbed him.

That my appeal was not allowed by the judges on the grounds that in the original trial I was not identified, and that therefore there could be no case of mistaken identity.

Wherefore your Petitioner prays that your honourable House will urge the Secretary of State for the Home Office to consider this miscarriage of justice and take action to right it.

And your Petitioner, as in duty bound, will ever pray, etc.

Martin Foran,
H.M. Prison Gartree,
Market Harborough,
Leicestershire.

To lie upon the Table.

He had hoped his hunger strike would also have drawn the attention of the media to his plight but, unfortunately, IRA detainees in Northern Ireland were also on hunger strikes and the media were more interested in these. The second such protest took place in 1981 and was a showdown between the prisoners and the Prime Minister, Margaret Thatcher. One striker, Bobby Sands, was elected as a Member of Parliament during the strike, prompting media interest from around the world. The strike was called off after ten prisoners had starved themselves to death, including Sands, whose funeral was attended by 100,000 people. Although Foran's hunger strikes were, in some cases, longer than those of the IRA members, the media's attention was not to be deflected, as a result of which Foran was to receive scant attention.

He made countless attempts to tell the press of his beatings and to plead his case. He spoke with priests, the Board of Visitors and with the governor of the prison but to no avail.

He had engaged solicitors, Frisby & Small, to try and get his appeal heard with a view to having his conviction quashed and decided to ask them to fight for a consultant from outside the prison to visit him so he could receive the proper medical attention which was being denied him. On 28th May 1981 he received the news that the Home Office had granted permission for him to be visited by his own consultant. It also added that the prospects for his appeal hearing were also very promising. This elated him and he waited patiently for the consultant's visit.

After waiting the whole of June, he wrote again to his solicitors on the 1st July. He was sure there had been dialogue between the MO of Gartree and the Derby Royal Infirmary, where the consultant was based and that it was this which was preventing his examination.

These fears were confirmed in his solicitor's reply on the 3rd July when he was told the surgeon had not responded to their letter.

Both these letters follows.

R. G. FRISBY & SMALL

29 MAY 1981

R.G. FRISBY
B.T.C. SMALL, M.A.
G.C. JONES

SOLICITORS AND COMMISSIONERS FOR OATHS

TELEPHONE
LEICESTER (0523)
555282 (4 LINES)

OUR REF | YOUR REF

CK/AG

5 DE MONTFORT STREET
LEICESTER LE1 7GT
(AND AT BEDWORTH AND BROUGHTON ASTLEY)

WHEN CALLING OR
TELEPHONING PLEASE ASK

FOR MR **Knight**

28th May 1981

Dear Sir,

Re: Your Claim

We thank you for your letter of the 27th May concerning the above.

The Home Office have granted permission for your own Consultant to visit you for the purpose of preparing a medical report. It is anticipated that a visit will be arranged by Mr. Firth of the Derby Royal Infirmary in the near future. Once his report is to hand further progess may be made.

The copy of the letter from Lord Belstead to Baroness Stedman appears encouraging and we hope that your case is referred to the Court of Appeal. Our firm will of course be pleased to act for you if you so require.

Yours faithfully,

R.G. Frisby & Small

Mr. Martin Patrick Foran,
C08627,
H.M. Prison Gartree,
Market Harborough,
Leicestershire, LE16 7RP.

R. G. FRISBY & SMALL

R. G. FRISBY
B. T. C. SMALL, M.A.
G. C. JONES
R. S. WHITING, LLB.

SOLICITORS AND COMMISSIONERS FOR OATHS

5 DE MONTFORT STREET
LEICESTER LE1 7GT
(AND AT BEDWORTH AND BROUGHTON ASTLEY)

OUR REF | YOUR REF

CK/AG |

TELEPHONE
LEICESTER (0533)
556282 (4 LINES)

WHEN CALLING OR
TELEPHONING PLEASE ASK
FOR MR   Knight

3rd July 1981

Dear Sirs,

<u>Re: Your Claim</u>

We thank you for your letter of the 1st July concerning the above.

The delay in conducting your medical examination has been due to the Surgeon who has failed to reply to our letters requesting that he visits you.

Our Mr. Knight telephoned the Derby Royal Infirmary on the 25th June and was told that the Consultant in question was on leave at present but would conduct an examination upon you upon his return two weeks later.

Please let us know if meanwhile you are transferred to another prison.

Yours faithfully,

Mr. Martin Patrick Foran,
008627,
H.M. Prison Gartree,
Market Harborough,
Leicestershire. LE16 7RP.

As he expected, it would be too late as he was transferred from Gartree prison in Leicestershire to Nottingham prison before any examination could take place.

By June 1982, his feelings of desolation and helplessness at the impossibility of getting anyone to listen to him increased daily. After all, he was a man sentenced to 10 years in prison for crimes he had not committed. He had served one year prior to his trial and another 4 years since conviction and suffered regular beatings throughout.

He knew more had to be done to draw attention to his situation and he conceived a daring plan.

He noticed that in one of the exercise yards a large pipe, about a foot in diameter, ran from ground level all the way up the wall to the roof of the prison, which was about 80 feet from the ground. It came from the ovens situated in the kitchens and was used to pipe hot steam throughout the prison for heating purposes. The pipe was boiling hot so posed no risk as far as the prison guards were concerned, but Foran had other ideas.

He managed to get hold of some scouring pads from the kitchens and stitched them to the outside of a pair of gloves to cover the palms of his hands. He also stitched some to the knees of his trousers. Once he had completed his preparations, wearing just a pair of trainers, he decided the time was right and in his own words, 'I just went for it'.

Somehow he managed to climb the entire length of the pipe, despite it being anchored to a smooth wall, until he reached the roof. During his 10 minute climb, the other inmates watching him were cheering him on. A prison officer tried to reach him and grabbed hold of the pipe but had to relinquish the task when he burned his hands. The pads which Foran had stitched to both his gloves and trousers were scorched through and both his hands and knees were burnt by the time he arrived on the roof.

Although he was 38 years old and relatively fit in those days having lost a lot of weight during his hunger strikes, the feat was nevertheless a significant one.

He had confided his plan to only a few of the inmates and they had agreed that if he succeeded in getting on the roof, they would arrange for bread to be passed up.

When he got onto the roof, he dropped a line over the edge above the cell windows where he knew they were, and the inmates would attach loaves of bread for him. Unfortunately, they were spotted almost immediately and moved to another cell, so his ingenious food supply arrangements were thwarted.

His intention was to stay there for as long as possible so he wore three T-shirts and two pairs of trousers to stop him getting burnt and he was also passed a jacket. These were his sole protection for what was to come.

The roof was very steep and he came close to sliding off or being blown off on several occasions. He also had to devise a method to prevent him slipping down at night when he fell asleep. There was a chimney nearby with a lightening conductor running up the side of it so he removed one of the T-shirts, twisted it into a rope and tied one end to the lightening conductor and the other around his waist.

Having survived the first few nights he began to get the publicity he wanted and the media were beginning to report on his rooftop escapade. Supporters gathered outside the prison and protested his innocence.

From her coalhouse roof, Mrs Sandra Woods, who lived near to the prison, could see Foran about 100 yards away. Valerie had travelled to Nottingham after hearing about her husband's protest and Mrs Wood invited her to stay with her so she could talk to her husband by shouting back and forth.

Sandra Wood & partner on the coalhouse roof overlooking the prison.
Taken by Valerie from her bedroom window.

Seeing and hearing Valerie's voice was a great boost to Foran and increased his determination to stay on the roof as long as possible to maximise the publicity for his case. There was also another reason. He knew that if he gave up without achieving something in return, he would be punished more severely than ever once he was returned to his cell.

With his added determination to remain on the roof and his supplies having been cut off, his most urgent job was to find a way of surviving and obtaining food and water.

THURSDAY JULY 8 1982 **THE TIMES**

Foran waves from his roof while Mrs Sandra Wood watches from hers

An inside-out chat between roofs

From Arthur Osman Nottingham

From the roof of Mrs Sandra Wood's coalhouse it is possible to conduct an extraordinary conversation at a distance of 100 yards with Martin Foran, the prisoner protesting his innocence on the roof of Nottingham Jail.

He will have been there for five weeks tomorrow and has become one of the sights of the city. There is a noticeable increase in traffic at weekends, it was said yesterday, as people come from miles around to watch him on the steeply-pitched roof of B Block.

Mr Foran achieved the 60ft climb at the cost of badly blistered hands via an internal kitchen flue, since concreted up to prevent a repeat trip. Unless his physical or mental state deteriorates alarmingly, he is likely to be there for some time yet, it was said yesterday. Friends have abandoned plans to float food to him on helium-filled balloons, because of cost.

Foran went up from his job as a machinist in the mailbag shop only hours after the Pope left Britain, on the day one of our Vulcans was impounded in Brazil, the climax of the Falkland crisis was still to come as was the Royal birth and Wimbledon. He has followed a momentous news month on the tiny transistor radio he took with

One thing he could not have anticipated was the wettest June on record. He has two plastic bags to cover his head and arms against the elements.

Yesterday he told me, his Southern Irish accent losing nothing over the distance between us, that he now felt "very rough", he last ate four days ago. A fellow prisoner named Phil had passed him a tomato sandwich via a string Mr Foran lowered to his cell. He said he was sorry that Phil had since been moved to Manchester and his cell was now empty.

He declined a suggestion by the prison doctor to continue his hunger strike indoors. Mr Foran told him he preferred to stay on the roof. "I said I had protested my innocence on six previous occasions, all to no avail. This time it is until death, there will be no giving up", he roared from the rooftop.

Foran has served nearly half of a ten-year sentence imposed at Birmingham on four charges of armed robbery. It was said he and another man had terrorised their victims with iron bars. He has previous convictions. He would have been eligible to apply to the parole board in October.

The last time he went on hunger strike was for 58 days

in Gartree Prison, Leicestershire, which damaged the kidney and astonished prison authorities by its length.

Mrs Wood, aged 30, has become his link with the world and she has given his wife, Mrs Valerie Foran, of Kingshurst, Birmingham the use of her coalhouse roof whenever she needs it. Mrs Foran, who has three children, spends most weekends in Nottingham shouting to her husband for hours on end.

Another neighbour, Mrs Ruth Poyzer, gives her lodgings. Mrs Wood's daughter, Carol, aged 12, also gives him occasional dancing displays on the coalhouse to cheer him up.

Mrs Wood, of Gunthorpe Close, Sherwood, said: "Two of the children took an umbrella for him to the prison but, of course, it was refused. We feel we can keep him in touch with life although some people in the road disapprove of what we are doing.

"The day starts at 7.30 am when he is washed and shaved in rainwater, which he also drinks from the guttering. He sleeps in the angle of the roof and chimney. Apart from his radio and razor, the only other thing he has is a Bible, which he reads a lot.

"When Carol has gone to

can call it that — and after tea we keep it up until it is dark. He is always grateful."

Mrs Wood has raised a petition of 1,600 signatures which has been sent to Mr William Whitlock, MP for Nottingham North, asking the Home Office to review the case. She said: "Many people think it unlikely the such hardship if there wasn't something in his claim."

Major Douglas Martin, the governor, said yesterday: "He is causing us no problems. He is behaving himself and is not doing any damage or costing us any money.

"He has no spite towards me or the prison department, it is purely against the police in Birmingham. Every time I see him he apologizes and says he is sorry, but 'A man has got to do what a man has got to do'. He is quite placid and he is not aggressive in any way.

"I could have starved him out by now but he said he would jump off or start ripping up the roof. My regional director is a bit concerned that we might lose a category B prison and with overcrowding as it is, he is not prepared to risk it.

"Foran is a very determined man. There is no question of using force and the only time I would do that was if I thought he was physically or mentally at

irman over pits

Editor, Inverness

displacing 600 men, a £3m investigation of reserves takes place. ...ion is committed to ...ial action if the board ...to impose the

...is first public address ...union since becoming chairman, Mr Siddall ...ed the miners against ...off potential cus-...by heedlessly putting ...price of coal or ...ning to cut off sup-...it is the cash from the ...er that pays the wages ...industry — and the ...he spends will ulti-...decide how many ...we can afford to

...whether loss-making ...uld have to close, he ...later: "These are ...ns we must discuss ...and not by ...at one another from ...ce. Most of the pits ...talking about have ...problems or they ...not be making losses. ...one time there is no ...is a subject for ...al discussion, ...people agree there is ...sible way out, that is ...of the road."

NCB chairman dis-...public investment in ...ustry through grants ...ms from the Govern-...ould amount this year ...m — more than one-...of all the total needs of ...tionalized industries. ...er industry gets more ...ment help than we ...concluded.

...iddall was accorded a ...ception by delegates ...words seemed to ...little impact. They ...dutifully and then ...on to castigate the ...ment's energy policy, ...ncing of the industry ...s plan to switch ...ingly towards nuclear ...stations. The miners ...urged coal to be ...doubled to 200 million ...a year, with no pit ...closed except on the ...of seam exhaustion.

...issue of jobs was ...to the Government's ...ial relations laws by ...s in a debate that ...d a unanimous call ...C opposition to Mr ...Tebbit's forth-...Employment Act ...delegates promised ...ion singled out for ...under the new mea-...ould receive immedi-...incial, industrial and ...nport from the NUM

In order to provide a source of water, he decided to take the dangerous measure of sliding down the roof to the gutter, which he cleaned out and blocked so he could collect the water from any rains.

He didn't have to wait long. Despite it being summer, the nights were cold and one night they had a snowfall, the worst ever experienced in Nottingham for 50 years. With little protection he hid behind the chimney

Food now became a priority. There was only one source available to him and that was the pigeons which would congregate on the roof during the day, at night they would gather near the chimneys and fall sleep. This gave Foran the opportunity to catch them and put them into a carrier bag he had brought with him. I was interested to know if he ate them raw but no, he also had this worked out. He would pluck them, remove the gizzard and entrails, wrap two at a time in newspaper and set light to it. He only had about three newspapers so had to be frugal in their use and therefore cooked several at a time

From his vantage point on the roof he could also observe what was going on elsewhere in the prison. At that time there was a major breakout of prisoners from a hostel unit within the prison and he was able to see them make their bid for freedom. They shouted to him and asked if he wanted to go with them but he told them that if he did, it would look as though he was guilty so he declined, thanked them and wished them luck.

He remained on the roof for 7 weeks and still wonders to this day how he did it. By this time the national press, radio and television were covering his demonstration. The governor of the prison was interviewed about plans to remove him and replied that no one would try to remove him physically. He also added that he believed that Foran was very determined and he wondered if there had indeed been a miscarriage of justice, as someone so resolved to have his case heard must be convinced he was wrongly convicted, so perhaps the case should be re-examined.

In addition to his determination to remain on the roof until he achieved a review of his case, Foran was also concerned that once he came down he would be given another beating and be moved from Nottingham making it even more difficult for Valerie to see him. He communicated this to Valerie who decided to take the matter up with the Board of Visitors at Nottingham prison, to which end, she sought to arrange a meeting.

The meeting was scheduled for the 21st June 1982 at which the Board agreed to seek a review of his case, ensure he was treated fairly, and confirmed he would not be moved from Nottingham if he agreed to come down from the roof.

This is a copy of their letter to Valerie agreeing to her requests.

Nottingham MP, William Whitlock, also decided to take his case into Westminster and received assurances from the Home Secretary, Patrick Mayhew, that he would review the case if any new evidence was produced.

Both these decisions were relayed to Foran through his solicitors who said they had new evidence and believed it would be sufficient for his case to be reviewed and have him acquitted. On this basis, after 49 days on the roof of Nottingham prison, Foran agreed to come down.

Extracts from Whitlock's speech are as follows: -

"While the House has been sitting, Mr. Martin Patrick Foran has entered his forty-seventh day on the roof of Her Majesty's prison, Nottingham. It is a demonstration that is intended to bring to public notice his statement of his innocence of the crimes for which he has been convicted.

"The evidence given by witnesses who were victims of the robberies that Foran was not among the robbers didn't seem to matter.

"The evidence given in court that he was at a house in Ladywood at the time of one of the robberies was thought to be of no consequence. Nor did it matter, apparently, that the absence of Foran's fingerprints at any of the scenes of crime was not made known to the defence. Everything in his favour was brushed aside.

"As I have said, there was a lack of evidence, identifying Foran as participating in the robberies but that lack of evidence was considered to be of no importance. Because that view was taken at the trial, the Court of Appeal in effect stated that identification was unnecessary and waived aside the evidence on Foran's side that had not been made available at the trial.

"I find that absolutely perverse. If that kind of logic is always adopted by our legal luminaries, my previous faith in British Justice must disappear."

Extracts from the Home Secretary's response are as follows: -

"I have listened with care to what the Honourable Member for Nottingham North said about the case of Foran. I shall study the report of the Hon. Gentleman's speech in the Official Report."

He then went on to read the entire notes of Lord Justice Donaldson's summary at the Court of Appeal including the following: -

"On 3rd April 1978, two police officers interviewed Mr. Foran at Leicester prison, when they read Campbell's statement to him. Their evidence was that he thereupon admitted that he had taken part in the Apechis and Trikam robberies as well as that at the jeweller's shop.

"At the trial, however, Mr. Foran denied entirely that he had confessed to any of the offences at any time, said that the police had fabricated all the evidence and, indeed, said that they had beaten him up for refusing to confess.

"When Mr. Foran sought leave to appeal against his conviction and his sentence, he sought leave to call Mr. Apechis and Mr. Trikam to give evidence. Mr. Apechis had said in a letter before the Court of Appeal that he was sure that Mr. Foran was not present. However, the full court refused the application, principally because the case against Mr. Foran had rested not on identification, for there was none in the case of the Apechis and Trikam robberies, but upon his confession to the offences."

Clearly, the Home Secretary had dismissed Foran's account that he had never confessed, and the fact that both the victims of the robberies had said he was definitely not the man. He preferred to believe the officers who said he had confessed despite the fact it was supported by only their own notes, and there was no corroboration from a senior officer, no signed confession or recordings of the alleged interview at which they claimed he confessed his guilt.

In a fair trial this would all have weighed heavily in Foran's favour, indicating that he was indeed telling the truth and had never been interviewed or confessed.

Mayhew also ignored the fact that three out of four people had failed to identify him during the identity parade and preferred to use the one person who claimed he was there (subsequently discredited) as sufficient evidence that Foran was likely to have been involved.

He then summarised as follows: -

"It must always be borne in mind that the Home Secretary must not usurp the function of the jury or that of the Court of Appeal. Against that

background I have carefully considered the case, including the fingerprint argument. I have been unable to find any new evidence or other material factor not already considered by the courts or previously available to the defence that would justify the Home Secretary seeking to intervene."

The full transcript from Hansard of the exchanges between William Whitlock MP and Patrick Mayhew, the Home Secretary, is attached as Appendix 1.

This was yet another blow to both Foran and his solicitors, who had become optimistic that the probability of his appeal leading to an acquittal had improved significantly.

He would go on to protest throughout his confinement by ongoing hunger strikes in many of the prisons to which he was sent, and made repeated appeals to have his conviction overturned, all of which were refused.

CHAPTER 5

THE AFTERMATH

Despite the reassurances from the Board of Visitors, on coming down from the roof Foran was taken to his cell where he received a savage beating. A few days later he was removed to Lincoln prison.

He was in agony when he arrived at Lincoln. They would watch him closely and this, together with his failing health, made the chances of him doing another rooftop vigil impossible.

He decided all routes to protesting outside the prison had been closed off so the only thing he had left was to use his body and it was then he decided to go on another hunger strike. This would be the longest of all his hunger strikes and would take him near to death.

It went on for over 6 weeks during which time he received visits from countless people, all asking him to stop: but after repeated disappointments and broken promises he was becoming a defeated man, and began to think it would be better if he just died. He later discovered that there had been an empty coffin waiting in the next cell.

One of his visitors was Cardinal O'Fee, who was then Roman Catholic Primate of all Ireland and Head of the Church in both the Republic of Ireland and Protestant-dominated Northern Ireland. He was also an ardent Irish nationalist.

On visiting Foran, he asked him to stop his hunger strike to assist the protest and appeals of the Birmingham Six. He was worried that the attention Foran had been receiving was detracting from the media coverage of their appeal process. This was focusing on the fraud and false evidence of the West

Midlands Serious Crime Squad which had led to their miscarriage of justice. He also told Foran that if he agreed, he would throw the weight of the church behind him and his family to help fight his conviction.

As a result, Foran agreed to stop his hunger strike, as the assistance of the church to support both his case and Valerie could well be compelling. However, he was to be disappointed yet again. The Birmingham Six gained their review and subsequently won their appeal with the help of significant media coverage, but the church did nothing to support Valerie and would play no part in assisting Foran with his appeal.

The effects of these hunger strikes and the regular beatings he would later receive would cause him to suffer a rectal prolapse which would cause his health to steadily deteriorate for the rest of his life.

He became too much for the prison officers and Governor of Lincoln prison to handle, and was moved to Franklyn prison in Durham. He believes the reason he was moved frequently was because none of the prisons to which he was sent wanted him to die there so they moved him to another.

To this day he is suffering ill health resulting from the hunger strikes but he was also to pay the price for a story printed in the Evening Mail which stated he was involved with the Birmingham Six. Had they been the bombers, Foran would have had a death sentence on his head and he is positive it was the SCS's way of getting rid of him; getting others to do their dirty work.

Despite his utter despair, he continually says it was Valerie who kept him going. She was the only person he could rely on to help prove his innocence. She was still as determined as ever and wrote to MPs and anyone who would listen. She also went on the BBC TV programme "Kilroy", a daily show involving lively studio discussion on topical issues, hosted by Robert Kilroy Silk. This gave the Foran case a full and very public airing, which brought his case into the media spotlight once again. After the programme he received letters of support from all over the world. However, none of this would have any effect on the applications for an appeal or an acquittal. He was destined to spend the rest of his sentence in prison.

Valerie's determination also spurred Foran to continue his own protests. He lost a lot of remission as a result but he couldn't shake off the injustice of spending so many years behind bars when he had done nothing to deserve it.

During the media exposé of the Birmingham Six, the officers involved were named, and this confirmed Foran's suspicion that the same officers were instrumental in concocting the evidence in his own case. This further increased his determination to clear his name and ensure they got their just desserts for all they had done to him.

Thirty-seven years later his persistence would pay off, and on the 9th January 2014 he was granted leave to appeal on the grounds that his conviction was 'unsafe'. This appeal is covered in Chapter 24.

CHAPTER 6

THE JOY OF RELEASE BUT IT WAS TO BE SHORT LIVED

He was released from prison in February 1984. His time in prison awaiting trial was taken into account so he had served almost 7 years of his 10 year sentence.

With no money and needing some provisions, he risked a journey in their car, which had no tax and insurance, and was caught behind the wheel in July. Knowing he had become a marked man because of his refusals to co-operate with the police, he was sure they were going to make an example of him. He needed a solicitor to assist him with his defence in the magistrates' court and an appointment was made to meet Ron Parker of Boyars Solicitors in Birmingham at two o'clock on the 10th September, 1984.

He was desperate to start a new life as Valerie was now pregnant with twins. They needed to borrow £200 to tide them over and to purchase a much needed pram. The Provident Building Society had agreed to lend them the money but it could only be provided by cheque, which would then need to be cashed at their bank. He decided, therefore, to combine the trip and collect the cheque, go to the bank, buy some provisions and then go on to the solicitor. It was this simple journey that would end up destroying his life forever.

Case 5 – 2 charges of robbery & conspiracy to rob

At approximately 4.30 am on the 9th September, the police were called to the Trident public house in Birmingham. The licensee, Frank Clowes, was asleep in his flat above the premises when he was woken by a youth who stood over him with a knife. A second person was described as wearing a balaclava and holding, what appeared to be, a 2-3 foot long bar. A third person was rummaging around in the room. The licensee was asked where his money was and the three men left with £1,700.

On that same day, Foran took his teenage daughter Joanne, niece Julie Masters, and two friends to the ice skating rink in the centre of Birmingham. He arranged to meet them on Hurst Street, at the Riviera café, at eleven o'clock to take them home. After collecting them his car broke down, and two men helped him push it to the side of the road. One was white and the other black and he later discovered they were called Paul Addison and Andrew McKenzie.

The following account is that of his niece, Julie Masters, who was then 16 years old, and was called to give evidence in court.

She explained that she, her cousin Joanne and their two friends were told to sit in the café and talk to no-one while Foran called the RAC to get the car fixed. She describes the café as being a seedy place and remembers a grey-haired elderly man sitting at one of the tables who she thought resembled Ernie Wise from the 'Eric and Ernie' television series.

She then said her Uncle Martin walked them to the bus stop and the two lads walked along with them 'chatting them up'. They didn't know their names but one was white and the other black. The bus stop was located outside the Law Courts in Birmingham City Centre and when they arrived there the last bus had gone. They then went to the nearby Digbeth police station to ask them to inform Foran's wife what had happened, let her know the girls were safe and that they would be late home. When they arrived outside the police station one of the lads told Julie that he wasn't going in because he was wanted by the police.

When they came out, they crossed a car park to get back to Foran's car and while they were crossing, one of the lads said to Julie that they would steal a car and get them home but

Julie told them not to be silly and that in any case her uncle would not allow it.

On arriving back at the car they waited for the RAC to arrive and her uncle hailed a taxi to take the girls home. He didn't have any money but left his details and said he would call in to pay them the following day while visiting his solicitor. They eventually arrived home safely at around half past one in the morning.

The next thing Julie knew was that her uncle had been arrested.

Her account supports that of Foran; he takes up the narrative explaining what happened next.

He had in fact called both the RAC and the AA, and it was the AA which eventually arrived at around quarter to two that morning. As the mechanic worked on the vehicle, Foran thanked the two men for helping them and told them he had an appointment the next day to see his solicitor at two o'clock. If they were around at three o'clock he would be happy to buy them a cup of tea and something to eat at the Riviera café, which they agreed to do.

The mechanic got his car started but could not keep it running so after driving for a few hundred yards Foran had to park it near Digbeth police station. At between two thirty and three o'clock he again went into the police station to inform the police what had happened and where he had left the car. Foran then remained in a nearby café until he got a lift home from his friend Barry Parker, arriving home between four and four-thirty in the morning.

At ten to twelve on the morning of 10th September Paul Addison was arrested by the police on suspicion of being involved in the robbery at The Trident public house. He was interviewed by DC Preston and PC Conn during which they claimed that Addison made a statement admitting he was involved in the robbery along with two other men, naming Andrew McKenzie and a third person who he knew only as 'Martin'. He said that 'Martin' had gained access to the pub by removing beading around the window using an iron bar and said that McKenzie had threatened the licensee with a knife to his throat.

According to the police evidence subsequently read to the court, Addison had said that the guy he only knew as 'Martin' had told him about a post office job he was going to do that day and that he would pick them up at the Riviera café at three o'clock. He also described the car in which 'Martin' was going to pick them up.

On the same day Foran set out for the city and collected the cheque from the Provident Building Society which he then cashed at his bank. Just up the road was a butcher where he purchased six pounds of mince before making his way back to the car. As he was leaving the car park for his two o'clock appointment with his solicitor he noticed police were stopping cars as they left. He was also stopped and on enquiring what the problem was the uniformed officer told him they were looking for some robbers. He then heard the voice of a CID officer behind say, "He's fucking Irish, he'll do," and he was dragged out of his car in the car park and searched.

During the search and on being arrested on suspicion of being involved in the burglary of The Trident public house, he asked the police woman present to take the cash he had just received from the bank and give it to his wife, explaining that it was money for a pram. However, she refused to take it, whereupon the male officer took the bundle and put it into his pocket. Foran would later learn the officer concerned was called Matthews, who features repeatedly during the saga of each of his convictions.

At that moment Sharon Laing, a friend, was passing and on seeing the commotion, approached the police and asked what they were doing. Foran told her what was happening and asked her to phone his wife and let her know and for her to get in touch with the solicitor who he should have been with by this time. He was then taken to Bradford Street police station and locked in a cell.

His wife received the call and immediately contacted the solicitor to explain what had happened. Meanwhile, while Foran was waiting in his cell, the door opened and an officer put his head round the door and said; "That's it, you've confessed," and shut the cell door again, whereupon Foran simply laughed.

He became concerned as to whether his wife had contacted the solicitor and he needed to know the whereabouts of the money which had been confiscated. He also wanted to know when his solicitor would be arriving so he asked to see the duty inspector, DI Reid.

At approximately four o'clock his solicitor arrived, and Inspector Reid began the interview with his solicitor present. However, he opened by saying that, as Foran had not been interviewed by the officers concerned at the time of his arrest 'on suspicion of robbing the public house', he was unable to discuss that matter but could discuss the missing money. He said he would look into it and let Foran know the outcome. However, no information was ever provided, the money remained missing and was never returned. The police account of the missing money during the trial would be found to be untrue when a letter dated 4th June 1985 from the Crown Court in Birmingham 'appeared' much later after the trial had finished. This letter confirmed that Judge Potter had made an order that £131.55 be returned to Foran;'s wife. A copy of his letter is shown in the next chapter dealing with the court hearing.

According to the police statement subsequently read to the court, DI Matthews, DC Preston, DC Jisra, DC Bartoszewicz, PC Conn and PC Shelley told the court that, based on the claims made by Addison, they waited outside the Riviera café for Foran to arrive which they said he did at five minutes past three. They went on to say that they arrested him on suspicion of robbery and attempted robbery and that he had a bundle of cash on him which he tried to dispose of while getting out of the car. They said they recovered a knife, two screwdrivers, two crowbars and a crash helmet from his car.

It is at this point that the evidence of the police and Foran's description diverge. Foran made it clear that he had not been anywhere near The Trident and protested that the police evidence could not conceivably be true as the timings could not possibly be correct: also that there were witnesses to verify his account.

While giving evidence, the officers said they had arrested and interviewed him at five minutes to three. However, both his solicitor's and Inspector Reid's notes made it clear that no interview had taken place. Furthermore, as he was on his way to his two o'clock appointment at his solicitors at the time of his arrest, he must have' been arrested before two o'clock and not at three o'clock as they had claimed. Furthermore, the custody records showed he arrived at Bradford Street police station at 3.12, which was at least forty-five minutes later than he actually arrived. If their account was correct, it would also have meant the trip from Hurst Street to Bradford Street took less than seven minutes, which was impossible.

Despite all the evidence to the contrary, he was subsequently charged on 31st December 1984 and committed for trial at the Magistrates' Court in respect of allegations of robbery and conspiracy to rob.

The misleading and downright dishonest evidence given to the court by the police in this case is detailed later.

CHAPTER 7

SECOND TRIAL

The trial commenced on the 29th April 1985. The police said Addison had been interviewed by PC Conn and DC Preston on the 10th September and had signed a statement admitting his involvement in breaking into The Trident public house; also that he said he did it with two other people, one called Andrew McKenzie and the other only known as 'Martin'.

On being asked how they had entered the pub, Addison said that 'Martin' had used an iron bar to remove the wood from around the window while he watched as guard. He went on to say that 'Martin' and McKenzie had gone upstairs and called back down to him telling him to go up and get the money. When he went up to the room he said 'Martin' was threatening the licensee with the iron bar and McKenzie had a knife to his throat.

He also said that before they broke into the pub 'Martin' had told him about another job they were planning on doing later the same day. He said it was a post office where they could get £16,000. The statement went on to say that on being asked how it was going to be done Addison said that 'Martin' and McKenzie were planning to pick him up at three o'clock that day at the Riviera café and they were going to break into the Post Office, while his job was to keep watch, for which he would get £1,000. He then gave the details of 'Martin's' car as being a white Allegro which, of course, he had seen the previous evening.

Despite Foran's denial of having ever been at The Trident and that any interview had ever taken place: which could easily have been confirmed by DI Reid as he had been unable to discuss the robbery with him when Foran's solicitor arrived at four o'clock, DI Matthews produced his official note book written up by him purporting to provide an account of the interview held with Foran at four o'clock on the 10th September in the presence of DC Preston.

In his account he said he told Foran that Addison had made a full confession and implicated Foran in the burglary. He went on to say they had recovered two iron bars and a knife from the car which he believed had been used in the burglary. These were subsequently sent for examination.

His notes also stated that he had recovered just £60 from Foran at the time of his arrest, which, after the trial had finished, would be shown to be untrue.

Matthews' full handwritten notes with typed transcript have been reproduced. Foran has always maintained these were concocted afterwards to use as evidence at his trial and there is substantiating evidence revealed later to support this. Firstly note the dates on which the note book was issued and returned: the book covers a full 6 years, and it was not handed back until 5 years had elapsed after the statement had been recorded.

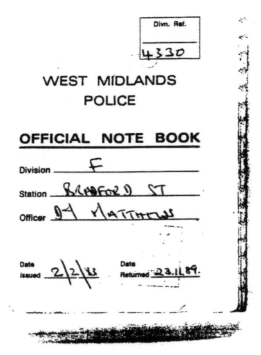

126

been bleaching.
Me What do you mean bleaching.
H. I haven't slept for a few days. You start to lose track of the days.
Me Where were they staying
H Nowhere than just a couch as well.
10.G Concluded.
10.35 Do you wish to make a statement about the robbery. You can write it yourself or I can write it for you.
H Ok, you write it the toast down

127

statement at dictation
DC Walder asked certain questions recorded. Signed and completed by Hammill in my presence.
Concluded 11.0pm
10th Sept 84.

16.00 Saw Martin Foran in cell at Bradford St P Stn will DC Preston.
Me Martin you know why you have been arrested its about the robbery at the pub in Shard End on Saturday night. Caution.
F I wasn't anywhere

10th Sept 84

16.00 Saw Martin FORAN in cell at
       Bradford St P Stn with DC
       Preston.

Me   Martin you know why you have
       been arrested its about the
       robbery at the Pub in Shard
       End on Saturday night.
       Caution.

F   I wasn't anywhere

128

129

near there on Friday anyway
I have ~~had £60 stolen out of~~
my money.

Me   Martin I took possession of
your money and it has been
counted thats all thats
there.

F   You've had £60

Me   If you wish to pursue that
allegation then ask to see
the uniform inspector but I
am interested in what you
were doing on Saturday night.
Not Friday

F   I don't want to say.

Me   Where did you get whatever
amount of money you say you
had on you today.

F   I borrowed it a few weeks ago

Me   How much

F   £200

Me   Where from

F   Provident I've got the card.

Me   Martin we have arrested Paul
Allison and he has made a
statement implicating you in
the robbery at

114

130

131

the pub and also in conspiring
to commit a robbery this
afternoon at a post office in
Water Orton you were going to
meet him when we arrested you.

F   I don't believe you thats
     fanny.

M   I have here a copy of the
     statement he has made, I will
     read it through to you and you
     can follow it as I read.
     Read statement

at conclusion. Caution.
What can I say to all there
isn't it.

Me   It is correct then

F   Im not saying anything. Look
     I know about it you know I help
     the police I can get the
     coloured lad for you.

Me   At the moment its your part
     I am interested in.

F   Im not saying anything you cant
     charge me on just that.

Me   We have recovered

132

[handwritten notes]

133

[handwritten notes]

two iron bars and a knife
from the car what about those.

F   I've told you I'm not saying
anything I want a brief.

Me   Anybody in particular

F   Yes Ron PARKER

Me   Very well if you want to see 6.15
me with your solicitor let
me know.

F   I won't want to you've got 7.30
fuck all evidence.

Me   If you want to persue your
allegation of theft. You
can request to see the

Uniform inspector or your
solicitor can make the
allegation on your behalf but
in any event you will be
charged with the robbery and
conspiracy to commit robbery
concluded   -
      Christopher Preston DC627
End   A/Det Supt
10/9/84

116

58

Foran never wavered in his denial that any interview had taken place, similarly that he had not seen any statement made by Addison.

He was sure his innocence could be proved and there were several issues that supported this view.

- In Clowes' (licensee) statement he had described Foran as West Indian with a Birmingham accent whereas Foran was white with a heavy Irish accent;
- The fact that he had visited the Provident Building Society and obtained £200 could be substantiated;
- The taxi driver could prove his whereabouts that night;
- His daughter, niece and their friends could verify his story;
- His solicitor could prove the time of their interview with DI Reid;
- Sharon Laing could prove the car park to be the place where he was arrested;
- Forensics on the equipment in the back of his car could show they were not used.

As he was powerless while confined, he decided to hire a private investigator to find witnesses to the robbery and the time he was at the Riviera Café in order to bolster his case. He also requested legal Counsel through his solicitors Eagle & Boyers and told them he required a full and detailed defence to be prepared so defence witnesses could be called, together with any supporting evidence contradicting the police statements.

It became clear Eagle & Boyers did not agree with Foran's plans but they did write to Counsel to obtain their opinion as to whether or not a full defence was necessary. However, in their brief to Counsel they made the following comments:–

- In their view because the witnesses were either members of Foran's family or friends, their evidence would be 'less compelling';
- They also said that when his previous conviction and imprisonment was revealed for similar offences it would count against him;
- They stated: 'Foran has an appalling record having served 10 years imprisonment for robbery';

- They recommended Foran should give no evidence at the trial;
- They described Foran in the brief as 'a suspicious and demanding individual who needs careful handling';
- They instructed the private investigator hired by Foran to take no further action until Counsel had considered the case (see below).

John F. Hope
Investigators & Solicitors Agents

P.O. Box 33, Smethwick, · Room 215 Gazette Building,
Warley, 168 Corporation Street,
West Midlands B67 5ER. Birmingham B4 6TF.

Tel: (021) 420 3547 (24hrs) Tel: 021 233 4340

Please reply to: BIRMINGHAM.

Our Ref: JFH/SIM. Your Ref: Date: 25th January 1985.

Mr. Martin Foran, C51796,
H.M. Prison,
Winson Green Road,
Birmingham, B18 4AS.

Dear Mr. Foran,

I have received further communication from Mr. Parker, who informs me that at the moment we are waiting from an opinion from Counsel as to the points that have been raised by yourself.

Mr. Parker has asked me if this matter can be left in abeyance for the time being but that he will let us know the position as soon as possible.

Basically what this means is that the Brief who will be in Court wants to decide what steps have to be taken.

Yours faithfully,

JOHN F. HOPE.

Members of
West Midlands Chamber of Commerce & Industry
Bund Internationaler Detektive E.V.
World Association of Detectives.

Clearly, they were trying to discourage Foran's request for a full defence. Foran knew nothing of this and didn't see their brief but Counsel did agree to speak to him, during which meeting they said they would do their best to get him acquitted.

The trial date duly arrived, and after the first day his Counsel sought a meeting with the presiding Judge. Later he approached Foran saying he had 'good news'. He explained that he had reached an agreement with the Judge that if Foran pleaded guilty, the Judge would sentence him to just three years.

Foran was incensed at this and fired his barrister on the spot saying that they had obviously not believed in his innocence from the outset and that he was certainly not going to plead guilty to something he took no part in. He then elected to run his own defence using the same solicitor.

Unfortunately, the lines were drawn preventing the introduction of new evidence and witnesses so he had to rely on challenging existing statements. He also had no idea of the briefing his solicitor had given counsel.

The judge was informed of this dramatic change in circumstances and allowed him to run his own defence using Eagle & Boyars as instructing solicitors. Even if Foran had known about their lack of confidence in him and his case, it would have been difficult, if not impossible to instruct new solicitors at such a late stage and he wanted to get the trial over and done with as soon as possible.

During the remainder of the trial, Foran claimed repeatedly that he had been framed by the police for both his first conviction and now this one. He cross-examined DI Matthews and DC Preston on the grounds that the interview described by them had not, in fact, taken place.

He went on to challenge them about the money which he claimed had gone missing and about the times they gave for his arrest and their arrival at the police station. Neither of these times, he said, could possibly be true [for the reasons described previously].

There should only have been one custody sheet, which the police acknowledged. Yet, in his case, there were two.

Furthermore, that these were fraudulent and not the original ones. The evidence to prove this only subsequently became clear as we now have copies of both the fraudulent ones which are clearly different, and obviously had been changed to suit their evidence. They have been reproduced at the end of this chapter: the insertions and changes can be clearly seen. Foran has always maintained that neither of these was, in fact, the real one which they must have destroyed as it would have falsified their account of the timing of his arrest and arrival at the police station.

He also cross-examined Addison who withdrew his allegation that the person he referred to as 'Martin' was in fact Foran and confirmed to the Court that he definitely wasn't.

His solicitor, Mr Daniels, who attended the police station, then gave evidence and maintained that he had arrived at the police station at least thirty minutes before the police records showed he had.

Foran's niece, Julie, was called to give evidence at the Crown Court and, during my interview with her, she explained what happened and the evidence she gave as follows:

She said that she had to remain outside the courtroom with a lady solicitor as she was not allowed to have contact with the defendant or any of the other witnesses at the trial. While she was waiting with her solicitor the 'white lad', who she recognised from the previous night when her uncle's car had broken down, walked past, and when he saw her she said he looked shocked. All she remembers at that point was that there was a bit of a commotion and her solicitor talked to someone, who she thinks was his solicitor, who remarked that the 'white lad' wanted to change his evidence. Clearly the fact he had seen her there had troubled him.

After giving her evidence, she remained in the court and listened to the remaining witnesses being cross-examined and she recognised the grey man, who had been sitting in the Riviera café who was able to verify Foran's account. She says she listened as his account was 'ripped apart' by prosecution counsel.

She also attended court during the sentencing and said she could not understand how the jury could come to the conclusion that he was guilty. She said the whole thing resembled a fairy story which she knew to be untrue, having been with her uncle on the night in question together with his daughter and their friends.

What we do know from subsequent court evidence is that Addison had changed his evidence on more than one occasion as this was mentioned in the Judge's summing up to the jury when he told them they should regard Addison's evidence with caution as he was a youth 'who had told lies and frequently changed his story'.

He also said that Foran's interview with the police was extremely important, saying that he was making 'the usual kind of complaint against the police'.

Twenty years later, during the appeals, both of these directions were described as prejudicing Foran's defence.

The taxi driver, Foran's daughter and their friends were not called to give evidence, and Barry Parker, who eventually took him home, was also not called. However, the grey haired man who Julie had seen sitting in the Riviera café was called and he confirmed he had seen Foran in the café at the time of The Trident robbery.

Foran knew that he had an arrangement to meet with his solicitor and thought that Eagle & Boyars would be able to uphold this claim. However, they told the police they had no record of having asked him to contact them to arrange an appointment. Foran became suspicious at this time that there must be collusion in some way between his solicitor and the police. He would later discover that one of the firm's female solicitors was the girlfriend of a member of the SCS and he maintains to this day that much of the evidence that he was using in his various cases against the police were being leaked to them beforehand so they knew every detail of his defence.

It was months later that the letter asking him to make an appointment was eventually found by Valerie.

Most significantly, no forensic report on the tools in the boot of Foran's car was produced by the police as evidence of his involvement. The reason for this would only become clear long after he had served his sentence, when their report would be 'found'. The 'discovery' was twenty years later during his appeal and would show the tools could not have been used in the robbery. This would prove to be one of several pivotal issues which would eventually quash his conviction.

Years later, long after the trial had finished yet another piece of evidence would surface. Judge Potter, who presided at the hearing, ordered that money to the amount of £131.55 should be returned to Foran's wife. This shows that DI Matthews' statement that only £60 was recovered to be blatantly false.

The documents which were 'unavailable' to be used during his trial but were eventually 'uncovered' follow.

Fig. 1

Solicitors	Commissioners for Oaths

Boyars

John A. Eagle
Alan L. Boyars
Ron Parker LL.B.
Alan P. Parker LL.B.

St. Martins House
10 Bull Ring
Birmingham B5 5DR
Telephone 021-643 3186

Our Ref. 4/5192-3-4/DF/JP   Your Ref.

20th August 1984

Mr Martin Foran
32 Acacia Avenue
Kingshurst
Birmingham

Dear Martin

Just a brief line to confirm that the motoring summonses against you at Birmingham Magistrates Court were adjourned until the 14th September 1984 at 2.00 pm.

Could you please telephone me and make arrangements to see me some time before that date so that I can take full instructions from you.

I look forward to hearing from you.

Kind Regards.

Yours sincerely

Dot Flanagan

Letter showing the solicitors knew an appointment had been requested

7/f
20/9/84

Officer i/c
PC 1550 Conn
Bradford Street

KEITH GRAHAM BARNETT MSc LRSC

over 21

Forensic Scientist

1

xxxxx

20   September 1984

On the 13th September 1984 the following items were received at

the laboratory from PC Conn, of the West Midlands Police, 'F' Division:-

TC1   Crow bar

TC2   Crow bar

TC3   Screwdriver

TC4   Knife

TC5   Screwdriver

JP1   Wooden beading

The wooden beading JP1 bears a number of instrument marks which

could have been made by a screwdriver. However, none of the screwdrivers

or other items submitted could have made these marks.

THE CROWN COURT
2nd Floor Victoria Law Courts Corporation Street
Birmingham B4 6QA

Telephone 021-236 9751

From the Chief Clerk

Mr. M. P. Foran,
C/o H. M. Prison,
Winson Green,
BIRMINGHAM B18 4AJ.

Your reference

Our reference BR/ADD

Date 4th June, 1985.

Dear Sir,

With reference to your letter received in this
office on 29th May, 1985. I confirm that on the 10th
May, 1985. His Honour Judge Potter made an order that
the money (£131.55) referred to as Exhibit 5 in the
above case, be returned to your wife.

This money should be claimed from the police.

Yours faithfully,

B. Roulstone (Mrs)
(for Chief Clerk)

The following letter from Foran's solicitors shows they had the
receipt for the money he received from the Provident building
Society, which the police had said was the proceeds from the
burglary.

Solicitors		Commissioners for Oaths

| **Eagle & Boyars** | John A. Eagle
Alan L. Boyars
Ron Parker LL.B.
Alan P. Parker LL.B. | St. Martins House
10 Bull Ring
Birmingham B5 5DR
Telephone 021-643 3186 |

Our Ref. 4/RP/AF   Your Ref.

Mr. M P Foran
C51796
H.M. Prison Winson Green
Winson Green Road
BIRMINGHAM
B18 4AS.   21st January 1985

Dear Martin

Thank you for your recent letters regarding your case. I have indeed heard from the Enquiry Agent, and have advised Mr. Hope that it will be a matter for Counsel initially as to his instructions.

In respect of your comments regarding your previous Trial and the use of identical words by the Officer, I of course would have no comment to make in terms of you obtaining a copy of any statement, but I must of course make the obvious comment that to produce such a document in evidence will tell the Jury quite clearly that you were involved in that previous Trial and its nature. I would have thought that it was at the least debatable whether that was in your best interests.

In respect of your previous letter, I acknowledge receipt of the Provident receipt together with a copy of the receipt from the Garage. I note your comments regarding detained property which will be taken up with the appropriate quarter.

I can confirm that the papers will shortly be delivered to your Barrister, and I trust that an early conference can be arranged. I note your comments regarding the pressure upon your wife and yourself contained in your last letter, and will do all that I can to assist. I trust this will be satisfactory.

Kind regards

Yours sincerely

Ron Parker

pRon Parker.

When calling or telephoning on this matter please ask for M

The following witness statement would be produced showing that he had called out the AA to attend his vehicle at the time he stated.

STATEMENT OF WITNESS

(C.J. Act 1967, s.9; M.C. Act 1980, s.102; M.C. Rules 1981, r.70)

NAME:.....MERIEL ELIZABETH NEWMAN.............................

AGE:......18.....................DATE OF BIRTH:..16.5.66..............
OCCUPATION:.....SECRETARY.....................................

ADDRESS:...C/O EAGLE & BOYARS, SOLICITORS, ST. MARTINS HOUSE,

........10 BULL RING, BIRMINGHAM B5 5DR.....................

TELEPHONE NUMBER:......021.643.3186............................

This statement consisting of   pages each signed by me is true to the best of my knowledge and belief and I make it knowing that, if it is tendered in evidence, I shall be liable to prosecution if I have wilfully stated in it anything which I know to be false or do not believe to be true.

Dated this   day of   1985

Signed:......................

Signature witnessed by:......................

I am employed by Eagle & Boyars, Solicitors, as a Secretary.

On the 17th October 1984 I was instructed by my Principal to telephone the A.A. Records Department and request certain information.

I spoke with a Mr. John Reeves at the A.A. and asked him to check the records for the evening of the 8th September/morning of the 9th September 1984, and confirm whether or not an A.A. Engineer attended vehicle registration no. HDA 104N Austin Allegro (white) in Hurst Street, Birmingham.

I explained that the information was needed by Eagle & Boyars as they were acting on behalf of a client charged with a criminal offence alleged to have been committed at a time when he was waiting for the A.A. to attend his broken down motor vehicle.

I exhibit herewith my original handwritten telephone message, taken at the time of the conversation with Mr. Reeves.

Signed:................ Signature witnessed by:................

But all this was too late for Foran. The trial started on Tuesday, 29th April and lasted three days. On 3rd May 1985 Foran was convicted on two counts of robbery and conspiracy to rob and on the 10th May, he was sentenced to 8 years imprisonment. This was later increased to 14 years for reasons described in chapter 11.

STATEMENT OF WITNESS

(C.J. Act, 1967, s.9; M.C. Act 1980, s.102; M.C. Rules 1981, r.70)

Continuation of statement of ....MERIEL ELIZABETH NEWMAN.............

The telephone message reads:

"17.10.84, conversation with Mr. Reeves of A.A. at Dog Kennel
Lane, Halesowen, Phone 550 4858. Re: Martin Foran. Yes, they
have a call logged from a M. Foran of 32 Acacia Avenue, Kingshurst.
The call was logged as coming in at 1.18 a.m. on the 9th September
1984. The Engineer who dealt with matter reported back in
at 2.14 a.m. The car was a white 1300 Austin Allegro, HDA
104N. Meriel".

The telephone message was then handed to my Principal, and
subsequently filed.

I am willing to attend Court if necessary.

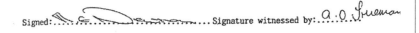

Signed:................................Signature witnessed by:..a..o. Freeman

Foran went on to endure his second term of imprisonment,
another 11 years, in circumstances that can only be described
as 'a living hell'.

The doctored evidence of Foran's arrest

The following arrest and charge sheets are the ones that were
used as evidence, neither of which is likely to be the original.
The changes that were made to suit the evidence of the police
officers are clear on close examination.

In order to make them easier to follow we have set out
page one of each document first and then page two. The areas
of obvious discrepancy which demonstrate they could not
possibly be copies of the same document are ringed, and if you
look closely at the two documents you will be able to spot
many more.

The two documents are clear forgeries but for reasons
unknown, the lawyers acting for Foran did not review them or
call for them to be used as evidence in Foran's defence.

First arrest sheet page 1

No 1

EST MIDLANDS POLICE

DIVISION ___ F.

SUB. DI

N

1 PERSON DETAINED

NAME	Surname. FORAN.
	Forenames. MARTIN PATRICK
ADDRESS	32 ACACIA AVENUE.
	KINGS HURST BIRMINGHAM
ADDRESS Verified by:	DC. O'CONNOR
NEXT OF KIN (Mr/Mrs/Miss)	
INFORMED BY	Time
OCCUPATION	UNEMPLOYED.
DATE & PLACE BORN	23/2/44 EIRE. Sex M.
Height	5'9. Build STOCKY
Eyes	BROWN Complexion CLEAR.
Marks & Peculiarities	OPERATION SCAR ON STOMACHE

Indicate if person detained holds Firearm/Shotgun/Explosives Certificate or Licence. (If so Firearms Department, Headquarters to be notified) — YES/NO

Indicate if wanted on warrant (See S.O. G.1.) — YES/NO

2 ACTION

ARRESTED By Whom	PC 1550 CONN.
Place	HURST STREET.
time	1505 date 10/9/84.
Signature and No. of arresting officer	PC 1550
ARRIVED AT STATION time	1512. date 10/9/84.
Signature & No. of Stn. officer accepting person detained	R J Williams PC6714.
FORMALLY CHARGED/ CHARGE REFUSED time	2100 AM date 10.9.84
Signature & No. of station officer	P Craig A/PS. 3/10
BAILED/LIBERATED time	
Signature & No. of Stn. officer	date

4 PE

SEARC

THIS F

Prisone

Witness (Signat

VARIA

Time & Date

VARIA
Time & Date

1910.

15/7/8

2250
10/9

3 REASON FOR ARREST/DETENTION ROBBERY

BRIEF DETAILS OF OFFENCE
(e.g. S.18. Wounding, Theft)

(*Give details in Section 5)

√		
	Arrest and charged with offence	
	Arrest on warrant — attach warrant	
*	Arrest and charge refused	
*	Arrest and bailed pending further enquiries S38(2)	
	Arrest and released pending decision as to process	
*	*Arrest and handed over to another Force	
	Absconder/Escapee from Prison/Borstal /Mental Hospital	
	Absentee or deserter from HM Forces	
	Juveniles taken into custody in need of care	
0	Arrest under Mental Health Acts	

31/
/12

5 OT

RE

CD

First arrest sheet page 1 cont.

RECORD OF PERSON IN CUSTODY (amended 1.81)

...SIONAL No. F2/884/84. LOCK-UP No.

...SONAL PROPERTY FOUND ON PRISONER ... 12.5mm N/9

...ED BY: CONN. RANK & NO: PC 1550. TIME: 1513 DATE: 10/9/84.

...CORD OF MY PROPERTY IS CORRECT

CASH 00

PERSONAL PROPERTY OTHER THAN CASH — As detailed below

Item No: 1–6.

Signature (REFUSED) TO SIGN.
CASH IN CDP 200424 (£131·55)

...ON MOVEMENT AND DISPOSAL OF CASH

Reason for variation movement or disposal	Amount £ p	Signature of prisoner & police officer	Balance £ p
		New Seal number	
		New Seal number	
		New Seal number	
		New Seal number	

1   BELT
2   IRISH DRIVING LICENCE
3   VEHICLE REG
4   MOT
5   COMB
6   6 CASSETTE TAPES IN CASE
    X REFUSED TO SIGN.

17 ✓
18 ✓
19
20 ✓
21 *
22
23

6 lb. S. Mince meat

ON MOVEMENT AND DISPOSAL OTHER THAN CASH

Reason for variation movement or disposal	Item No:	Signature of prisoner & police officer	
Mr. S. Smith SOL: for.	10.		New Seal number
Sealed Bag TO L/U			New Seal number
HMP.	1.2. 3.4 +6	REFUSED. 9420 C1951.	New Seal number
			New Seal number

Seal Security number 002613

6 PROPERTY SUBJECT OF CHARGE
Crime Property Book Ref. F2/200424/84

7 DO SPECIAL WARNINGS APPLY — YES ✓ NO
e.g. tends to violence, suicide, escaping, mental/physical illness, false allegat
IF "YES" AFFIX GUMMED DISC AT RIGHT CORNER OF SHEET and enter details at "other information" overleaf.

8 FORMS ISSUED TO PRISONER
Notice of Charge/Bail by: .... Date: ....
(WG 421)
Legal Aid form by: .... Date: ....
Liability for deportation (WC 343) by: .... Date: ....
WG 582 (S.62 CRIMINAL LAW ACT 1977)
Issued by: 674 Time: 1517 Date: 10/
Reason for any delay in complying with request for intimation of applica

...ER INFORMATION – Reasons for Refused Charge etc.

...INED) ITEM 5.
F2/200424/84 TO (SAFE)

...en would not sign because
...ed all property including
A.P. item

NO REQUEST

"Reasonably named person" message sent.

Second arrest sheet page 1

WEST MIDLANDS POLICE

DIVISION F

No 2

1 PERSON DETAINED

NAME
Surname: FORAN
Forenames: MARTIN PATRICK

ADDRESS
32 ACACIA AVENUE
KINGSHURST BIRMINGHAM

ADDRESS Verified by: X O'CONNOR

NEXT OF KIN (Mr/Mrs/Miss)

INFORMED BY — Time

OCCUPATION — UNEMPLOYED

DATE & PLACE BORN — 27/2/44 EIRE — Sex M

Height — 5'9" Build — STOCKY

Eyes — BROWN Complexion — CLEAR

Marks & Peculiarities — OPERATION SCAR ON STOMACH

Indicate if person detained holds Firearm/Shotgun/Explosives Certificate or Licence. (If so Firearms Department, Headquarters to be notified) — YES/NO

Indicate if wanted on warrant (See S.O. G.1.) — YES/NO

2 ACTION

ARRESTED By Whom — PC 1550 CONN

Place — 19 HURST STREET

time — 1505 date 10/9/84

Signature and No. of arresting officer — CONN P. 1550

ARRIVED AT STATION time — 1512 date 10/9/84

Signature & No. of Stn. officer accepting person detained — WILLIAMS PC6714

FORMALLY CHARGED/ CHARGE REFUSED time — date

Signature & No. of station officer

BAILED/LIBERATED time — date

Signature & No. of Stn. officer

3 REASON FOR ARREST/DETENTION

BRIEF DETAILS OF OFFENCE
(e.g. S.18, Wounding, Theft)

(*Give details in Section 5*)

1	Arrest and charged with offence
2	Arrest on warrant — attach warrant
3*	Arrest and charge refused
4*	Arrest and bailed pending further enquiries S33(2)
5*	Arrest and released pending decision as to process
6*	Arrest and handed over to another Force
7	Abscondee/Escapee from Prison/Borstal /Mental Hospital
8	Absentee or deserter from HM Forces
9	Juveniles taken into custody in need of care
10	Arrest under Mental Health Acts

Second arrest sheet page 1 cont'd

First arrest sheet page 2

FORAN

VISITS TO AND MOVEMENTS OF PRISONER

To commence with time of arrival at Station, where detained, movement within the Station, time placed in cell, meals, visits of solicitors, doctors or removal to court or Lock-Up, remand to and from Prison, committal, liberation, etc.

Date & Time	By Whom	Remarks	Date & Time	By Whom
1512	PC 1550	TO DOCK + SEARCH	10/9 2210	7494
1520	6714	TO CELL	10/9 2243	7494
1600	DC MATTHEWS DC PRESTON	INTERVIEW IN CELL	10/9 1050	7494
1615	2916	INTERVIEW CONCLUDED		
1635	2916	REQUESTED SOLICITOR	✓	
		DI MATTHEWS - INFORMED		
1700	PC 1550	MR PARKER EAGLE + BYAS X INFORMED		
1755	6714	INTERVIEW IN X CELL WITH SOLICITOR X (MR) DANIELS ✓		
1828	2916	INTERVIEW TERMINATED ✓		
1836	2916	FURTHER INTERVIEW BY X SOLICITORS		
1843	2916	INTERVIEW TERMINATED		
1847	2916	TO INTERVIEW ROOM WITH		
		INSP REA'S SOLICITOR		
1910	2916	INTERVIEW TERMINATED		
		RETURNED TO CELL		
1912	6714	GIVEN MEAL + WATER X		
1923	1550/2916	CLEANED F/C + PHOTO'D		
		ALL OTHER DETAILS		
2015	2916	PLACED IN ORDER		
2100	2916	CHARGED		

OTHER INFORMATION — Details of any illness, injury, any arrangement

DETENTION OVER 4 HOURS
REASON FURTHER ENQUIRIES
AUTHORISED BY INSP
INSP
Time 1920HR Date 10. 9. 84.

74

First arrest sheet page 2 cont

No 1

r persons, interviews.

Prisoners should be visited at least once each hour. In the case of drunken persons visits should be made at not less than half-hour intervals. More frequent visits may be necessary. (See Standing Order G4, Paragraphs 7 - 14).

Remarks	Date & Time	By Whom	Remarks
asleep on bench.			
asleep onself.			
C/up			

VARIATION MOVEMENT AND DISPOSAL OF CASH *Continued from overleaf*

Time & Date	Reason for variation movement or disposal	Amount £ p	Signature of prisoner & police officer	Balance £ p
			New Seal number	
			New Seal number	
de for escort etc.			New Seal number	

VARIATION MOVEMENT AND DISPOSAL OTHER THAN CASH *Continued from overleaf*

Time & Date	Reason for variation movement or disposal	Item Nos.	Signature of prisoner & police officer
			New Seal number
			New Seal number
			New Seal number

Second arrest sheet page 2

MOVEMENTS OF PRISONER

with time of arrival at Station, where detained, movement within the Station, time placed in cell, meals, visits of solicitors, doctor, court or Lock-Up, remand to and from Prison, committal, liberation, etc.

Date & Time	By Whom	Remarks	Date & Time	By Wh
1512 ¼/x	PC 1550	(TO) DOCK + SEARCH	10/9 22 10	7.1.11
1520 x	6714	(TO) CELL	10/9 2147	7.1.11
1600 x	DE MATTHEWS x DC PRESTON	INTERVIEW IN CELL	x	
(1615)	2916	(INTERVIEW CONCLUDED)		
1635	2916	Requests Solicitor	✓	
		D.I. MATTHEWS - INFORMED		
1700 –//–	PC 1550	MR PARKER EAGLE + BYNS INFORMED	x	
1755 –//–	6714	INTERVIEW IN CELL WITH SOLICITOR (MR) DANIELS.		
1828 –//–	2916	Interview Terminated		
1836 –//–	2916	Further Interview by Someone		
1843 –//–	2916	Interview Terminated		
1847 –//–	2916	To Interview Room when		
–//–	x	his Cell, Solicitor		
1910	2916	Interview Terminated		
–//–		Returned to Cell		
1912	6714	Given Meal y water		
1923	1550/2916	Received files, Photos.		
		As other Details.		
2055	2916	Checked In Order		
2100	2916	Charged.		

OTHER INFORMATION — Details of any illness, injury, any arrangem

DETENTION OVER 4 HOURS

REASON Further Enquiries to Cell

AUTHORISED BY: INSP. [illegible] INSP.

Time 1920 hrs Date 10. 9. 84

40

Second arrest sheet page 2 cont'd

CHAPTER 8

HIS FIRST SUICIDE ATTEMPT

Winson Green

O nce again, on 10th May 1985, the doors of Winson Green prison clanged shut behind him. Depression and demoralisation would not adequately describe his feelings at this time. He was still very ill with ulcerated colitis from the treatment he had received during his first conviction, but he maintains that it was not just the physical maladies that affected him. In addition to the hunger strikes and beatings he received, he said prisoners would receive water with diluted aspirin in it but, in the case of the Irish prisoners, they would put Jeyes Fluid in theirs, and he believes this was the main cause for his prolapse and the acidic liquid that would seep from his wound following his eventual colostomy.

He simply could not come to terms with the fact that he was to serve another long term of imprisonment for a second conviction inflicted on him by the police. He was, by now, a broken man and after the first day of the trial he concluded he was going to lose the case and remembers what happened next vividly.

On Tuesday, 30th April 1985, after the first day of the trial had ended, he arrived back in his cell and was at his lowest point. Having heard the evidence from the police, he sensed his word would not be believed against those of the representatives of the Serious Crime Squad. What had been exultation at experiencing his freedom for the first time in years and with a new beginning to his life looming; being able to re-join his family to take up his responsibilities as a father, once again, it looked like being snatched from him. He kept asking himself: 'Why me?' 'What have I done to deserve this?' Nothing seemed to make sense. All he did know was that the West Midlands Serious Crime Squad was out to get him no matter what. With these dark thoughts, sitting in his cell alone, and with the next few days of the trial still to come he made a decision.

He grabbed the note book he had brought with him and began to write: firstly a note to his wife, followed by another to his daughter Joanne. He then wrote one to his son, Martin, and another to his daughter Valerie. Two further letters were written to his brother and mother and, finally, he wrote one to his sister, Irene.

He put the note book down and took a sheet from his bed and ripped it into strips. He tied one end to the bars of his cell window and climbed onto the sill. Wrapping it tightly around his neck, he jumped. To his dismay, the sheet tore and he hit the floor.

Undaunted, he decided if the sheet was wet it would be stronger, so he soaked it in the basin in his cell and tried again but it failed once again. However, after this second attempt, his rectal prolapse dropped through his back passage and he was hopping round the cell in agony. While hopping around the floor he caught sight of himself in the reflection in the green cell door and, suddenly and unaccountably, he found himself beginning to laugh in the middle of his agony. He couldn't understand what was happening: how or why he was laughing in the midst of such pain, or how it was he had survived two attempts at taking his own life.

However, a surreal explanation would be provided about two years later while embarking on another of his many hunger strikes. He experienced something which would affect him for the rest of his life. It was a moving experience of which he has never spoken until now other than to his wife Valerie, and is described later in Chapter 14. He knew that, alongside his instinct to go on fighting and the unquestioning deep love and fighting spirit of Valerie to keep going, there was now something extra, different and inexplicable to him, that was telling him not to give in.

The letters he wrote were kept secret from everyone, including his family, but he has authorised their inclusion for which I am delighted. They are not only very moving but explain better than any words I could write his mental state at that time. A copy of his shortest letter is reproduced here so you have an indication of how he was feeling at that time: the full text of all his letters is shown at Appendix 2.

CHAPTER 9

HIS FIRST 'HOSTAGE'?

Winson Green

The agony of his prolapse and lack of proper treatment while at Winson Green caused him severe depression and almost became too much for him to bear during 1985. However, there was something to look forward to, in that his eldest son Martin's birthday was coming up on 8th December and he couldn't wait to put his arms around him and give him a birthday hug.

On the 12th December Valerie and their son visited the prison. The anticipation overcame everything, including the pain from his prolapse, which had still not been treated. On learning of their arrival he was taken to the visitors room but was horrified to see they had taken him to a Category 'A' visitors room instead of the usual one. These were in separate cubicles with a chair and table on Foran's side of a glass screen and the same on Valerie's side so they were unable to touch each other.

In addition, when Valerie and his son saw the state he was in they were concerned and wanted to provide some comfort to him. After talking for about ten minutes, the difficulty they had in hearing each other and the inability to touch caused both Valerie and their son to become upset, and Foran desperately wanted to hug his son after his birthday.

He asked the prison officers why they had been brought to a Category 'A' room instead of the normal visitors' room and the response he received was simply that he had ten minutes so he'd better get on with it. Foran explains what happened next as, simply, 'something just snapped inside me'.

He stood up, took hold of his chair and threw it through the glass screen, then jumped through and cuddled them both. He said, 'I just had to do that so I could be close and talk to them.'

He barricaded them in the room to prevent the prison officers removing him. Valerie also intervened and demanded to see the Medical Officer and prison Governor as she wanted some questions answered as to why he was not being treated properly for his medical condition.

Foran said that he would come peacefully if one or both of them came to explain to his wife why he had not received the necessary treatment.

The Assistant Governor arrived and asked him to release his hostages but both Valerie and their son told the Governor that they were not hostages but were there of their own free will, and required answers.

The Assistant Governor eventually called for Dr Martin, the Medical Officer, to come and arrange for him to be assessed whereupon Foran left peacefully.

As Dr Martin's letter shows, he did escort him away and examine him and said he would arrange to have him further examined by a specialist. He also spoke to Valerie and her son in the presence of a member of the Board of Visitors to explain what he planned to do. It is also clear from Dr Martin's letter that Valerie had not felt in the least bit threatened and she was delighted she had achieved her objective of getting her husband the treatment he needed. However, Dr Martin's letter to the Governor also made it clear they wanted rid of him.

Some weeks later, Foran learned from Valerie that after the incident, she was taken to the ordinary Visitors room and asked to press charges against him for taking her hostage. Obviously, she refused any such suggestion.

This, of course, would have been a serious charge and would have led to an extension of his prison term. As it was, it cost him the remission he might otherwise have been granted.

However, this did not stop the prison entering into his records that he had taken his wife and son hostage and this would be a further offence that would follow him throughout his transfers from prison to prison.

MEMORANDUM

From Dr J P Martin
Medical Officer
H M Prison
Birmingham

Telephone 021-554 3838

Extension 216

To The Governor
H M Prison
Birmingham

Your reference

Our reference JPM/MMW

Date 13 December 1985

REPORT ON HOSTAGE SITUATION 12.12.85.
C51796 - Martin Patrick FORAN

At approximately 4.00 p.m. on 12.12.85. I was called to the Secure Unit visiting area where Foran was holding his wife and son hostage. Within half an hour of my arrival Foran had released his hostages and came out of his own volition. This was due to talking to the Assistant Governor.

At the Governor's request I escorted Foran to 'D' Wing where I examined him and found there were no marks of injury but he was discharging per rectum with a blood stained discharge which was more copious that I have ever known from this patient. I recorded this and then went to see Mrs Foran in the presence of a member of the Board of Visitors, at the request of the Governor. Mrs Foran and her son did not seem unduly worried about themselves and did not appear to want me to examine them, so I did not persist in this. I tried to reassure her as much as possible and promised her that her husband's medical needs were being adequately treated. I did not make any comments about allegations made about the early part of the day and the reasons why Foran had acted in this manner. Mrs Foran seemed to accept this.

I then felt in view of the copious blood stained discharge I would seek an independent medical opinion from Dudley Road Hospital. I arranged for Mr J Randall, FRCS, Surgical Registrar, of that Hospital to visit Foran. He arrived at approximately 5.45 p.m. He examined Foran and felt that he was suffering from a possible ulcerative proctitis after examining him with a proctoscope.

He suggested that we restart the Salazopyrin and for him to start Predsol enemas. He also offered to expedite an appointment with a Consultant and suggested he would ask Mr Donovan, in whom Foran has the greatest faith, to see him urgently. I had also made arrangements for Foran to have a high fibre diet, an adequate supply of towels, and be allowed a bath. By this I am not saying that these were not already available, but I made sure they were.

I feel that the future disposal of Foran - i.e. transfer to another establishment - is a matter also for the Senior Medical Officer of Birmingham Prison to discuss with the Governor and no decision should be made until Dr Rahman is consulted.

(J P Martin)
MB ChB
Medical Officer

CHAPTER 10

POLICE COVER-UPS

Winson Green

Foran was planning to bring a case against the five officers who had committed perjury in order to secure his conviction, in particular DI Matthews, who he regarded as the prime motivator. He was determined to show that the police involved had concocted their evidence, and there were two key pieces of information he had gained to strengthen his case.

He discovered that Matthews had been suspended from duty as a result of disciplinary enquiries against him and he let this be known, as he wanted to use it as a strong part of his appeal to have his conviction overturned.

Having been in contact with members of the 'Birmingham Six', Foran also made it clear that some of the officers he had cited as being involved in his conviction were the same officers who were involved in the fraudulent evidence which led to their wrongful conviction. He therefore contacted William Whitlock MP, who had been sympathetic to his plight previously, and made this fact known to him.

What was to follow would be more attempts by the police to cover their tracks, this time by top ranking officers who also joined in the cover-up.

As a result of Foran's claim that Matthews had been suspended, the Criminal Appeal Office wrote to the Chief Constable of the West Midlands Police on the 14th April 1986 seeking confirmation that this was the case. Three days later they received a response assuring them that this was not true and that there was no likelihood that such an event would take place.

Copies of both these letters follow:

CRIMINAL APPEAL OFFICE

Royal Courts of Justice

Strand, London WC2A 2LL Tel 01-936 6388

If telephoning please ask for: Mr(s) Miss ....

or .... Section, Listing Room ext ....

The Chief Constable
West Midlands Police
P.O. Box 52, Lloyd House
Colmore Circus Queensway
Birmingham B4 6NQ

All letters should be addressed
to THE REGISTRAR

Our reference: 3250 C2 85
Your reference:

14th April 1986

Dear Sir,

Regina v Martin Patrick Foran

On 3rd May 1985 in the Crown Court at Birmingham the above-named was convicted of robbery and conspiracy to rob. On 10th May he was sentenced to a total of 8 years imprisonment. He now seeks leave to appeal against his conviction.

One of the prosecution witnesses at the trial was Detective Inspector Paul Joseph Matthews.

In his grounds, the applicant alleges that this officer has since been suspended from duty.

As the Court may wish to know more about this would you please let me know if what the applicant says is correct and, if it is, supply brief details of the complaint against the officer and the outcome of any disciplinary proceedings, and say whether there is to be, or has been, a prosecution.

Yours faithfully,

T S G Midia

```
                                                    32-3 02 35
   to De                                                 
   Office                                            777/24/211 223
   Royal Courts of Justice
   Strand
   LONDON                                            17 April 1986
   WC2A 2LL


   Dear Sir

   REGINA v MARTIN PATRICK FORAN

   I refer to your telephone conversation today with
   Superintendent Franklin, Complaints and Discipline
   Department, regarding Inspector Paul Joseph Matthews and
   confirm that he has not been suspended and there is no
   likelihood of this event taking place.

   I trust that this information will be of assistance to you.

   Yours faithfully


            Assistant Chief Constable
```

In fact this was totally false and in my view, criminally misleading. Matthews was, in fact, the subject of several disciplinary enquiries as his behaviour had given the Force considerable cause for concern.

Eight months earlier, on 12th August, 1985, Matthews had been transferred from detective duties to uniform administrative duties at Birmingham Lock-up. However, he said he would be unable to undertake the duties assigned to him due to an arthritic condition, and he immediately reported sick.

After being examined by the Force Consultant Surgeon he was deemed fit to return to work but Matthews did not return.

He was again examined by the same doctor who passed him fit for duty and he returned on the 24th February 1986 but reported sick the following day with arthritis.

At the time the Assistant Chief Constable provided the assurance to the Criminal Appeal Office that Matthews had not been suspended from duty, he had not been at work for 8 months and it would be just 5 months later that he was dismissed from the Force.

Foran continued to apply pressure, which caused Matthews' full disciplinary sequence to come to light as follows:

RE:D.C.PRESTON AND OTHER OFFICERS OF THE
WEST MIDLANDS POLICE SERIOUS CRIME SQUAD

COMPLAINANT : MARTIN FORAN

Copy/ CHRONOLOGICAL HISTORY RE: RESIGNATION
OF D.I.MATTHEWS

EX-POLICE INSPECTOR 6863 MATTHEWS

During the early 1980's MATTHEWS was a Detective Inspector at Bradford Street Sub-Divisional Police Station. In this period he was the subject of several complaint/disciplinary enquiries which did not, taken separately, amount to very much. However, when put together they clearly gave cause for concern. The following schedule is the result of action taken in response to that concern :-

12.8.85 : Transferred from detective duties to Uniform Administrative duties at Birmingnam Lock-up, Steelhouse Lane.

12.8.85 : MATTHEWS informed Superintendent WILLIAMS that it was not his intention to work in Lock-Up as this would be deterimental to an arthritic condition he was suffering from.

He reported sick that same day and remained certificated sick until 23 February 1986.

27.11.85 : MATTHEWS examined by Force Consultant Surgeon who concluded that the officer, whilst not fit to perform full active duties, would be fit to perform the tasks he would be expected to perform in the Lock-Up.

4.2.86 : MATTHEWS again examined by the Force Consultant Surgeon who confirmed his opinion that MATTHEWS would be fit to perform duty in the Lock-Up.

24.2.86 : MATTHEWS returned to duty.

25.2.86 : MATTHEWS reported sick with arthritis. No sick notes nor sickness giros were submitted by the officer and at a subsequent interview, in June 1986, he acknowledged he had not sought medical advice.

28.2.86 : A report of this date was submitted by MATTHEWS in which he stated that he did not consider Lock-Up work was suitable and he would not attend work. He also indicated that he was seeking medical retirement.

19.3.86 : MATTHEWS failed to attend an appointment with the Force Consultant Surgeon.

25.3.86 : MATTHEWS failed to attend an appointment with the Force Consultant Surgeon.

1.4.86 : A written directive from the Deputy Chief Constable was given to Chief Inspector ARNOLD to serve on MATTHEWS ordering him to report for duty at the Lock-Up on the 7.4.86.

Despite several attempts, Mr ARNOLD was unable to serve the document.

11.4.86 : Chief Inspector ARNOLD served MATTHEWS with a letter from the Deputy Chief Constable (dated 8.4.86) ordering him to return to work on 14.4.86.

After reading the letter MATTHEWS repeated his request for a medical discharge and stated he would not return to work. He subsequently failed to do so.

- 2 -

10.6.86 : MATTHEWS was examined by the Force Consultant Surgeon who concluded that he was still fit for the duties to which he had been posted and could find no reason why he should be granted a discharge from the police service on medical grounds.

13.6.86 : MATTHEWS was interviewed by Superintendent FRANKLIN who subsequently recommended that disciplinary proceedings be instituted against MATTHEWS.

4.8.86 : MATTHEWS served with written order from the Deputy Chief Constable ordering him to report for duty at 9.00 am on 5.8.86. MATTHEWS failed to report for duty.

23.9.86 : MATTHEWS appeared before the Chief Constable and dealt with under the Police (Discipline) Regulations, 1985. He pleaded 'Not Guilty' but was found 'Guilty' on all charges as follows :-

    (1) DISOBEDIENCE TO ORDERS
    Disobeyed a lawful written order from the Deputy Chief Constable :
    Reduced in rank to Constable

    (2) NEGLECT OF DUTY
    Without good and sufficient cause absent without leave from duty.
    Reduced in rank to Constable

    (3) NEGLECT OF DUTY
    Without good and sufficient cause failing to work duties.
    Reduced in rank to Constable

    (4) DISOBEDIENCE TO ORDERS
    Disobeyed a lawful written order from the Deputy Chief Constable
    Required to Resign forthwith

P Battison
Inspector

This evidence is conclusive that the cover-up was endemic right to the top of the Force.

During the same period, William Whitlock wrote to the Home Secretary, Patrick Mayhew, notifying him that Foran's conviction had relied on evidence provided by the same people who were involved with the Birmingham Six.

He received a reply from the Home Office (below) assuring him than none of the officers who Foran had accused had, in fact, been involved with the Birmingham Six case.

HOME OFFICE
QUEEN ANNE'S GATE
LONDON SW1H 9AT

PARLIAMENTARY UNDER
SECRETARY OF STATE

Dear Mr Whitlock

Thank you for your letter of 16 April enclosing this one from Mr Martin Foran, who is in Gartree prison. I am replying in Patrick Mayhew's absence from the office.

Mr Foran refers to the cases of those prosecuted for the Birmingham pub bombings and those convicted of the murder of Carl Bridgewater. I can confirm that the Carl Bridgewater case is being investigated because fresh information has become available; no allegations have been made against any police officers. None of the police officers about whom Mr Foran has earlier complained appears to have been concerned in the case of the Birmingham pub bombings.

Mr Foran has made two formal complaints against the police officers who dealt with his case. These were investigated in 1978 and 1980 but were not found to substantiated.

Yours sincerely

(THE LORD ELTON)

William Whitlock Esq

The following is a list of the officers directly involved in the fraudulent conviction of the Birmingham Six which clearly shows four of the officers were also instrumental in the wrongful conviction of Foran.

		Statement No.	Page No.
	MORRIS, Colin (Det. Sgt.)	M.147	185 – 200
	WOODWISS, Terence (Det. Con.)	W.206	201 – 217
	MILLICHAMP, David (Det. Sgt.)	M.148	218 – 242
	BELL, Douglas (Det. Con.)	B.268	243 – 269
	POWELL, Colin (Det. Ch. Insp.)	P.125	270 – 272
	HIGGINS, Peter (Det. Sgt.)	H.208	273 – 277
	BUXTON, Alan (Det. Con.)	B.261	278 – 282
1 CASE	HORNBY, Michael (Det. Sgt.)	H.213	283 – 285
	BRYANT, Richard (Det. Sgt.)	B.269	286 – 288
1 CASE	DAVIES, John (Det. Con.)	D.110	289 – 291
	BUNN, Roy (Det. Sgt.)	B.270	292 – 296
six CASE	MATTHEWS, Paul (Det. Con.)	M.149	297 – 301
	BALL, Roger (Det. Sgt.)	B.271	302 – 304
six case	READE, George Roland Sturgess (Det. Supt.)	R.102	305 – 322
	ROBINSON, Harry (Det. Ch. Supt.)	R.104	323 – 324

The extent of the corruption and fraud within the West Midlands Crime Squad and their police accomplices was now becoming clear, and had it not been for the determination of Foran, despite his maltreatment and failing health, it might never have come to light.

CHAPTER 11

HIS SECOND HOSTAGE

Maidstone and Wandsworth

In early 1986 he was transferred from Birmingham to Maidstone prison. It would be difficult to find a more remote prison for his family to visit. While there he frequently requested essential medical treatment but, each time, it was refused. After only a few months at Maidstone he was moved again, this time to Wandsworth prison in London.

He was examined by Dr Somasundaram, the Medical Officer at Wandsworth prison who wrote to Mr J. Kirkham, Consultant Surgeon at St James' Hospital, asking him to examine Foran whose condition was deteriorating. Prior to this, several doctors had expressed their concern that the pain and distress he was suffering was causing him to become depressed and experience mood swings, which could, in extreme circumstances, become violent. Dr Somasundaram also confirmed this in his letter.

Unfortunately, Dr Somasundaram's actions and letter were not communicated to Foran who assumed that, yet again, nothing would happen as had been the case countless times before. The diagnosis concerning the effect his medical condition was having on his mood swings also proved to be correct.

On April 9th, in a desperate attempt to draw attention to his plight and the pain he was in, he took regrettable action, which could only be described as that of a desperate man.

When prison officer Richard Pike was on duty and visited Foran's cell, Foran detained him and barricaded both of them in his cell. When the alarm was raised Foran tied a noose made from sheets round the officer's neck, held a broken bottle to his throat and threatened to kill him unless the prison medical officer promised to allow him access to a consultant so he could receive the necessary treatment for his rectal prolapse. In order to keep the other prison officers at bay he stuck glass on the end of a broom handle to use as a spear.

Foran had no intention of harming Pike: it was a desperate attempt to draw attention to his plight so he could get the necessary surgical treatment to rid him of his continual pain.

It worked, and on the 9th April he was referred to Mr J. Kirkham, Consultant Surgeon at St James' Hospital for a full assessment.

On the 29th April, Kirkham's registrar, Dr Talbot, wrote back to the medical officer at Wandsworth prison expressing concern that he had not attended for his appointment with Kirkham, and the importance of sustained medical treatment. He also recommended he should not be moved until he had received the necessary, proper treatment.

Unfortunately, this concern expressed by two senior medical experts was all too late for Foran, as he had already left London. The Governor had seen fit to move him the day after he had been referred to Kirkham and before the treatment could be administered.

He was moved to Parkhurst prison on the Isle of Wight on the 10th April, 1986.

Dr Somasundaram's letter and the reply from Kirkham's Senior Surgical Registrar follow and clearly display the urgency they attached to getting Foran the necessary treatment.

Home Office
H M PRISON WANDSWORTH
P.O. Box 757 Heathfield Road London SW18 3HS
Telephone 01-874 7292   ext   348

Mr J Kirkham   *Please reply to the Senior Medical Officer*
Consultant Surgeon
St James' Hospital   *Your reference*
Sarsfeld Road
Balham SW12 8HW   *Our reference*   VS/JN

                                          Date   26 March 1986

Dear Mr Kirkham

re: C51796 Martin Patrick FORAN   Dob 27 2 44

I would be obliged if you could see this unfortunate man and suggest some
way of relieving his intractable problem which is constant mucous discharge
from the rectum. This discharge continues throughout the day, is sometimes
blood stained and occasionally mixed with faeces, which has resulted in
him wearing pads though the day and night!

His problem started as a rectal discharge, frequency of defaecation following
a hunger strike in prison. On EUA in August 1981 at Leicester Royal Hospital
no cause was found but he subsequently developed a solitary ulcer, the cause
of which was thought to be anterior rectal prolapse. He subsequently had a
Well's operation in December 1983 with insertion of Ivalon sponge. Post
operative recovery was good and the discharge stopped.

When he was seen in Dudley Road Hospital by Mr Donovan in January 1985 for
recurrence of his symptoms, he was thought to have a narrowed area with faeces
above it. There was evidence of some discharge in lower rectum and the
sphincter was normal. Subsequently when he was seen by Professor Keighley
in June 1985 it was noted that he had a grossly patuous anus, poor sphincter
tone and diffuse abnormality of rectum and lower sigmoid, the picture not
being typical of ulcerative colitis. He was put on Salazopyrin and topical
steroids.

Colonoscopy and biopsy in January 1986 did not show any significant abnormality
and confirmed no evidence of inflammatory bowel disease.

Inspite of the above expert treatment his problems have continued unabated and
this discharge is producing psychological effects on him and the amount varies
with his mood state. I would be quite happy to provide all the details of his
past treatment for your perusal, when you are ready to see him.

Yours sincerely

V Somasundaram
Medical Officer

ST. JAMES' HOSPITAL
SARSFELD ROAD
BALHAM
LONDON SW12 8HW

Dr V Somasundaram
Medical Officer
H M Prison Wandsworth
PO Box 757
Heathfield Road
LONDON SW18

29th April 1986

Dear Dr Somasundaram

Re: C51796 Martin Patrick FORAN dob 27.2.44

Thank you for asking Mr. Kirkham to see this
unfortunate man in the rectal clinic.
For one reason or another he did not attend
for this appointment.

One of this man's biggest problems is that he
is being assessed periodically at different
hospitals by different if eminent surgeons
and not attend any one place long enough for
them to come to grips with the problem.

It would be advisable for him to stay put long
enough for this matter to be sorted out. To this
end if he is going to stay at Wandsworth for any
length of time please make another appointment
for him to see us when it is convenient for the
prison service.

Yours sincerely

R TALBOT   FRCS
Senior Surgical Registrar to Mr J S Kirkham

Worse was to come. Foran freely admitted taking Pike hostage in order to make someone listen to his desperate pleas for help. However, this explanation would not cut any ice and he was prosecuted for taking the action and, as an example to other inmates who might consider taking similar action, the judge added a further 6 years to his 8 year sentence.

The following month, on the 10th May, 1986, the senior prison officer of the block Foran was in at Parkhurst, Mr D. Sheppard, wrote to the Governor of the prison expressing concern at Foran's worsening condition and stressed it was putting him into a desperate state of mind.

Three days later Dr B. D. Cooper, the Principal Medical Officer at Parkhurst, also wrote to the Medical Officer of the Prison Service, Dr D. Doherty, expressing concern that Foran should be in hospital receiving urgent treatment. He also supported the likelihood that the 'great distress' caused by his prolapse was affecting his temperament and was the likely reason for him taking the prison officer hostage.

However, although Dr Cooper confirmed that he needed urgent medical attention, significantly, he was also suggesting he was moved again, which was against the medical advice from St James Hospital and indeed no reasonable doctor would have suggested such a thing when they had their own hospital unit at Parkhurst. The reason he gave in his letter for not admitting him to their unit was because there were dangerous inmates there, one of whom was involved with him during the hostage taking at Wandsworth. This was totally untrue as there was no-one else at all involved in the Wandsworth incident, just Foran.

Nevertheless, as a result of Cooper's letter and the Governor's unshakeable determination to move him, Foran was sent to Liverpool prison's secure hospital unit at the beginning of June 1986.

The letters from Senior Prison Officer Sheppard and the prison medical officer, Dr Cooper, follow:

From S/O SHEPPARD. D.
HMP PARKHURST

'''''' for information,

Telephone

Extension

To THE GOVERNOR
HMP PARKURST

Your reference

Our reference

Date 10TH MAY 1986.

RE:- C51796 FORAN

Sir

C51796 FORAN, WAS RECIVED IN THE SEG UNIT ON THE "10TH APRIL 1986", AND HAS HAD CONSTANT MEDICAL TREATMENT FOR A BOWEL DISORDER, WHICH REQUIRES THE WEARING OF PAD'S, FOR HIS BACK PASSAGE, AND THE TAKING OF MEDICATION.

TO-DAY THE "9TH MAY 1986", A DOCTORS CALL UP IN OUR HOSPITAL, WAS REQUIRED BECAUSE OF HIS CONDITION WORSENING. WHEN THIS HAPPENS IT IT AFFECTS HIS MENTAL CONDITION. I HAVE HAD LONG CONVERSATIONS WITH FORAN, DURING HIS STAY IN THE SEG UNIT AND TO-DAY, AFTER YET AGAIN ANOTHER LONG CONVERSATION EVEN I, AS A LAYMAN WOULD SUGGEST HE IS ONCE AGAIN APPROACHING A MENTAL STATE, IN WHICH HE WOULD BECOME A VERY DANGEROUS MAN.

THIS MAY BE DISCRIBED BY SOME AS SOME SORT OF TRY ON, FOR HIS OWN BENIFIT. I PERSONALLY DO NOT BELIEVE THIS TO BE TRUE.

ALL OF HIS ANXIETY IS DUE TO HIS PRESENT MEDICAL PROBLEM.

(signature). (S/OFFICER).
D. SHEPPARD

1384P (Rev)
31541 2/85 XLYQ737

Dr B D Cooper
Principal Medical Officer
HMP Parkhurst
Newport
Isle of Wight

0983 523855

Dr D Doherty
RPMO
Cleland House

cc: Governor, HMP Parkhurst

BDC/JL

12 May 1986

C51796 - FORAN Martin Patrick

This man was transferred to Parkhurst on 10.4.86. Prior to his transfer
he had been involved in a Hostage Incident at Wandsworth in which he had
tried to pressure the SMO there to give him access to a consultant.

FORAN's medical problems started following a period of food refusal in
prison. This was followed by continual rectal discharge. It was investigated
at Leicester Royal and subsequently he had a Wells operation for a rectal
prolapse in December 1983. He was seen in Dudley Hospital by Mr Donovan in
January 1985 for recurrence of his symptoms and subsequently by Professor
Keighley in June 1985. At that time it was noted that he had a grossly
patuous anus with poor sphincter tone. Biopsy in January 1986 did not show
any sign of abnormality. His problems have continued unabated, and if anything
the rectal discharge has increased. There is undoubtedly a relationship
between his physical condition and his psychological state.

I feel he could quite easily attempt to take a hostage again.

Although FORAN is located in the Segregation Unit he really requires to be
located in a hospital setting but I am loath to admit him to our hospital where
we have several dangerous inmates including one who is alleged to have been
involved with him in the incident at Wandsworth.

Could this inmate be transferred to the Midlands Region? He lives in Birmingham
and was sentenced in the Birmingham CC, and arrangements by the relevant
consultant at Leicester Royal where the original operation was performed. Our
surgeons are reluctant to become involved in such a situation and until FORAN
is seen again by surgeons at Leicester Royal, he presents a difficult and
potentially dangerous problem.

B D Cooper
Principal Medical Officer

CHAPTER 12

LIVING HELL

Liverpool

By the time he arrived in Liverpool his life was in danger and after extensive examinations of his abdomen and the condition of his prolapse, they decided to perform a colostomy.

He had the operation at around eleven o'clock on the 4th June, 1986, and after the operation he was returned to a cell to recuperate.

On Sunday, 29th June, while still recovering, Foran went downstairs to the canteen to collect his food and take it back up the stairs to his cell as he had done several times before.

As soon he entered the canteen he knew something was wrong: other prisoners were serving the food but this day there were fewer than usual and the canteen itself was empty except for about 4 hospital prison officers, one of whom he recalled was tall with a beard. Foran was on vegan milk at the time and asked for it as usual, when one of the officers shouted: 'you're not getting the milk'. Still weak from the operation and in no mood to argue, he decided to go back to his cell but shouted back to the officer, 'sod the milk'. As he turned to leave, the officer jumped on him from behind and pushed him up against the pantry door. In the process the colostomy bag was ripped off and he fell to the floor screaming in pain. The next thing he remembers was four officers dragging him to the strip cell along the corridor. Once in the strip cell he was roughly stripped of his clothing as he struggled and shouted that he had just had a colostomy, but one of the officers lifted his legs and began kicking him and another jumped on his stomach. They left him barely conscious and doubled up in pain.

He remained on the floor for a while, covered in blood and thinking he was going to die. When he came to, he rang the bell for assistance and the tall bearded officer returned with a mop and bucket and began mopping him down to remove the blood from his body and the floor.

While on his own, still writhing in agony, the prison Roman Catholic priest, Father Moran, entered the cell. This was unusual as it was not the normal time for the priest to visit but it would save his life. He went to Foran and turned him over. Certain he was about to die, he whispered to the priest to tell his wife what had happened and that he did not want to die. The priest called for the Medical Officer who visited him but said it would be difficult to do a full examination because he was covered in blood and mucus from the open wound where his colostomy bag should be.

Foran insisted on seeing the prison Governor who happened to be taking Messrs Calderwood and McFall, two members of the Liverpool Prison Board of Visitors, round the prison at the time. When they arrived, Foran told them what had happened; that he had been savagely beaten and wanted to talk to the police. One of the visiting Board Members wrote details of the incident down and informed the Governor that the police should be called immediately.

Father Moran had done as Foran requested and contacted Valerie, who immediately made arrangements to visit Liverpool the next day. She insisted on seeing the Governor and wanted a full explanation of what had happened.

While being escorted to the governor's office, several prisoners approached her and whispered that she must insist on seeing Foran's stomach. On arriving at the Governor's office she asked to see Foran but the Governor told her it would not be possible as he was receiving medical attention. Valerie was not going to be deterred and said she would not leave the prison until she had seen her husband. She also threatened to go to the press.

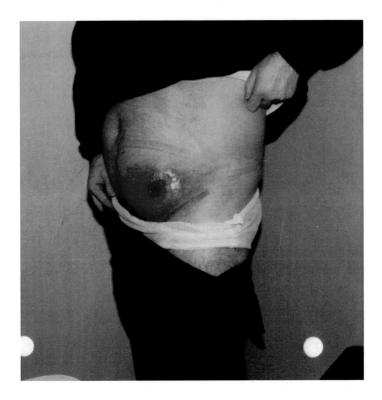

The Governor eventually relented and when she saw the state her husband was in and heard his explanation she decided to take action.

However, the next day, on the 1st July, 1986, before a thorough examination could be made and before any police could become involved, he was removed from Liverpool and taken back to Parkhurst prison on the Isle of Wight. His condition was now serious but there was something else that caused him even more concern and made him fear for his life.

He was sealed in the back of a prison van and could not see where he was going; all he knew was that the journey was taking much longer than he expected. Peering through the cracks he could just make out they were nearing Oxford Prison, which was not on the authorised route to the ferry for the Isle of Wight.

He could hear the escorts talking in the front cabin and in the conversation he overheard they were asking each other what they should do next. He was sure they had something planned for him, and he looked around for something he could use as a weapon if necessary.

By this time several hours had elapsed and when he next looked through the cracks it seemed to him he was in a small airport but he really had no idea where.

Shortly afterwards, he heard a police siren and a police car drew up outside the van and started questioning the escorts in the cab. He heard the police officers asking them what they were doing and told them they were six hours late and a long way off course. When prisoners are escorted from one prison to another they have a prescribed route from which they mustn't deviate, and the police are informed. When they hadn't arrived at the ferry by the allotted time, the officials at Parkhurst had rung the police and they had started to search for the van.

When Martin overheard this conversation he was certain they had planned to dispose of him somewhere en route and what he had overheard in the conversation was them discussing their plan and what story they would tell the authorities.

It should be said at this point that not all prison officers were sadistic or inhuman in their treatment of him. There were some who privately would tell Foran that they did not agree with the way he was being treated.

To emphasise this, one day, before being removed from Liverpool prison (HMP Walton), a prison officer at the prison passed Foran a handwritten note. The signature of the person who issued it is not clear but it is obviously a high ranking officer at the prison. The note clearly shows that Foran was a targeted man and that there was a conspiracy to prevent him receiving any help or assistance. The officer who passed him the note was obviously very concerned about his welfare.

Foran smuggled it out through his wife who passed it to his MP who used it in a letter to the Home Office as evidence of the way he was being treated. The Home Office replied saying it was a fake. Judge for yourself.

REG. No. C51796 NAME Foran

12

Continuous Medical Record

These pages are intended to provide a continuous medical record passing from one sentence to another. The Medical Officer at each establishment through which an inmate passes should record details of each consultation. Both medical and nursing staff should record any salient medical features or occurrences.

Establishment and date	
H.M.P. Walton 29/6/86	*All members of staff dealing with this inmate are reminded that he took hostage a hospital officer & in order to deter others from engaging in such incidents, are to allow his situation to serve as a lesson, nothing should be done to aid and comfort this individual.*

Because the copy of the handwritten note is poor quality, the following is a typed transcript.

Reg. No. C51796 Name FORAN

Continuous Medical Record

H.M.P. Walton

29/6/86

All members of staff dealing with this inmate are reminded that he took hostage a hospital officer. So in order to deter others from engaging in such incidents and to allow his situation to serve as a lesson, nothing should be done to aid and comfort this individual.

MEDICAL IN CONFIDENCE

CHAPTER 13

THE LIVING HELL CONTINUES

Parkhurst

On arriving back at Parkhurst, the Chief Officer demanded to know why they were so late arriving and requested the escort provide an explanation. Prison Officer Naylor wrote the note below in reply, which clearly shows there had been an inadequate explanation as to why they were 6 hours late arriving at Parkhurst.

Dr Kahn examined him, at around nine o'clock in the evening of 1ˢᵗ July, 1986 and expressed no real concern over his condition. Additionally, Dr Khan's diagnosis did not seem to agree with Naylor's observations.

Dr A Khan
Medical Officer
HMP Parkhurst

The Governor
HMP Parkhurst

HCPs AK/SJ
11 July 1966

C51796 - FORAN

I was called to see the above at about 9.30 pm on 1 July 1986. He was received at Parkhurst from HMP Liverpool having arrived here at about 8.45 pm. He was seen and examined in a room on EIII Landing in the presence of HPO Seager and HSO Jenkins.

He was cooperative and answered to the point and gave an account of being assaulted by staff at HMP Liverpool.

The circumstances preceding these events need not be factual and, therefore, I cannot comment on them.

On examination, he was cooperative, civil and in a clear state of mind. He was not showing any evidence of mental disorder.

He was noted to have several bruises all over his body, these looked a few days old and some were beginning to resolve.

The following bruises were noted:-

LEFT KNEE: (No effusion and full range of movement. No obvious joint involvement). Tender left shin without swelling.

Bruises over left thigh and left buttock and right iliac fossa. A small bruise over the right iliac crest. Several small bruises on sacrum and one small one on the left shoulder and left upper arm.

A small bruise on the left side of the chest and another one above the left eye. There was no injury to his eyes and his vision was grossly normal. No bruises or swellings were noted on his head. He was not particularly distressed. His chest was clear.

CNS: There were no abnormal signs.

ABDOMEN: Clinically, there was no evidence of internal injury. There was no major injury to his colostomy apart from minimal excoriations around the colostomy and slight blood around it. There was no evidence of any bony injury and, therefore, no need for X-Raying him.

The Governor - HMP Parkhurst   11 July 1986

C51796 - FORAN (CONT'D)

His cardio vascular system was grossly normal and he was given
no specific treatment other than to be observed overnight. He
was referred to Consultant Surgeon, Mr T Walsh who, after thoroughly
examining him, was satisfied that there was no need for this man to
undergo treatment for his injuries.

He appears to have recovered from his injuries and will be under
review by the Surgeon with regards to his colostomy which, at the
moment, is functioning quite satisfactorily.

A Khan
Medical Officer

Dr Khan's full medical report issued to the governor is reproduced at Appendix 3.

Two days later Sister Moul spoke to Foran and he explained the injuries he had suffered during his beating in Liverpool's hospital wing to her, after which she wrote the following note to Dr Cooper:

MEMORANDUM

From

Senior Sister Moul .

Telephone

Extension

To   DR Cooper .
H.M.P Parkhurst.

Your reference

Our reference

Date   3/7/86 .

Sir

On the 2/7/86 at approx 15.00hrs —
— I was talking to cs1796 Foran in E III room 11
regards his colostomy as instructed by Dr
Khan

whilst discussing the problems he stated he
had a cut in his colostomy. He proceeded to
show me where it was He then started to
relate to how the injury had occured. He
stated that he had been kicked in the area
? the colostomy.

Ac Moul   3/7/86 .   —

After visiting her husband in Liverpool prior to his transfer and seeing his injuries, Valerie got in touch with solicitors who wrote to the Governor requesting an explanation. They received a response that the Governor had held an internal enquiry during which the officers concerned had said that Foran had tried to assault one of the officers while in the canteen and had to be restrained. The tall man with the beard was identified as Charlton and another was named Robinson, who was the Hospital Senior Officer.

The Governor said there was no record of having received a complaint or a request from Foran to call the police.

MEMORANDUM

From

Governor
HM Prison
Liverpool

Telephone   051 525 5971

Extension   427

To

P3 Division
Room 613
Cleland House

Mrs Age Mony

For the attention of J/W Watts

Your reference
PDP/F 0523/8/9

Our reference
WG/SGM

Date

11 September 1986

<u>C51796 FORAN Martin Patrick</u>

Despite Foran's reference to July 6th it would appear that the allegation he makes in his letter dated 16 July 1986 is the one he withdrew on 30.6.86. Regarding your other queries:-

(i)   I enclose the Principal Medical Officer's report.

(ii)   I enclose all statements relating to the incident.

(iii)   F213 enclosed (Further information may be in the hospital case paper still at Parkhurst).

(iv)   Although Foran did say to Assistant Governor Temple (see official C14/80 warning) that he wanted his "Full Legal rights", there is no record of him asking to see either the police or a solicitor.

GOVERNOR

As so often happens in Foran's history, many years later a letter dated 30th June 1986, written by Messrs Calderwood and McFall of the Liverpool Board of Visitors was 'uncovered'. This clearly stated that they had received an allegation from Foran of assault. Furthermore, as shown in Dr Todd's report to the prison Governor, which follows, he had been examined by the Senior Medical Officer at HMP Liverpool on the 30th June. It would be stretching the imagination too far to believe the Governor could have forgotten both an encounter with a man bleeding profusely and calling for assistance and also forget a subsequent medical report

(2)

BOV

BOARD OF VISITORS

SHEET N°: - 2/3

X9

RECORD OF ROTA VISIT

at Liverpool Prison

Date 30ᵗʰ June 1986

Visitor(s) M.T. Calderwood and R McFall

We next visited the gardens and greenhouses. There appear to be very well cared for; and look splendid. We next visited the Hospital.

Saw C51796 FORAN in the strip cell. Foran made allegations of assault, and said he wished to see the Police. He has been seen by a doctor today. He was to follow normal procedure and make a formal complaint. While we were discussing FORAN with the Chief Officer, H/a TE come to the hospital to enable FORAN to have the facilities to make a formal complaint. We understand that he was di So. Also in Strip cells saw, H 26468 Johnson who con had set c/me to bedding in his cell. Understand he is prison c/w ARSON. He was not, apparently, injured in the ce fire. Also saw P54533 Jones who seemed in good sp and was about to be returned to normal location.

Visited next to G Wing and visited P50101 McMullen regarding his request for terminal home leave. Informed him that his length of sentence did not qualify him But understand also that he is awaiting a reply to inspection on a matter

F 312

109

Strangely, also uncovered was an internal note which confirmed they knew Foran had made an allegation of assault by prison officers. The Governor of Liverpool Prison had written a memorandum on the 7th July confirming the fact but said the accusation had been withdrawn so he decided not to pursue it. Of course Foran never withdrew the allegation and had indeed been fighting hard to have it heard and acted upon. A copy of Governor W. J. Ginn's letter is reproduced below.

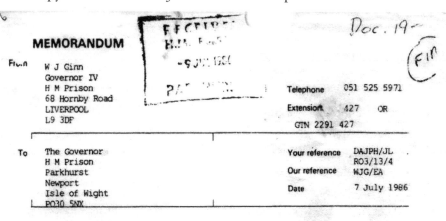

MEMORANDUM

Doc. 19

From W J Ginn
       Governor IV
       H M Prison
       68 Hornby Road
       LIVERPOOL
       L9 3DF

Telephone   051 525 5971
Extension   427 OR
GTN 2291 427

To   The Governor
     H M Prison
     Parkhurst
     Newport
     Isle of Wight
     PO30 5NX

Your reference DAJPH/JL
                RO3/13/4
Our reference   WJG/EA
Date   7 July 1986

RE: C51796 - FORAN : ALLEGATION AGAINST LIVERPOOL STAFF

Thank you for your memo dated 4 July 1986.

Foran did submit a written Statement of Allegation here which he subsequently withdrew following a warning in accordance with CI 14/80.

Notwithstanding his decision to withdraw I called for written statements from all staff involved in the incident which gave rise to the allegations.

Having studied these statements I decided not to pursue the issue further. I see no need for further enquiries at this stage.

W J GINN
GOVERNOR IV

cc. North Regional Office, Manchester
     South East Regional Office, Surbiton, Surrey

It is difficult to believe that a man, having just had a serious operation just 3 weeks earlier, with a colostomy bag fitted and experiencing regular discharges from both his anus and the site of the colostomy would be in a position to assault or even wish to assault a prison officer. Unaccountably, the supporting evidence of his inability to do this does not seem to have been sought or provided by the medical consultant. However, amongst the papers Foran was able to smuggle out was an additional medical report issued 2 months later by Dr Todd, the Principal Medical Officer.

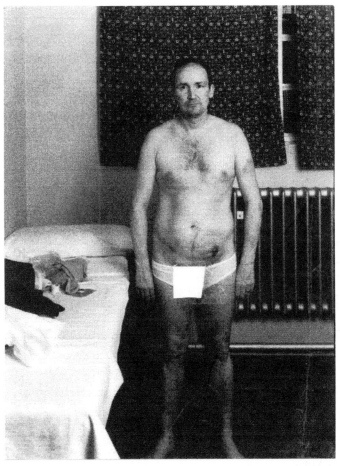

The photograph above shows the picture taken of his injuries and accompanied the following report by Dr Todd, the Principal Medical Officer for the Governor follows:

MEMORANDUM

Dec. 20

From

Dr A J Todd
Principal Medical Officer
H M Prison
Liverpool

Telephone

Extension

To

The Governor
H M Prison
Liverpool

Your reference

Our reference
AJT/RD
Date
9 September 1986

RE: FORAN Martin Patrick C51796

Further to the memo from P3 Division with reference to the above named prisoner: Our Hospital Case Paper is still at Parkhurst Prison so I may be unable to answer fully all queries raised in the memorandum. However I can 1) confirm that the operation of colostomy was carried out and that there were no complications as a result of this operation.

The purpose of the operation was to relieve Foran of bleeding from the back passage which had continued for some time. He was also made aware that this bleeding would continue after the operation but would gradually subside. It was noted that he was able to obtain blood from his back passage and smear it over his body in order to make statements that this had been done by the staff whilst trying to injure him.

2) Following the alleged assault Foran smeared his body with blood in the method described above. He refused to be examined by Dr Benett and continued to be abusive and threatening. On the following day (30.6.86) he continued to be abusive and threatening, refusing treatment. By the afternoon he had calmed down and he was interviewed by the Senior Medical Officer who found the following injuries :

He had various bruises, notably on the outer side of his left eye, on the side of his left cheek, on the right upper side of his abdomen, on his right knee, his left groin and his left shin. These were all small and of a minor nature. In addition it was also noted that he had rubbed the site of his operation which was bleeding and had contributed towards the blood that he had smeared on his body. I enclose a photocopy of F213. Apart from normal minor dressings to the site of his operation he required no special treatment for the bruises.

A J TODD
PRINCIPAL MEDICAL OFFICER

What is of concern in Dr A. J. Todd's report to the prison Governor of the 9th September is that he did not confine his comments to the medical aspects of Foran's colostomy operation and treatment but went on to say that Foran had been able to obtain blood from his back passage and smear it over his body. Dr Todd repeated this a second time in his letter yet he had not been present when Foran was assaulted by the officers so why would he include such comments unless it was a direct attempt to support the defence of the prison officers?

Despite everything, Foran decided to bring an action against prison officers Charlton and Robinson and through his wife, Valerie, George E. Baker & Co., solicitors, was instructed. Foran was clearly demonstrating that, despite being a very sick man, he was determined not to let the prison officers get away with it and he was going to hold them to account.

It was 18 months later, in January, 1988, that the defendants would produce an interview with the Governor of Liverpool prison dated 15th December, 1986 giving their version of what had happened. This was carried out 6 months after the event, and claimed Foran had assaulted them and they were simply trying to restrain him. They also said that he had deliberately smeared his own blood all over his clothing and body.

With the officers denying any knowledge of an incident in the first instance and then documents emerging subsequently to show otherwise, I have included the full minutes of the interviews with Foran, Charlton and Robinson conducted by W. A. Martin, governor of Leeds prison so readers can make up their own minds as to which version of events they believe. These are shown in full at Appendix 4.

Foran was put into solitary confinement for 23 hours a day with no contact with the other inmates. His illness and isolation were not assisting his mental state; he was again becoming desperate for anyone to listen to his pleas of innocence and requests to treat him humanely – and medically – for the continual pain he was experiencing.

Sensing his determination to seek redress through the courts against prison officers, and his evident distress and frustration at being locked in solitary, the Governor was convinced he had become a liability and decided to move him yet again.

A few months later, on 17th October 1986, Foran was transferred to Long Lartin prison in Worcestershire, supposedly at the behest of Dr Wool, one of the Parkhurst medical officers.

Disabled prisoner attacked

Following a hunger-strike three years ago, Martin Foran suffers from an incurable bowel illness. He requires clean clothing twice daily and showers three to four times, as well as specific medical attention.

In December 1985 whilst very ill, Martin was moved from Winson Green to Wandsworth the day before he was due to see a specialist. He was put in the prison hospital and again booked to see a specialist. The day before this appointment was due he was moved again. Back to Winson Green. From there to Maidstone where a specialist *did* examine him and recommended immediate hospital treatment.

In March 1986 Martin was transferred to Wandsworth where he was put on a waiting list for treatment at St Mary's hospital. Before this appointment could take place he was told that he was being transferred on GOAD (good order and discipline) to the block at Parkhurst. No reason was given.

Martin demanded to see a doctor as he was too ill to move. This right was denied

him for two hours during which time Martin repeatedly warned that he would take a hostage if forced to. Martin held a prison hospital officer hostage for *13 hours* before he was finally granted a medical examination.

The prison doctor who examined him insisted that nothing was wrong and Martin was moved to Parkhurst where for four weeks he received no medical attention. Eventually the prison officers on the block complained to the governor and things suddenly began to move. Martin was rushed to Liverpool prison hospital for an emergency colostomy. Whilst recovering from this operation he was violently assaulted by six officers who dragged him into a padded cell, kicked him repeatedly and rushed him back to Parkhurst.

Martin is now at Long Lartin where he is

being held in the segregation unit because 'normal location' cannot cope with his condition. Other inmates confirm the continued brutality of his treatment and the rapid deterioration of his condition. They fear he may die. He is in constant pain. The colostomy was not successful due to the beating which followed it and infection is now spreading to his groin and legs. Martin himself has written to *FRFI* and tells us he is 'locked up 23 hours a day on GOAD, with a colostomy, in an airless cell, with hot pipes, inhuman, degrading, a pig can't live like this.'

Nicola Jameson

Messages of support and solidarity should be sent to: Martin Foran C51796, HM Prison Long Lartin, South Littleton, Evesham, Worcs, WR11 5TZ.
Urgent letters of protest should be sent to the Governor at Long Lartin and to the Home Secretary, Douglas Hurd at the Home Office, Queen Anne's Gate, London SW1.

Drawing by Andrzy Jakubczyk (HMP Winchester)

Worcestershire newspaper article following the assault

CHAPTER 14

AN AMAZING ENCOUNTER

Long Lartin

On arrival at Long Lartin, he was put into the hospital wing where he was examined by their Medical Officer, Dr Greaves. After a short time he was moved, once again, into the segregation unit.

He was sitting at the end of his bed contemplating when to start his next hunger strike and went to the basin to pour himself a beaker of water. On turning round to walk back to his bed he saw something that caused fear to course through his veins and he dropped the beaker. What happened next is something he never revealed to anyone until much later and then only to his wife, Valerie.

Foran is not a religious man but sitting on his bed was the figure of a Monk aged in his sixties, with greying hair and a beard, and dressed in his robes. He had no idea who the man was or how he had got into his cell. He checked the door and looked out of the small window into the passageway and turned again to see if his imagination was playing tricks but he was still there. He became frightened and started shouting, 'How the hell did you get in here?'

The Monk replied quietly, 'Calm down and listen to what I have to say. Why do you think the sheet broke?' he asked.

Foran looked at him trembling. It was years ago and he had never told anyone about it, not even his wife, so how did this man know?

'Why do you think it broke the second time when the sheet was wet?' continued the Monk.

Foran was now completely stunned. The Monk even knew he had made two attempts with both a dry sheet and a wet one. Only he knew this.

The Monk continued, 'You will never die in prison. Your wife and family will never desert you, and you will survive your prison sentence – and after you have left prison you will win your cases.'

Foran just gazed at him blankly, shocked at what he was hearing.

'Once you have won your cases, you will die shortly afterwards in your sleep,' the Monk said.

Foran became rigid, continuing to stare at the man as he talked calmly. Who was he? Why was he talking about him winning his case when he had to face many more years yet in prison?

Before he disappeared, the Monk finished by saying, 'You will shortly find out who I am.'

Foran was sure he must have been hallucinating and couldn't mention it to anyone including his wife and family in case they thought he was losing his mind. He himself was not entirely sure if that was not the case.

Those few moments were etched in his mind and never left him during his term in prison. To this day he doesn't talk about it in case people think he suffers from an over-active imagination.

It was 6 months later that he would realise he had not imagined it. Valerie came to see him on one of her regular visits and she was clutching a letter. It had come from Brazil from someone she had never heard of and was correctly addressed to their home in Birmingham. She couldn't understand it but assumed it must have been a contact known to her husband. She passed it to him and he opened it up to find it contained a short note, a rose, and a music tape, together with a photograph and description of a Monk by the name of Padre Pio.

Foran's mouth dropped open: he couldn't believe the picture he was staring at. He recognised the man immediately; it was the Monk who had been in his cell six months earlier.

He then told his wife for the first time about his experience when the Monk visited him and sat on his bed. It was also at this point that he first told her about his attempted suicide.

Picture of Padre Pio received by Valerie

Padre Pio was born of simple, hardworking farming people on 25 May, 1887 in Pietrelcina, southern Italy. He was tutored privately until his entry into the novitiate of the Capuchin Friars at the age of 15. Of feeble health but strong will, with the help of grace he completed the required studies and was ordained a priest in 1910.

On 20 Sept. 1918 the five wounds of our Lord's Passion appeared on his body, making him the first stigmatized priest in the history of the Church. Countless numbers were attracted to his confessional and many more received his saintly counsel and spiritual guidance through correspondence. His whole life was marked by long hours of prayer and continual austerity. His letters to his spiritual directors reveal the ineffable sufferings, physical and spiritual, which accompanied him all through life. They also reveal his very deep union with God, his burning love for the Blessed Eucharist and Our Blessed Lady. Worn out by over half a century of intense suffering and constant apostolic activity in San Giovanni Rotondo, he was called to his heavenly reward on 23 September, 1968. After a public funeral which attracted almost 100,000, his body was entombed in the crypt of Our Lady of Grace Church. Increasing numbers flock to his tomb from all parts of the world and many testify to spiritual and temporal graces received. On 20 March, 1983 the informative process on his life and virtues began. Let us pray so that it will conclude successfully and quickly with the beatification and canonization of the venerated Padre for the glory of God and the good of souls.

Those who wish to make known graces or favours received through Padre Pio's intercession are asked to write directly to the address given below.

Years later, after his release, the predictions of Padre Pio would continue to have special significance. After years of trying to get his appeals heard, his second conviction was referred to the Court of Appeal and they acquitted him. His first conviction was subsequently referred back to the Court of Appeal and he was acquitted on all charges for this conviction too. Both these appeals and the bases of overturning the original verdicts are detailed later in chapter 24.

However, as a result of the predictions during the visitation of the monk, Foran was concerned that his final prediction would also come true. Although he knows he is dying, the thought of doing so in his sleep after the second case was won in the Appeal Court and before he could embark on achieving compensation, had caused him to think of rescinding the appeal.

It is of the utmost importance to Foran that he lives long enough to continue his fight for the compensation due for his wrongful conviction and the years of incarceration which caused enormous hardship to his wife and family. His dying ambition is to clear his name and secure their future.

Although not a religious man, he has visited priests to get their views on what happened in his cell. He told me that although they were listening, he could tell they were looking for another explanation. This became clear when one asked him if he ever took drugs, which is something he has never done in his life.

He was certain about one thing though. There was no way the sheets he had used in his suicide attempt could have torn the way they did. He was very sure of that.

CHAPTER 15

SUMMONS AGAINST THE SCS

Long Lartin

Over the next few months, as he sat alone in his cell with nothing to do but contemplate his plight, his thoughts drifted through his life, and he wondered how he had come to be incarcerated for a second time for something he hadn't done. With nothing to do but fight for justice, he decided to take an action against the SCS police officers whose perjury and fraudulent evidence had convicted him in the first place.

Prior to his move from Parkhurst, Foran had written to the Magistrates Court in Newport to enquire how he went about commencing criminal proceedings against the West Midland Police officers. They responded saying they could only hear cases if the offence had been committed on the Isle of Wight or if the accused were resident there, and advised him to bring the action where the event took place. Their response is shown

However, before he received that reply and thinking he probably would not be given any responses, he wrote another to the Magistrates' Court in Evesham, where he was now located. He received a similar response from them: that he should start the proceedings where the trial took place.

H. M. IRELAND, M.A., LL.B.

BARRISTER

CLERK TO THE JUSTICES
ISLE OF WIGHT PETTY
SESSIONAL DIVISON

TEL. NEWPORT 524244-5

Magistrates' Clerk's Office,

Guildhall,

Newport, Isle of Wight.

PO30 5BB

My ref : HMI/JCH

Your ref :

2 May 1986

Dear Sir,

In a letter dated April 21 you say that you wish to commence criminal proceedings against 4 police officers whom you name.

This court would only have jurisdiction to issue a summons if either the alleged offence was committed on this island or the accused resided or were present here.

I think it unlikely that this is so, and would suggest therefore that you make your application instead to the Clerk to the Justices for the area in which your trial took place.

Yours faithfully

Clerk to the Justices

Foran C51796
c/o The Governor
HM Prison,
Parkhurst,
NEWPORT
Isle of Wight

TELEPHONE NO. 2140

D. CLARE
Acting
Clerk to the Justices
EVESHAM DIVISION
PERSHORE DIVISION

OUR REF. PH/AC
YOUR REF.

Magistrates' Clerk's Office,
106, High Street,
Evesham, Worcs.
WR11 4EJ

16th June ~~XXXXX~~ 1987

Mr M Foran
Number C51796
H M Prison
Long Lartin
South Littleton
Evesham
Worcs
WR11 5TZ

Dear Sir

Thank you for your letter requesting advice as to how to proceed with a private prosecution against members of the West Midlands Police Force.

I am afraid that I am not in a position to give you the advice that you require as it is a matter for you and your solicitor as to whether or not you have sufficient evidence to justify a private prosecution and whether bringing such a prosecution would be the best course of action to take. I note that you do not wish to instruct a solicitor, and although it is, of course, a matter entirely for you whether you do or not I would strongly advise that such a course be taken.

If you choose not to be legally represented I can only suggest to you that you write to the Clerk of the Magistrates Court which dealt with your committal proceedings and ask to be allowed to issue a summons returnable at that court as it is necessary for your summons to be issued in the area where the offence was committed.

Yours faithfully,

Acting Clerk to the Justices

He was not going to be deterred so he then wrote to Birmingham Magistrates' Court who confirmed in a letter to the Governor of Liverpool prison dated 23rd June 1986 that he should be allowed to make an application for the process to be started by making a statement to a visiting Justice of the Peace in Liverpool prison.

Whether or not this also acted as a trigger for his rapid return to Parkhurst we can only surmise.

Something must have alerted the Magistrates' Court to think their letters weren't being passed to Foran as they followed it up a few days later with another.

1x Parkhurst, 1. 7. 86

Birmingham Magistrates' Court

Victoria Law Courts
Birmingham
B4 6QA

All communications to
be ar[?]essed to the
CLERK TO THE JUSTICES
Telephone No. 021-235   4951/2

When phoning or calling
please ask for   Mr Butler

MY REF   LRB/CSH
(which must be quoted
in all correspondence)   YOUR REF

27 June 1986

The Governor
HM Prison
68 Hornby Road
Liverpool
L9 3DF

[stamp: D[?]'CF [?] OFFICE — 1 – JUL 1986 — H.[?].[?] [?]OL]

Dear Sir

Re: Foran C51796

I have received, at the above Court, several letters from the above named and each time a reply has been sent to him advising of the correct procedure for the issue of process he is desirous of taking against some West Midlands Police Officers. I shall be glad if you will advise me if copies of the correspondence, always enclosed with my letters, have been handed to Mr Foran as some of the questions crop up in each letter to the Court. Will you please confirm that Mr Foran has been given the opportunity of making an application before one of your visiting Justices to issue the process required.

An early reply to these questions will be apreciated.

Yours faithfully

Clerk to the Justices

The above was given letters in the presence of a J.P. and the slips were signed by Foran and returned to the mags Court. ∅

His attempts to bring the action had now gone full circle so he therefore began the process again at Long Lartin.

However, instead of a visiting JP, he received a visit from Glyn Jones, a probation officer at Long Lartin who, on hearing what Foran wished to do, realised he did not have the qualifications to advise Foran on his case. He wrote to the Prison authorities to let them know he was not qualified to take it any further.

memorandum

HM PRISON SERVICE

From

Telephone

Extension

Date

To *Whom it may concern*

Your reference

From *Glyn De Jones*
Probation Officer
Long Lartin Prison

Our reference

In a letter to Mr M Foran C51796 from the Clerk to the Justices, Birmingham magistrates court he is being advised to see a probation officer "... with a view to obtaining legal advice.". I am not a legal advocate nor do I have any legal training I am not therefore, as a probation officer, to give any legal advice to Mr Foran over this particular issue.

Glyn De Jones July 1st 1987.

Finally, on the 7th July 1987, he was visited by Margaret Legg, a Justice of the Peace, to whom he made a full statement. This was a private summons against the five officers who had conspired to pervert the course of justice. His full statement follows:–

I WISH TO TAKE OUT A PRIVATE SUMMONS AGAINST THE THE FOLLOWING POLICE OFFICERS OF WEST MIDLAND POLICE:–

1) PAUL JOSEPH MATHEWS,
DETECTIVE INSPECTOR,
WEST MIDLANDS POLICE,
BRADFORD STREET POLICE STATION,
BIRMINGHAM.

2) CHRISTOPHER PRESTON
DETECTIVE CONSTABLE 6270
WEST MIDLANDS POLICE,
BRADFORD STREET POLICE STATION,
BIRMINGHAM.

3) DAVINDRA KUMAR JISRA,
DETECTIVE CONSTABLE 3841
WEST MIDLANDS POLICE,
BRADFORD STREET POLICE STATION,
BIRMINGHAM.

4) TERENCE CONN,
POLICE CONSTABLE 1550,
WEST MIDLANDS POLICE,
BRADFORD STREET POLICE STATION,
BIRMINGHAM.

5) STEFAN JAN BARTOSZEWICZ,
DETECTIVE CONSTABLE 3776,
WEST MIDLANDS POLICE,
BRADFORD STREET POLICE STATION
BIRMINGHAM

I WISH TO BRING THE FOLLOWING CHARGES:–

CONTINUED (2)

1) THE ABOVE MENTIONED CONSPIRED TOGETHER
ON MONDAY 10th SEPTEMBER 1984 TO PERVERT
THE COUSE OF JUSTICE IN THAT THEY KNOWINGLY
FALSIFIED EVIDENCE BY ALTERING THE TIME OF
ARREST ENTERED IN "THE PRISONER IN CUSTODY
BOOK" I.E. CHANGED THE TIME OF ARREST re
MARTIN FORAN FROM 2.12 p.m. TO 3.12 p.m. AT
BRADFORD STREET POLICE STATION.

2) THE ABOVE MENTIONED COLLUDED TO FABRICATE
EVIDENCE TO THE EFFECT THAT M. FORAN WAS
PRESENT IN HURST STREET, BIRMINGHAM FROM
3.05 p.m. ON MONDAY 30th SEPTEMBER 1984
CONTRARY TO POLICE RECORDS WHICH INDICATED THAT
HE WAS IN POLICE CUSTODY AT 3.12 p.m. AND DUE
TO DISTANCE INVOLVED BETWEEN HURST STREET, AND
PLACE OF DETENTION COULD NOT HAVE BEEN AT HURST
STREET AT TIME STATED.

3) THE ABOVE MENTIONED CONSPIRED COLLECTIVELY TO
COMMIT PERJURY AT THE TRIAL OF M. FORAN VIZ.
SWORE ON OATH THAT AT THE TIME OF ARREST OF M.
FORAN HE DID NOT HAVE IN POSSESSION BAG'S OF
MEAT, DESPITE THE FACT THAT THE ABOVE NAMED
OFFICERS HAD SIGNED TO THE EFFECT IN THE "PRISONER
IN CUSTODY BOOK" THAT THE PRISONER HAD IN
POSSESSION BAG'S OF MEAT AT TIME OF ARREST.

4) THE ABOVE MENTIONED OFFICERS CONSPIRED WITH
'PAUL ADDISON' TO PERVERT THE COUSE OF JUSTICE.

5) THAT THE ABOVE NAMED OFFICERS CONSPIRED TOGETHER
ON DATES UNKNOWN BEFORE THE TRIAL OF M. FORAN
IN APRIL — MAY 1985 TO COMMIT PERJURY BY
KNOWINGLY MISLEADING A JURY BY SWEARING UNDER
OATH THAT HE WAS AT HURST STREET AT 3.05 pm. ON
MONDAY 10th SEPTEMBER 1984.

> I MARTIN FORAN DO SOLEMNLY, AND SINCERELY DECLARE, AND AFFIRM THAT THE CONTENTS OF THIS DECLARATION ARE TRUE TO THE BEST OF MY KNOWLEDGE AND BELIEF, AND I MAKE THIS SOLEMN DECLARATION CONSCIENTIOUSLY BELIEVING THE SAME TO BE TRUE, AND BY VIRTUE OF THE PROVISION OF THE STATUTORY DECLARATION ACT 1835.
>
> *[signature]*
>
> Margaret *[signature]*.   J.P.   July 7 1987.

He heard nothing as to what happened next but in his own words, he said, 'it proceeded to go round in circles and at the end of the day nothing further was done.'

Once again he had been thwarted and his frustration grew. After all, it was the West Midlands Police officers who had falsified their evidence resulting in the start of his 40 year fight for justice.

He would never let this case go, and he continued to fight to have the officers prosecuted for a further five years.

What he didn't know was that Dr Greaves, the Medical Officer at Long Lartin, had written to Dr Cooper, the Medical Officer at Parkhurst, on the 27th April recommending that he be transferred back to Parkhurst. Staggeringly, in his letter, he also said that he thought Foran's medical condition and behaviour were self-induced and that he should be placed on their Category 'C' Wing. This would mean he would again be put into solitary confinement and be generally ignored, which was in stark contrast to the best medical advice obtained from outside the prison service who had said he should be kept under close medical supervision.

From   Dr B Greaves
        Medical Officer
        H M Prison
        Long Lartin

Telephone

Extension

To   Dr David Cooper
     Principal Medical Officer
     H M Prison
     Parkhurst

Your reference

Our reference   BHG/WJA

Date   27 April 1987

Re: C51796 FORAN M P

We discussed this man in our telephone conversation of 22 4 87.

He has been here for six months since October 1986, following his transfer from HMP Parkhurst at the request of Dr Wool.

He continues to have problems managing his colostomy which disgorges copious volumes of liquid faeces, giving rise to exoriation of the stomal mucosa and peristomal skin. He has been investigated by a local gastro-enterologist who now feels that serious consideration should be given to closure of the colostomy as no underlying colonic pathology has been demonstrated, despite which he continues to produce mucous discharge from both stomal operatives and from the anus.

His behaviour continues to be disruptive and threatening so that he has now had to be located in the segregation unit of the prison as we have not the requisite manpower to maintain a full time watch on him in the prison hospital ward.

He was seen by a consultant psychiatrist here who ventures the opinion that his whole condition might be self-induced, and that this would fit with his long history of disruptive and subversive behaviour and his hysterical and inadequate personality.

While I would seek an early transfer to your hospital for assessment for possible closure of his colostomy I suggest that, in view of the need for close and continuous supervision of this inmate, because of his history of disruptive and threatening behaviour and because of the possibility that his 'medical' condition is self-induced, that he be considered for location in 'C' Wing at Parkhurst.

B H Greaves
Medical Officer

CHAPTER 16

FORAN WINS HIS FIRST CASE

Parkhurst

F oran continued with his case against the four officers who had assaulted him at Liverpool. He began with the first two, who he knew were primarily responsible for the beatings, namely, Charlton and Robinson.

Eventually, his, solicitors, Baker & Co, acquired the assistance of Martin Strutt, a Barrister in London, who prepared a case against the four officers involved in the beatings. However, just before the case was due to be heard, additional medical examinations showed that the planned reversal of his colostomy at some point in the future could never be performed because the muscles at the base of his spine no longer worked. The doctor who examined him said that the nerve damage at the base of his spine was consistent with him having been kicked. Strutt asked for an adjournment of the original planned hearing date because he considered these findings would increase the quantum of any damages should the case succeed.

The detailed letter to the court from Strutt describing the medical findings is shown at Appendix 4.

Before the trial began, Foran's solicitors received a document from the defendants' solicitors which they asked him to sign, which purportedly detailed the 'facts' of the case. To all intents and purposes it was a document giving Charlton's own account of what happened and if Foran had signed it, it would have destroyed his case. The documents follow:

: -

IN THE WESTMINSTER COUNTY COURT   Case No. 8715181

B E T W E E N:

MARTIN PATRICK FORAN	Plaintiff
- and -	
CHARLTON (Male)	First Defendant
- and -	
THE HOME OFFICE	Second Defendant

NOTICE TO ADMIT FACTS

TAKE NOTICE that the Second Defendants in this action requires the Plaintiff to admit, for the purposes of this action only, the several facts respectively hereunder specified.

AND the Plaintiff is hereby required within seven days after receiving this Notice to admit the said several facts, saving all just exceptions to their admissability, as evidence in this action.

Dated the   20th day of January 1988

Treasury Solicitor

Treasury Solicitor
Solicitor for the Second
Defendant.

To: Messrs George E. Baker & Co.
       Solicitor for the Plaintiff.

The Facts, the admission of which is required, are set out in the attached schedule.

4.   At the time of the alleged incident the Plaintiff was convalescing in the hospital at H.M.P. Liverpool after a colostomy operation on or about 4 June 1986.

5.   At or about 8.10.am. on 29 June 1986 the Plaintiff was let out of his cell to join the queue of inmates waiting to be served breakfast; this queue was being supervised by the First Defendant.

5.   On reaching the front of the queue and on seeing his food the Plaintiff complained aggressively and then threw his food tray towards a group of inmate cleaners, narrowly missing one of them.

6.   The First Defendant then ordered the Plaintiff to return to his cell and followed him as he walked towards it, without restraining him in any way.

7.   Before reaching his cell the Plaintiff lashed out with a clenched left fist at the First Defendant but the First Defendant deflected the blow by putting his left arm up and then tried to restrain the Plaintiff by putting his right arm over the Plaintiff's right shoulder and chest and by pulling him to a sitting position on the floor.

8.   The Plaintiff lashed out with both arms and both legs and three other officers came to assist the First Defendant, seizing the Plaintiff's arms and legs.

9.   Once the Plaintiff had been adequately restrained he was lifted and carried to the room identified in the Particulars following paragraph 2 of the Particulars of Claim as "a Strip Cell" but which is

- 2 -

properly described as Silent Medical Room No. 9. He was placed there
on the floor and stripped, there being a suit of clothes in the cell
for him to wear.

10.   Following delivery of the Plaintiff to the said cell and
completion of the appropriate disrobing formalities the First
Defendant and the other officers left the cell which was then locked.
Before leaving the cell the First Defendant saw that the Plaintiff's
colostomy bag was still in place.

11.   Shortly afterwards the First Defendant and another officer
returned to the cell and the First Defendant saw that the Plaintiff
had removed his colostomy bag and had smeared himself with blood.

12.   At no time did the First Defendant or the other officers use
force other than when necessary and then no more than reasonable force
in order to restrain the Plaintiff from either assaulting the officers
or hurting himself and the First Defendant and the other officers did
not beat, punch, kick or pull the hair of the Plaintiff either as
alleged or at all.

13.   No admission is made as to the alleged or any injuries loss or
damage.

Served the 11ᵗʰ   day of May 1987
by Victor Mishcon and Company of
125 High Holborn London WC1V 6QP,
Solicitors for the First Defendant

- 3 -

The case was eventually heard on the 8th and 9th December at Newport County Court on the Isle of Wight.

After the first two days of the hearing Foran wanted to know from his Counsel, Martin Strutt, if it was possible to stop the proceedings in the event of a criminal action being brought by the police. He also wanted to know why the police had not been allowed to see him when in prison. He had to assume that there must have been some collusion to prevent it.

Nevertheless, the case continued and on the 16th December 1988 an award of £750 was made to Foran, with no acceptance of liability by the prison officers concerned.

Foran accepted the payment but would try to gain prosecution of the officers at a later date. Unfortunately, the fact the settlement was subject to the prison officers' 'no-liability' clause ultimately prevented him from doing so. This wasn't until after several attempts to lay charges by both Foran and Valerie, who continually pressed MPs and the Home Office.

(1)
BETWEEN   MARTIN PATRICK FORAN ....   PLAINTIFF

AND   CHARLTON & THE HOME OFFICE

CHARLTON   FIRST   DEFENDANT

THE HOME OFFICE   SECOND DEFENDANT

CASE No. 8802466

(1)
if in a
revi.
heading

BEFORE HIS HONOUR JUDGE GALPIN Q.C. SITTING AT THE GUILDHALL, NEWPORT, ISLE OF WIGHT ON 8TH, 9TH & 16TH DECEMBER 1988.

UPON hearing Counsel for the parties

AND UPON the Plaintiff and the First and Second Defendants having agreed to terms endorsed on Counsel's briefs and signed by Counsel for the parties and by the Plaintiff

BY CONSENT

IT IS ORDERED that:-

1) All further proceedings in this action be stayed except for the purpose of carrying such terms into effect.

2) Liberty to apply as to carrying such terms into effect.

3) There be Legal Aid Taxation of the Plaintiff's costs.

DATED

Address all communications to the Chief Clerk AND QUOTE THE ABOVE CASE NUMBER

THE COURT OFFICE AT

NEWPORT I.O. ... IELD COURT CENTRE
130/1 ... ...
NEWPORT I.O.W.
FO30 1TP

is open from 10 am to 4 pm Monday to Friday

134

from IAIN MILLS Member of Parliament for MERIDEN

HOUSE OF COMMONS
LONDON SW1A 0AA

25th May 1989

The Rt Hon Douglas Hurd MP
Home Secretary
Home Office

Dear Douglas,

I have been contacted by Mrs Foran, the wife of C51796, Martin Foran, presently at HM Prison, Frankland, Durham.

You may recall that I have written on other occasions regarding Mr Foran, and his continued concern about beating up by prison Warders which took place at HM Prison, Liverpool.

Mrs Foran has shown me photographs and these could be available to you should you wish.

I understand Mr Foran took Court action and was successful, and has an award for compensation of £700, but there has apparently been no disciplinary action against those concerned.

I would be grateful for your comments.

Yours sincerely,

While this was going on, Valerie was still pressing for his case to be reviewed on the grounds of tainted evidence from the West Midlands Serious Crime Squad, and she garnered the help of Robin Corbett, her MP for Erdington, Birmingham.

From: Robin Corbett, MP

HOUSE OF COMMONS
LONDON SW1A 0AA
01-219 5096

11 September 1989

Dear Mrs. Foran,

This is to confirm that statement which I dictated over the telephone yesterday concerning Mr Martin Foran:

The absence of a signed confession by Martin Foran makes this conviction unsafe.

His conviction rests solely upon the evidence of two police officers and the alleged confession by another convicted person who is said to have implicated Mr. Foran.

The disbanding of the West Midlands Police serious crimes squad, and the investigation into the events leading up to that, with allegations that officers tampered with written evidence and forced suspects into confessions, has created a climate where it is necessary to review all convictions based upon alleged verbal confessions to West Midlands police officers.

This case should be included in the current investigation of West Midlands Police under the supervision of the Police Complaints Authority.

I would be grateful if you would keep me in touch with the campaign.

And will you please also let me know whether Mr Foran is now getting the medical attention he needs. If you are uncertain about this, then I shall raise the matter with the Home Office.

Yours sincerely,

Robin Corbett
Birmingham, Erdington.

Mrs Valerie Foran
32 Acacia Avenue
Birmingham B37 6AQ

She also managed to get Ken Livingston MP to take up the case and pose a parliamentary question to the Attorney General.

PARLIAMENTARY QUESTION FOR PRIORITY WRITTEN ANSWER

ON TUESDAY 4TH APRIL 1988

QUESTION   MR KEN LIVINGSTON: To ask Mr Attorney General, whether he will prosecute for assaulting Martin Foran, the four prison

304 W   officers from Walton Prison against whom £750 damages were awarded in favour of Mr Foran at Newport County Court.

MEMBER'S CONSTITUENCY: BRENT EAST   (LAB)

ANSWER   THE ATTORNEY GENERAL: No. Such proceedings would not be in conformity with the Code for Crown Prosecutors. I add, in the interests of accuracy, that in the civil proceedings to which the Hon. Member refers the action was stayed upon terms that £750 be paid to the plaintiff, with costs. No admission of liability was made.

CHAPTER 17

YET ANOTHER MOVE

Frankland

On 9th February, 1989 he was moved to Frankland prison in Co Durham where he remained for about a year. During this time he again sought medical treatment for his worsening condition and engaged solicitors Meikle Skene & Co. to assist him..

On the 17th July, Consultant Surgeon Mr. A. Peel of North Tees General Hospital wrote, saying he would provide an independent medical report on Foran's condition and requesting his full medical records. On receipt, he complained the copies were of such poor quality that he requested further medical reports. He also said he would charge £125 for this report so Foran's solicitors sought legal aid from the Legal Aid Board for this examination to take place.

By September, this had still not been granted and, following excessive delays, they threatened court action as the medical examination was becoming urgent. In the end it took a writ and the intervention of several MPs before the Home Office agreed to the examination. The solicitors then wrote to Peel to tell him the examination could be done.

The full text of the exchange of letters now follows:

NORTH TEES HEALTH AUTHORITY
Chairman: Mr. D. J. Otter F.C.A.

 **North Tees
General Hospital**

HARDWICK, STOCKTON-ON-TEES, CLEVELAND TS19 8PE   Telephone: STOCKTON (0642) 672122

Consultant Surgeons
H. Brendan Devlin, M.A., M.D., M.Ch., F.R.C.S.
R. W. Thomson, F.R.C.S.
A. L. G. Peel, M.A., M.Chir., F.R.C.S.
I. L. Rosenberg, M.A., M.Chir., F.R.C.S.
E. Leslie Gilliland B.Sc. M.S.F.R.C.S.

ALGP/JL
YOUR REF LAP/F/36/MJC

17th July 1989

Mr Petterson
Messrs Meikle Skene & Co
Solicitors
8 North St
Market Place
Ferryhill
Co Durham DL17 8HX

Dear Mr Petterson

re: Martin Patrick FORAN

Thank you for your letter of the 13th July. I have perused the Press
Release dated 5th June 1989 together with the most helpful medical report
dated 6th October 1987. There is also supplementary information relating
to a letter of the 11th July 1986 from Dr Khan, a letter from Mr Talbot,
the photocopy being of the quality that I could not identify the date, and
a letter from Mr Cooper the photocopy being of such quality that it was
actually unreadable.

I would be prepared to provide an independent medical report on Mr Foran,
and the following would be advantageous - further medical reports and
details since the full report dated 6th October 1987, copies of any medical
notes and for Mr Foran to attend at North Tees Hospital so that he can be
examined fully, including sigmoidoscopy, and the expertise of the stoma
therapy department.

The preparation of a detailed report would be in the region of £125.00.

Yours sincerely

A L G Peel
Consultant Surgeon

SOLICITORS

Also under the style of
DAWSON, ARNOTT & PICKERING

8 NORTH STREET
MARKET PLACE, FERRYHILL
CO. DURHAM DL17 8HX

Telephone: Ferryhill (0740) 652811/2/3
DX60180 FERRYHILL
FAX (0740) 655854

Our Ref: LAP/F/36/MJC
Your Ref:
Date: 25th July, 1989

Dear Mr. Foran,

re: YOur Case.

We have now received a Legal Aid Certificate from the Legal Aid Board which is limited to the obtaining of a Medical Report and the Opinion in Counsel. Coincidentally, we have also heard from Dr. Peel indicating that the cost of the preparation of a Medical Report would be in the region of £125.00. We enclose photocopy of his letter of the 17th of July, 1989.

We also enclose an appropriate form of Authority enabling your notes to be released to Dr. Peel and perhaps you could sign this and return it to ourselves as soon as possible and preferably by return of post, indicating where your medical records are presently held. Presumably, they are with the Prison Doctors, but perhaps you could confirm that this is the case. In addition, will there be any difficulties about the Prison Authority making arrangements for you to be taken to North Tees General Hospital. We are writing to the Governor separately upon this matter but perhaps you could make enquiries yourself.

Finally, are there any further reports other than those indicated in the first paragraph of Dr. Peel's letter. If so, perhaps you could forward copies of these to me when replying.

Yours sincerely,

M.P. Foran Esq.,
Prison Number C51796
H.M.P. Frankland,
P.O. Box 40
Finchale Avenue,
Brasside,
DURHAM
DH1 5YD.

W. S. Skene, LL.B., E. T. Amos, LL.B.
R. A. Cruz, J. Roberts, LL.B.
M. G. Wilson, LL.B., L. A. Petterson, LL.B
T. B. M. Farrell, LL.B., Karin E. Welsh, LL.B

Also at:
2 Chole Terrace , Spennymoor. Tel. 814
7 High Street, Sedgefield. Tel
38 Horsemarket

THIS FIRM IS REGULATED BY THE LAW SOCIETY IN THE CONDUCT OF INVESTMENT BUSINESS

SOLICITORS

Also under the style of
DAWSON, ARNOTT & PICKERING

8 NORTH STREET
MARKET PLACE, FERRYHILL
CO. DURHAM DL17 8HX
Telephone: Ferryhill (0740) 652411/2/3
DX60180 FERRYHILL
FAX (0740) 655854

IAP/F/36/MJC

27th September, 1989

Dear Sirs,   URGENT

re: Reference No. 08/01/89/10511C - Martin Patrick Foran.

We refer to the above Legal Aid Certificate which was limited to the obtaining of a Medical Report and the Opinion of Counsel.

We have written to the Home Office on a number of occasions and enclose copies of correspondence passing between ourselves and the Home Office and more particularly the latter letter of the 20th of September, 1989. You will note that we allowed a seven day time limit asking for confirmation that our client can have facilities to be medically examined independently. We have received no confirmation of this request and the period expires today. We enclose photocopy of Rule 37A and an extract of Page 47 of Prison Rules (A Working Guide by Joyce Plotnikoff).

In the circumstances it is desired that an application to the High Court be issued as soon as possible to allow facilities for Mr. Foran to be independently medically examined. We believe that the Home Office are being deliberately obstructive.

In the circumstances, if it felt that you can amend the Legal Aid Certificate perhaps you could telephone us so that an urgent application can be made to the High Court.

Yours faithfully,
per pro MEIKLE, SKENE & COMPANY,

Legal Aid Board,
DX61005
NEWCASTLE UPON TYNE

W. S. Skene, LL.B.
R. A. Cole, J. Roberts, LL.B.
H. G. Wilson, LL.B., L.A. Ferguson, LL.B.
I. P. H. Farrell, LL.B., Kenn F. Wells, LL.B

And at:
2 Clyde Terrace, Spennymoor. Tel. 814338
7 High Street, Sedgefield. Tel. 20258
38 Horsemarket, Barnard Castle. Tel. 30255

FIRM IS REGULATED BY THE LAW SOCIETY IN THE CONDUCT OF INVESTMENT BUSINESS

SOLICITORS

Also under the style of
DAWSON, ARNOTT & PICKERING

8 NORTH STREET
MARKET PLACE, FERRYHILL
CO. DURHAM DL17 8HX

Telephone: Ferryhill (0740) 652811/2/3
DX60180 FERRYHILL
FAX (0740) 655854

Our Ref   IAP/F/36/MJC

Your Ref

Date   18th October, 1989

Dear Mr. Peel,

**re: our client Martin Patrick Foran Prison No. C51796
H.M.P. Frankland, Brasside, Durham City.**

You will no doubt recall that we wrote to you some time ago regarding the examination and report upon our above named client. After protracted correspondence and the issue of a Writ and the intervention of several M.P.'s the Home Office have relented and are agreeable (so we understand) to you seeing Mr. Foran. In connection with this we would suggest that you now write direct to the Prison Authorities (or better still to telephone them) to neadvour to fix a mutually convenient up. Should you encounter any difficulties, please do not hesitate to contact us.

Perhaps you could confirm to ourselves that an appointment has been arranged.

Yours sincerely,

Mr. A.G. Peel,
Consultant Surgeon,
North Tees General Hospital,
Hardwick,
STOCKTON ON TEES
Cleveland
TS19 8PE.

W. S. Skene, LL.B.,
B. A. Cone, J. Roberts, LL.B.
M. G. Wilson, LL.B., J. A. Pettersson, LL.B
T. B. M. Farrell, LL.B., Karen E. Wrim LL.B

And at:
2 Clyde Terrace, Spennymoor. Tel: 814235
7 High Street, Sedgefield, Tel: 20255
38 Horsemarket, Barnard Castle. Tel. (0833) 690505

THIS FIRM IS REGULATED BY THE LAW SOCIETY IN THE CONDUCT OF INVESTMENT BUSINESS

To their horror, Peel wrote back on the 26th October to say that, after consulting the Medical Officer of the prison, he declined to do the examination. There was no explanation as to why.

Z C

 **North Tees
General Hospital**

HARDWICK, STOCKTON-ON-TEES, CLEVELAND TS19 8PE   Telephone: STOCKTON (0642) 672122

Consultant Surgeons
H. Brendan Devlin, M.A., M.D., M.Ch., F.R.C.S.
R. W. Thomson, F.R.C.S.
A. L. G. Peel, M.A., M.Chir., F.R.C.S.
I. L. Rosenberg, M.A., M.Chir., F.R.C.S.
E. Leslie Gilliland B.Sc. M.S.F.R.C.S.

ALGP/SF

23 October 1989

Meikle, Skene & Co
8 North Street
Market Place
FERRYHILL
Co Durham
DL17 8HX

Dear Sir

RE: MARTIN PATRICK FORAN
     HMP FRANKLAND BRASSIDE DURHAM CITY

Thank you for your letter of 18 October 1989.

Since your letters of 1 August 1989, I have been in communication with the authorities at HM Prison and in particular their medical officers.

It would seem that it would be inappropriate for me to take matters further with effect to Martin Patrick Foran and I, therefore, decline to take any further action.

I have enclosed the photographs.

Yours sincerely

A L G Peel
Consultant Surgeon

Enc

SOLICITORS

Also under the style of
DAWSON, ARNOTT & PICKERING

8 NORTH STREET
MARKET PLACE, FERRYHILL
CO. DURHAM DL17 8HX

Telephone: Ferryhill (0740) 652811/2/3
DX60180 FERRYHILL
FAX (0740) 655854

Our Ref   LAP/F/36/SS
Your Ref

Date: 26th October, 1989

Dear Mr. Foran,

re: Your Case

Further to our recent meeting, completely out of the blue I have in this mornings post received correspondence from Mr. Peel and enclose photocopy of the same. This is the first indication that I have had that Mr. Peel would be unwilling to treat you.

In the circumstances, presumably, it will be necessary for us to instruct a new Consultant Surgeon. Perhaps, you could let me have your comments as soon as possible and preferably by return of post.

Yours sincerely,

P.S. We return copies of Extracts as requested.

Mr. M.P. Foran,
Prison Number C51796,
H.M. Prison Frankland,
P.O. Box 40,
Finchale Avenue,
Brasside,
DURHAM.
DH1 5YD.

W. S. Skene, LL.B.,
R. A. Coxs, J. Roberts, LL.B
M. G. Weiser, LL.B., L.A. Pickering, LL.E
F. N. M. Eward, LL.B., Karen E. Webb, LL.L.

And at:
7 Clyde Terrace, Spennymoor. Tel. 914338
Hugh Street, Sedgefield Tel. 20255
Marketways, Barnard Castle. Tel. (0833) 690505

THIS FIRM IS REGULATED BY THE LAW SOCIETY IN THE CONDUCT OF INVESTMENT BUSINESS

Fortunately, Mr Cook, the Consultant Surgeon at Dryburn Hospital, agreed to do the examination but asked for assurances that he would not be the subject of any litigation. Just what the prison medical officer had told the surgeons is anyone's guess.

SOLICITORS

Also under the style of
DAWSON, ARNOTT & PICKERING

8 NORTH STREET
MARKET PLACE, FERRYHILL
CO. DURHAM DL17 8HX
Telephone: Ferryhill (0740) 652811/2/3
DX60180 FERRYHILL
FAX (0740) 655854

Our Ref LAP/F/36/MJC
Your Ref
Date 1st November, 1989

Dear Martin,

re: Your Case.

We have recently received a telephone call from Mr. Cook, Consultant Surgeon of Dryburn Hospital. He advised that he was still perfectly willing to treat you and that you are approaching the top of the waiting list. However, he was not prepared to consider treating you if there was any threat of litigation pending. It is our understanding that Dr. Flood has been speaking to Mr. Cook and as a result of this Mr. Cook has contacted us.

We understand that during your last discussion with Mr. Cook you were quite prepared to receive treatment from him but obviously he requires some fairly definite assurance that he would not be the subject of litigation. In the circumstances, obviously we cannot give this assurance on your behalf and you would have to decide whether you are prepared to give confirmation that you would not wish to take any sort of proceedings against Mr. Cook arising out of past medical treatment.

In the circumstances, perhaps you could let us have your views upon this as soon as possible and preferably by return of post.

Yours sincerely,

Lawes Abson.

M.P. Foran, Esq.,
Prison Number C51796
H.M.P. Frankland,
P.O. Box 40
Finchale Avenue,
Brasside,
DURHAM
DH1 5YD.

W. S. Skene LL.B
P. A. Cook J. Roberts LL.B
M. G. Wilson LL.B I. A. Ferguson L.B
I. R. M. Farrell, M. R. Arnott Walsh LL.B

Also at
7 Clyde Terrace, Spennymoor Tel. 814336
2 High Street, Sedgefield Tel. 20255
30 Horsemarket, Barnard Castle Tel. (0833) 8902.

Eventually, another consultant vascular surgeon agreed to do the examination but by this time a year had elapsed. Considering the treatment Foran required was urgent when the original request was made in July 1989, it is staggering that neither the prison service nor the medical officers directly concerned attached any significance to the urgency. In fact, it would be easy to believe that they deliberately produced a stream of delaying tactics.

Trevor Layzell
Consultant General & Vascular Surgeon

17 Witton Way
High Etherley
Bishop Auckland
County Durham
DL14 0LR

(0388)-832857

TL/AMCK/6/90/F

29th June 1990

Meikle Skene and Co.
Solicitors
8 North Street
Market Place
Ferryhill
County Durham
DL17 8HX

Dear Sirs

Your Client Martin Patrick FORAN

I spent some 2 hours talking to your client at HMP Frankland on Thursday 14th June 1990.

I made it clear that I was there as a Medical Advisor, and your client seemed to accept this.

We had a long talk about his medical problems.

I suggested that I would consider what he had told me, and attempt to come up with a course of action which might alleviate the problems that he presently has.

Briefly, he needs to receive attention to his stoma, so that it is the easier for him to manage. He may well benefit from an abdominal support, with an orifice for his colostomy.

I have asked my secretary to contact the Governor to ensure that I might see your client again on the afternoon of Tuesday 3rd July 1990.

I reiterate that my aim is to be as helpful as I know how in the medical management of your client. Perhaps you could assure me that whatever appliances, medication, or whatever I prescribe, would be made available.

Yours faithfully

Trevor Layzell
Consultant General and Vascular Surgeon

SOLICITORS

Also under the style of
DAWSON, ARNOTT & PICKERING

8 NORTH STREET
MARKET PLACE, FERRYHILL
CO. DURHAM DL17 8HX
Telephone: Ferryhill (0740) 652811/2/3
DX60180 FERRYHILL
FAX (0740) 655854

Our Ref: LAP/F/36/SS
Your Ref:
Date: 2nd July, 1990

Dear Martin,

re: Your Case

We have now received correspondence from Mr. Layzell and enclose photocopy of the same for your information. I am writing to the Governor in connection with the final paragraph of the Report of Mr. Layzell and upon receiving a reply from the Governor, I will write to you again. In the meantime, I understand that you are to see Mr. Layzell on Tuesday the 3rd of July, next.

Yours sincerely,

Love

Mr. M.P. Foran,
Prison Number C51796
H.M.P. Frankland,
P.O. Box 40
Finchale Avenue,
Brasside,
DURHAM CITY
DH1 5YD

W. S. Skene, LL.B.,
Roberts, LL.B.
M. G. Wilson, LL.B., L.A. Petterson, LL.B.
T. B. M. Farrell, LL.B., Karin E. Welsh, LL.B.

And at:
2 Clyde Terrace, Spennymoor. Tel. 814336
7 High Street, Sedgefield. Tel. 20266
38 Horsemarket, Barnard Castle. Tel. (0833) 690505

In another unbelievable move, the Governor of Frankland arranged for him to be moved to York prison without having received the necessary surgery which was first requested 3 years earlier.

His solicitors then had to start the process again by writing to the Governor of York prison explaining the situation and requesting an independent medical consultant attend Foran. He received the following reply:

HM Prison
Full Sutton
York
YO4 1PS

Telephone 0759 72447
Fax 0759 71206

Meikle, Skene & Co
Solicitors
8 North Street
Market Place
FERRYHILL
Co Durham DL17 8HX

Your reference LAP/F/36/MJC

Our reference

Date 14 April 1992

Dear Sirs

MICHAEL PATRICK FORAN C51796

I refer to your letter of 30 March 1992. Dr Kumar has written to you separately on the question of Mr Foran's medical treatment and confirms that there is no objection to an independent consultant visiting here to examine Mr Foran.

As regards a move for Mr Foran, I have been exploring the possibility of a transfer to a less secure establishment nearer his home. I think this is desirable, the more so as Mr Foran approaches discharge.

Yours faithfully

J STAPLES
Governor

His solicitors then wrote to the Governor of York prison to arrange for the necessary surgery and sought assurances that he would be kept there long enough for it to be carried out.

SOLICITORS

Also under the style of
DAWSON, ARNOTT & PICKERING

8 NORTH STREET
MARKET PLACE, FERRYHILL
CO. DURHAM DL17 8HX

Telephone: Ferryhill (0740) 652811/2/3
DX60180 FERRYHILL
FAX (0740) 655854

Our Ref LAP/F/36/MJC
Your Ref
Date 6th May, 1992

<u>For the Attention of Mr. J. Staples.</u>

Dear Sirs,

<u>re: Martin Patrick Foran – Prison No. C51796</u>

Thank you for your letter of the 14th of April, 1992. We enclose copy of letter that we have written direct to Dr. Kumar. We understand that the Consultant Surgeon at York General Hospital is ready to carry out surgical treatment upon our client and we look forward to receiving your confirmation within the next seven days that our client can remain at Full Sutton until such time as this treatent has been carried out and that you will co-operate with the medical authorities.

Yours faithfully,
per pro MEIKLE, SKENE & COMPANY.

The Governor
H.M. Prison,
Full Sutton,
YORK
YO1 1PS

J. Roberts, LL.B. M. G. Watson, LL.B.
L. A. Petterson, LL.B. T. B. M. Farrell, LL.B.
Kevin E. Welsh, LL.B. J. S. S. Bona, LL.B.

And at
2 Clyde Terrace, Spennymoor Tel: 814336
7 High Street, Sedgefield Tel: 20255
38 Horsemarket, Barnard Castle Tel: (0833) 690935

THIS FIRM IS REGULATED BY THE LAW SOCIETY IN THE CONDUCT OF INVESTMENT BUSINESS

By this time, Foran was more in fear of the prison officers than the other inmates and he wanted to get away from the hospital cells and the segregation units and in among the other prisoners. He also contemplated another rooftop vigil to gain more publicity for the injustices he had suffered.

Martin Foran takes up the story from here:

'Later on, when I had recovered from the beatings, I tried to climb onto the prison roof but, unluckily for me, my body was still weak from the long hunger strikes and, upon trying to climb the pipe onto the roof, I broke my foot. I was half way up and couldn't get up or down and asked all the prisoners in the yard to support me to make sure I was not beaten up again. Yet again I landed up in another prison hospital but I was not further harmed, although, because of what had happened in Wandsworth, the staff did not like me.

'I was left in pain from my foot and from the colostomy, which was by now very sore. Otherwise, I was left alone as my illness got worse. I was moved out of the hospital and back to the prison wing. Life was bad for me and for the other prisoners.

'Months later, I was told that I would be seeing a London specialist to have an operation, but the biggest shock of all was when I was told that I would be released to make my own way to my home in Birmingham, and from there to make my own way to the London hospital. Can you try to picture what this news was doing to my mind? I was asking, what was going on? Everything went through my mind: was it a plan to kill me, by saying I'd broken out of prison, or was the plan to have me met by the SCS in Birmingham? My mind worked overtime. All my protesting, all my hunger strikes and still three years to do, yet they were saying I could go on my own?

'Every part of me was saying it's a set up, but I couldn't resist the thought of two days with my wife and children with no prison officers to say 'time up' after one hour. I had not held my daughter Valerie for more than a few minutes after she was born, while I was on remand in 1978. To spend a day with my children was like winning the pools, so no matter what danger lay in store for me, I wanted to be with my wife and children. I would risk walking over the burning fires of hell. My joy at this chance could never be expressed by words on paper, even if it meant my death in the long run.

'At the back of my mind there was still the danger of being killed. I, myself, have no fear of death. Even now, years later, I know my days are numbered as all my years of protesting are starting to drain me and I can hardly walk. I have to be pushed about in a wheelchair, but I have never feared death. My main concern has always been my wife and our children. As long as no harm came to them, they could do anything to me, just leave my family alone.

'So, the day came when I was let out, my joy overruled my fears and it helped rebuild our family life. No visits from the Crime Squad; I had been shown trust by the prison governor and I did not want to break that trust. The police left me alone while I was in Birmingham, so I turned up at the London hospital on time for my operation only to be told that while in the hospital, I would have a police guard.

'This did not feel right. I was trusted to make my own way to my home in Birmingham, stay there for two days, then make my own way to London, then to be told I would have police staying with me caused all my fears to come rushing back in a deluge. Was I being set up? Would they try to say I'd confessed to this and that while recovering from the operation? I thought of the great powers of the SCS and, all of a sudden, flashing into my head were warning signs.

'After the days with my family and the joy of freedom, what now did they have in store for me? In fear of the police, I ran out of the hospital doors and got in touch with my wife to tell her what was happening and that I was wondering what to do, when my daughter and son said; "Don't go back to prison, Dad, run away with us so we can all be together," so I did. I said I would carry on my fight for justice and then, later, hand myself back. So we started a life on the run, and continued our fight for justice. However, it almost got off to a very bad start when we went to live in Erith in Kent.

'Our plan was to buy a car with help from our friends to raise the necessary money. I bought a car and, while driving it the next day, the police stopped us in Erith. They said the car was stolen and I was arrested and taken to the police station. Before the police pulled us up, I had said to my wife that I would say my name was Andrew and not Martin. I decided to use my brother's name to see if I could talk my way out of it at the station.

'Once at the station, I explained where I bought the car and showed I still had the receipt for it. I gave them a full statement and prayed for bail as I was using Andrew's name. After the statement was taken, I was placed in a cell for about an hour and could hear them talking. The sergeant said, "there's a report here for a Martin Foran who is wanted but it says he has a colostomy, go and see if he has one." I thought; 'here we go, the game is up and I'll be parted from my wife and children again.'

'As the cell door opened I was just going to say; "yes, I have a colostomy and, yes I'm Martin", but before I could open my mouth the police officer asked me; "do you know what a colostomy is?"

'I said, "it's how you shit into a colostomy bag when you're ill". Oh the joy on my face when he asked me to remove my trousers and drop my underpants so he could see my backside. This I did, turning my back to him so he could see my backside.

"He shouted to the sergeant, "He has no colostomy," and told me to get dressed, locking the cell door.

'Try to imagine my joy about half an hour later, when I had been released on my own bail. Try to picture if you can, the look on my wife's face, as I came walking out of that police station.

'We had to leave an address where we were staying and I had a feeling they would soon discover that I was not my brother so we stayed in a caravan that night. The next morning, while going to get some milk, the police were raiding the flat we had been staying in. I was stopped and asked did I see anyone run from the flat. I said; "he's just run over there", pointing to a house and off went the police, running! I walked away, and got word to my wife, who was watching everything from the caravan, staying out of sight in case they saw her. We met up later, and made up our minds to go to Ireland.

'Firstly, we made our way to Scotland, planning to get a ferry from Stranraer. While waiting to board the ferry, the police came around checking all the cars: we hadn't used our real names when purchasing the tickets in case the ports were being watched for me. When the policeman got to us, my daughter was asleep on my lap. He asked our names and where we were going and then left us, but he was soon to come back. I said to my wife, "I think he knows".

'I was asked to get out and come over to the little police station. On walking over, he asked about my children and their ages. I knew then for certain that he knew who I was. He said, "are you going to run?"

'I said, "no, all I ask is that you let my wife and children drive home."

'He stopped and looked at me for a while, then said, "go back to your family, get on the boat and good luck to you!"

'I was shocked, and I asked "why?", because I had no love for the police.

'His words were to shock me even more when he said, "I know who you are and I know a little of your story. Don't paint all police with the same brush as the Serious Crime Squad. Now, get on the boat before you're seen and good luck!" and he walked away.

'That officer's words touched me in a big way and made me decide not to judge all police officers just because of the bad ones in the West Midlands Crime Squad.

'After returning to my family, my wife had woken up the children to tell them the police had Dad again so there was joy on their little faces as I told my wife what had happened. We got on that boat, and landed in Belfast, then drove to Limerick.

'After a few weeks, we were offered a house and we settled down for a few months. However, I could not forget the injustice I had suffered so I started to fight my case again and went on Irish TV to talk about it. Later on we knew we could not just walk away from it: we had to return to carry on the fight. However, that turned out to be a very bad mistake on my part.

'After a short time back in the UK, I was re-arrested while picking up my children from school and locked up in Winson

Green prison. A few days later, while my wife was waiting in the prison visiting room at Winson Green, I was already on my way to Parkhurst.

'In Parkhurst I was told I was not wanted there in case I went onto the prison roof. By now I was feeling very low as it was just coming up to Christmas but everything seemed to be just starting all over again.

'A few days later one of the prison Governors came to see me. We had met previously in one of the other prisons, and he asked if I was going to settle down and stop protesting.

'I said, "No, how can I when I'm innocent of the crimes I'm doing time for?"

'He said "It's about time you stopped fighting the prison service and start fighting with a pen and keep writing to everyone."

'He said if I met him halfway, he'd meet me halfway and I asked what he meant.

'He said, "Go to the prison wing, no protesting, no fighting, use the pen: prove you can do this and I will try to help you."

'The deal was that I was to stay out of trouble, no protesting, and he would try to get me moved to an open prison. Remember, I was only arrested a few weeks before so I trusted him and he turned out to be a man of his word.

'Two months later, on 14th February, I was granted home leave. What a wonderful surprise for my wife. Everyone told the prison Governor that there was no way I would return so I knew he had put a lot of trust in me. I knew he would be ridiculed and be the laughing stock of the other prison Governors and prison staff if I didn't return, so I wasn't going to let him down.

'Once again, he was true to his word and I was moved to a category C prison and later landed up in Spring Hill Open prison where I would finish my sentence.

CHAPTER 18

VALERIE

T his book would not be complete without hearing from the woman who has stood by her husband throughout his ordeal.

During his first 8 year sentence, following his wrongful conviction of robbery on four counts, she was his only link with the outside world and she fought for his freedom every day of his imprisonment despite having to bring up her five children.

After his second wrongful conviction he told her not to wait for him as she should not have to put up with further hardship and stress which she had endured following his first conviction. However, she only rebuked him for suggesting such a thing and, despite the effect on her own health, she spent the next 11 years continually telling him he mustn't give up while continuing her own fight for his release.

She has stood by him ever since and continues to support him during his present appeals. Such is her devotion to her husband that she has made it clear she will never stop her fight to restore his and their family's reputation.

Foran describes the support from his wife as follows:–

"What she went through was a million times worse than me. You have to remember it was the time of the backlash to the IRA bombings and all her family turned on her and told her to divorce me.

People in the area also turned on her and used to spit on her in the street. Where she got her strength from I simply don't know.

She was treated badly by everyone, including some prison officers and it became a nightmare for her.

No one should ever have to go through what she went through."

So desperate was her plight given the absence of money that he made an appeal to all his relatives, Valerie's family and all their friends and neighbours. He told them that for each loaf of bread they put on Valerie's table, he would repay them with £1,000 once he came out of prison, if he won his appeals and received compensation.

Believing that this would help her feed the children, he was horrified to learn later that, with just a single exception, none of these people took up his offer and Valerie received no loaves.

What follows is a transcript of my interview with Valerie:

....

How much did you know about Martin's past when you first met?

Not much, but it wasn't long before he told me. As far as I was concerned what happened in the past was in the past and it didn't stop me loving him.

Did he make any pledges that he would stay out of trouble?

After we had been together a while, I fell pregnant with our eldest daughter and he assured me he would not get into any further trouble.

What did your parents think of you marrying him?

My family didn't want me to be with Martin and in view of the problems being experienced with the IRA and Martin being Irish, it didn't help. Both Martin and I can be quite stubborn so we just decided to get on with our own lives. We even got married on our own as we didn't want to invite anyone who we knew would not want to be there.

When were you married?

We were married in 1975.

Wasn't that around the time you were both picked up at a jewellers shop for supposedly passing off stolen jewellery?

Yes, that's right. What happened was, my gran passed away in 1971 and she gave me her rings and a watch. Times were hard and we hadn't got much money and we thought we would see how much we could get for the rings if it became necessary. While at the jewellers, the next thing I knew the police were behind us saying they were arresting us for being in possession of stolen jewellery. To this day I never received my gran's rings or watch back.

What were your first thoughts and feelings when he was accused of this?

I was shocked. I really didn't think things like this could happen. What also shocked me was that when we were at Digbeth police station being questioned, I saw an elderly man being dragged in by his legs.

How did you feel when more and more things began to happen after this incident, and the police were gradually building a case against Martin?

They were on to Martin all the time. We had no peace from the police from that moment. There was a time when we went to the Social Security office to ask if we could get any assistance towards buying a bed as we didn't have one and the woman behind the counter said, 'Go and do what you normally do and steal one.' I left absolutely disgusted.

Was this sort of thing typical of the reaction you were getting from the people in Birmingham or was this an isolated incident?

The thing is that after the Birmingham bombings and the other things that were happening at the time, anyone who was Irish was abused and me, being English, walking down the street with an Irishman, I used to get called all sorts of names. It was a nightmare time that I would not like to live through again.

When Martin was on remand in Winson Green prison, how often were you able to visit him?

I could visit him practically every day. We used to stand in a queue on arriving.

Did it ever cross your mind that he would be found guilty?

Never, I was sure he would get off.

You must have been devastated?

I simply couldn't believe it and to make matters worse I was pregnant with Valerie by that time. I really do believe that it was all the stress surrounding this that caused her to be born deaf.

When Martin was eventually sentenced to 10 years for crimes you knew he hadn't committed, could you try to put into words your thoughts and feelings at that time as you had two very young children with a third on the way?

Oh dear, the emotions were just overwhelming, I couldn't stop crying, I didn't know what to do or where to go. I had no-one to turn to.

Would your family not help you?

This is the bit that hurts. They didn't want to know and I was completely on my own.

How did you explain things to the children?

What happened was that before he was eventually arrested the police would ransack the house without a warrant and they would empty all the drawers and the fridge and not tell us what they were looking for. So I had to explain to the children what was happening and what was going on. I've never ever held anything back from them.

How do you think all this affected the children?

Really badly and they also had a bad time at school with other children calling them names and saying, 'your dad's in prison.' There was nothing they could do, they just had to take it.

Did the neighbours rally round and help?

No, they didn't want to know. I was just on my own. There was one exception, an elderly lady said if I needed anything, she would try to help. She was a lovely lady. Martin told everyone that he would give £1,000 to anyone who put a loaf of bread on our table to feed the children. No one did it except this one lady.

What about the Irish community, did they get in touch to see if they could help?

No, not really. You have to understand that Martin was Irish and I was English and, generally speaking, the Irish didn't like the English so Martin and I used to keep ourselves to ourselves. The children also helped me to survive.

There must have been moments, particularly when Martin came out of prison and then almost immediately went back in again, when you thought, 'I can't go on with this'?

Well, naturally, you would think that. I thought, No, not again? Particularly as I was pregnant with twins when he went back inside for the second time.

Did you feel there must come a time when you had to live your own life and leave Martin in prison?

No way, no way. No!

That never even entered your head?

No, not at all. My thoughts were, this is another nightmare but the worst of the nightmares because he was sent to prison in September and the twins were born in October. That was hard, really, really hard. As for leaving Martin, there was no chance of that whatsoever, our love is stronger than that.

You have endured 19 years without your husband and another 20 years fighting for his convictions to be quashed. Nothing has gone right during that time until the success of the appeal for his second conviction in 2013 but still the compensation claim was refused. Are you optimistic about the next appeal?

I really don't know which way this is going to turn out, to be honest. We've had to fight for years and years to get this far. No amount of compensation could give us back our lives that we lost. We've also lost a lot health-wise. We've not been able to see our children grow up together. I really can't say more because we don't know how their minds [the judiciary] work.

It's not necessarily comforting for you but the Birmingham Six took ten years before they received their first offer of compensation, which was rejected, and it was a further year before they received their final compensation.

The problem is that Martin hasn't got that time left.

If for any reason Martin's health prevented him from seeing the compensation claim succeed, would you continue the fight?

I would say, I think I would continue but it would depend on if I had enough strength in my body to continue the fight.

What about the children, would they help you continue the fight?

Yes, I'm sure they would but I can't speak for them.

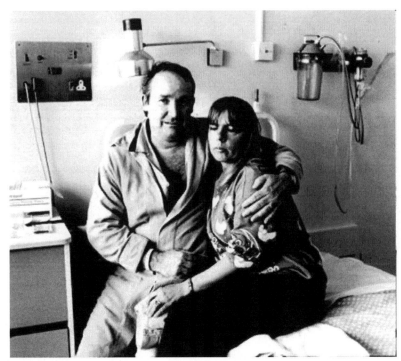

Above: During Valerie's visit to Kettering hospital in August 1992
Below: With daughter Valerie and twins Helen and Terry

CHAPTER 19

THE FAMILY'S EMOTIONS

Although Valerie was the family's tower of strength, I wanted to know more about the effect it was having on the children with their father being absent all the time.

We often don't give sufficient credit to young children who see more than we think and are affected in many ways either consciously or subconsciously when others are not happy. Often they can't or don't wish to express it.

I was continually recalling Foran's words telling me that, despite the horrendous treatment and pain he had endured during his 19 years spent inside prison, it was nothing compared to what Valerie had endured, and it made me want to get a glimpse of some of the issues and emotions they had to deal with within the family.

They are clearly a close, loving and private family and reluctant to reveal too many of their emotions to others. If ever a family showed resilience to devastating events and demonstrated the 'stiff upper lip', it is the Forans.

Among the papers I was sifting through, I came across a letter from their daughter, Helen, when she was a young adult. When I read it, it answered my questions perfectly and said everything that I could have possibly tried to say only much more poignantly. The family have given permission for it to be reproduced.

Twins Helen and Terry aged 7

Cheated

①

I was asked how I feel about my dads exposure, Injusticed is how I feel. Confused ~~from~~ about my childhood memories, Stolen from the life I ~~ee~~ Should have had, I'm inspired by my mothers Strenghth and deflated by my adults truth.

As a child you see life through Inaocence eyes. All my memories are now tarnished as I realised things were not as Percieved them.
Looking back as an adult I now feel my childhood memories have been Stolen from me. Nothing remains the way I Seen it through innocence new eyes ~~now~~ Im now Seeing a guilty world

life is now questions, Many un answered.

I'm amazed to realise how little help my mum had yet She was so strong. raising five kids alone is hard enough for any person to deal with and believe me, my ~~broth~~ twin brother and I was, quite a handful but to deal with my dads injustice and remain strong ~~for him and his family~~ while fighting for his freedom ~~and raising his kids wonderfully~~ I'm so proud to have been blessed with her as my mother and what a wonderful role model I have been given.

~~first~~ My mum is a new jewel stone, richer than gold as she is LOVE. In everyday life you dont always think about the past you try and focuse on the

3 ⊕

future but now I find I am
being made to face the
past and suddenly it doesn't
seem as fun as ~~J~~ I remember

~~Bike rides a~~
~~Exciting~~ memories of many
~~protest which~~ c

Past memories being changed
by my ~~d~~ adults ~~perspetive~~

Past feelings unfelt, not sure
how I feel ~~now~~
    fun bike rides and protest
~~with~~ + not understanding
what we were protesting for
or knowing what protesting
ment
    now becomes clear
memories that ~~we~~ once seemed
fun are now clouded by
the truth
    realisiation has just changed
my world * where ~~is m~~ has my child

<u>4</u>

– hood gone.

Can someone please
give me back my childhood

So I can look back
with my new adults eyes

and see it remains the
way I remember it.

Injustice and Stolen
moments and hurt
and pain is

now all I see.

Is that justice?

Not only was a mans life
taken from him but in
his cell with him was my
mothers heart and his
childrens childhood memories

With family during their many prison hospital visits
Twins Terry and Helen with daughter Valerie and son Martin

CHAPTER 20

THE "BIRMINGHAM SIX"

There are striking similarities between Foran's case and that of the "Birmingham Six". They had all been convicted in 1974, the same year that Foran was arrested. They were all Irish and accused of being members of the IRA, and they were all arrested and convicted by the same officers who were involved in Foran's case.

In March 1991 they walked free from jail after their convictions for the murder of 21 people in two pubs were quashed by the Court of Appeal.

Paddy Joe Hill, Hugh Callaghan, Richard McIlkenny, Gerry Hunter, Billy Power and Johnny Walker, who between them had served 96 years for a crime they did not commit, were released onto the streets outside the Old Bailey in London at five past four in the evening.

Paddy Hill said, "The police told us from the start they knew we hadn't done it."

On their release they were greeted by cheering crowds, as they punched their fists in the air and waved, celebrating their first taste of freedom.

Richard McIlkenny said, "We've waited a long time for this – 16 years because of hypocrisy and brutality. But every dog has its day and we're going to have ours."

Paddy Hill went on to announce, "For sixteen and a half years we have been used as political scapegoats," he said. "The police told us from the start they knew we hadn't done it. They didn't care who had done it."

The six had left Birmingham shortly before the bombs exploded in two city centre pubs in the bloodiest ever IRA attack. The Mulberry Bush pub and The Tavern were both destroyed in the blasts and 21 people were killed with more than 160 injured.

The men claimed in court they had confessed only after being beaten by police but the court did not believe them and so began their long battle for justice.

In January 1987, their first appeal was rejected, but the campaign for their release gathered pace headed by the Labour MP, Chris Mullin. A new inquiry by Devon and Cornwall Police into the original inquiry uncovered irregularities in the police case against the Six, which paved the way for their successful appeal.

New scientific tests showed statements made by the Birmingham Six were altered at a later date.

Scientists also admitted in court that the forensic tests which were originally said to confirm two of the six had been handling explosives could have produced the same results from the accused handling cigarettes.

The similarities go on. In a book about his 16-year struggle for justice, Hill described an attack on prisoners by officials at Winson Green prison in Birmingham.

He says, "I was punched and kicked across the room. Somebody grabbed me by the hair and smashed my head down on the top of the door. My nose burst apart and the blood ran from it like a tap."

They all appealed for compensation for the lost 16 years spent behind bars for something they didn't do. However, after 10 years they were still getting nowhere, as the British Government refused to acknowledge liability for the mistreatment of the Birmingham Six.

Lawyers for the Six continued to press for compensation and for a public apology from the Government for the men's treatment at the hands of the police and prison authorities.

Their solicitor, Gareth Peirce, wrote to Irish Foreign Affairs Minister Brian Cowen, urging him to intervene in the 'continuing unresolved injustices' over the British Government's refusal to acknowledge liability for their mistreatment. He said it was important to extract a full apology because "influential people continue to reiterate behind closed doors that the men were, in fact, guilty, and escaped life imprisonment only on a technicality."

Eventually, in 2001, Paddy Hill received an offer of £549,932 in compensation which he rejected. Although the full offer was over £900,000, the difference was to be withheld because of various reductions but Hill was still angry about the way he had been treated.

The amount was eventually recalculated and a year later a new offer in the region of £1m was made which Hill, reluctantly accepted. Each of the others also received a similar amount but there was no apology ever made for the distress and heartbreak their families had suffered. Hill still says that they all remain very angry as their families were 'torn to pieces'.

Following a full investigation of the West Midland Serious Crime Squad in 1999 it would be revealed that there were over 30 miscarriages of justice attributable to the Squad. Details of the full indictment are reproduced in Appendix 8

CHAPTER 21

SUPPORT FROM INSIDE AND OUTSIDE PRISON

Foran's case had attracted a great deal of media attention over the years following his many hunger strikes and rooftop vigils. As a result he received letters of support from both inside and outside prison.

- People outside would write to the Irish newspapers asking them to join a petition to have him freed;
- The leader of the Irish Government, Desmond O'Malley, gave an interview to the Irish News expressing his anger at the treatment Foran was receiving;
- The Minister of Foreign Affairs was in constant touch with the Irish Embassy in London and wrote confirming he was monitoring his case closely;
- Senator Hugh Byrne wrote direct to Foran when at Frankland expressing his support;
- The Irish Commission for prisoners overseas wrote to the Governor of Long Lartin while Foran was there asking for an explanation about a series of incidents;
- Even prisoners inside the prison at Parkhurst and Frankland wrote to the Governor expressing their concern at the treatment Foran was receiving.

Later in this book there are also examples of prison officers trying to offer some compassion for the way in which he was being treated.

Foran would discover on leaving prison that there had been hundreds of letters sent to the various prison Governors complaining of his plight.

Some of these letters follow and others are at Appendix 5.

IRISH COMMISSION
FOR PRISONERS OVERSEAS

7-8 Lower Abbey St., Dublin 1. Tel: 766482, 788177

Governor,
HM Prison Long Lartin,
South Littleton,
Evesham,
Worcs WR11 5TZ.

29th July, 1987

Re: Martin Foran C51796

Dear Governor,

I write on behalf of the Irish Commission for Prisoners Overseas, a subsection of the Bishops' Commission for Emigrants. Our concerns are the welfare of Irish prisoners overseas. (See information leaflet enclosed).

This Commission is seriously concerned about the condition of Mr Foran. We have been dealing with his case for some years now. He is claiming 2 things:

    (a) Wrongful conviction.,
    (b) Ill-treatment in prison - particularly in relation to medical help for a colostomy condition and continuous lock-up for 23 hours per day.

I have spoken with the probation and welfare people in Long Lartin and they tell me that Mr Foran is in the segration unit because the hospital cannot keep him. The officer with whom I spoke felt that the segregation unit was unsuitable for Mr Foran's medical condition.

This Commission has received a copy of a letter signed by at least 10 co-prisoners testifying to an allegedly deteriorating and inhuman situation. The Commission must take these allegations seriously, as they bear out what both Mr Foran writes and what one visitor has described to us. Therefore we are writing to you to seek clarification as to:
    (a) Why Mr Foran is in the segregation unit which, he says, means 23 hours per day lock-up?
    (b) What exactly is the medical condition of Mr Foran?
    (c) Why he is not receiving adequate medical treatment, as he and others claim?
    (d) Whether it is possible to have an independent medical expert examin Mr Foran, at the request of this Commission.

CHRISTOPHER BERNARD HAGUE L37455   94

My name is Christopher Bernard Hague and I am a serving prisoner doing a 15yr sentence for armed robbery. I have been allocated to C wing Frankland since 24th May 1989. I am in cell no. 24 which is opposite Martin Forans cell no 36 Martin has been so badly neglected medically that I have on numerous occasions heard prison officers being openly critical of the neglect he is being subjected to. I have mentioned the neglect to members of staff and they seem mystified why he is being obviously maltreated. They find it embarrasing to discuss because the abuse is so obvious it is indefensible. I overheard one medical officer say to Foran that "there seems to be a conspiracy not to give you proper treatment by the doctors". I have seen acid marks on Forans stomach to his groin. I have accompanied him to the sick hatch and heard a medical officer say that she had been told not to give him any treatment, although she herself showed concern she said she was acting under instructions.

Signed 19/6/89

[signature]

28th January, 1990.

Mr. Martin Foran,
No., C51796
HMP Frankland,
P.O. Box 40,
Finchdale Ave.,
Brasside,
Durham.
5YL.

Dear Martin,

Your friend Mr. George Dwyer has been in touch with me with your conviction and consequent jail sentence.

I have a particular interest in your case as I have in the case of the Guildford Four now released and the Birmingham Six and many other Irish Prisoners in British jails who were wrongfully convicted by a police force who have now being dicovered for what they are totally discredited.

It was not the Irish people or the Irish Government or any one in Britain that discredited this police force they discredited themselfs with the apparent good will of the british system. I have heard much about your case as I have about others and I would be most anxious for you to contact me as soon as possible with a view to me calling to see you or seeing members of your family.

Please be assured of my fullest co-operation and please let me hear from you as soon as possible.

Very best wishes,

Yours sincerely,

Senator Hugh Byrne,

Give Martin a helping hand

(From Mr. Seamus Mac Seain NW10)

Dear Sir

I enclose some background information about Martin Foran, a Limerick man in Frankland Prison in Durham.

Not everyone is aware of this man's stay in prisons through Britain.

Mr. Foran was convicted twice by the infamous West Midland serious crime squad and virtually all the police officers, who perjured themselves in the Birmingham Six case were involved in Martin Foran's conviction, also involved was Det. Reade.

Mr. Foran was convicted of robbery in 1977 and was imprisoned until 1984. During this time, he embarked on six hunger strikes to highlight his claim of innocents. Three of the hunger strikes he endured lasted 10 weeks, 60 weeks and 58 days.

In 1985, after serving his first sentence and while trying to prove he had been framed, Martin Foran was arrested and convicted again for armed robbery, again by the West Midlands serious crime squad. He was sentenced to eight years in prison.

During this second term which began in 1985, Martin Foran suffered from a serious bowel complaint and needed medical treatment as a result of previous hunger strikes, although obviously suffering pain he

did not get the attention he needed and indeed every time an appointment was made for him to see a surgeon he got transferred to another prison just before he was to have his appointment (ref. petition)! This happened seven or eight times before Mr. Foran, out of sheer pain and desperation, took a prison officer hostage, and demanded medical attention.

Only four weeks after the operation Martin was given a severe beating by prison officers who left him bloody and unconscious. He subsequently brought a civil case against the home office and was awarded £750 compensation although no criminal charges were lodged against the officers involved.

Martin Foran was later given a six years sentence for taking a prison officer hostage, on top of his original eight year sentence. Since 1985, Martin has embarked on "eight more hunger strikes". The tragedy is that his serious condition is due to his hunger strikes to highlight his claim of innocence. His situation has become complicated due to his colostomy moving close to his hernia.

Surgeons will not operate unless Mr. Foran is free from prison so he has a decent chance to recover from the potentially very dangerous operation.

It is at present the view of Martin Foran,

his wife, solicitors, Irish Commission for Prisoners (Fr. Paddy Smyth) and campaigners that people can help him by writing to the Home Secretary and asking him to consider releasing Martin Foran on parole on "compassionate grounds" for medical treatment, and that it is the most appropriate thing to do to help.

Please write to The Home Secretary, Kenneth Baker MP, but send the letter to Mark Phillips of Tyndallwoode of Millichip's (Solicitors) 5th Floor, Albany House, Hurst Street, Birmingham B5 4BD, England.

Mark Phillips who is dealing with Martin Foran's case will compile the letters before forwarding them to the home office.

Letters of support are needed soon before a decision on the petition for parole is made.

Minister for Industry Dessie O'Malley TD has called for Martin Foran's release and there are more and more people getting involved with the Irish Embassy in London doing all it can to help. The details of Martin Foran's case are almost too horrifying and tragic to think about. However, you can help Martin.

Yours Sincerely
Seamus MacSeain,
London NW10 1NR

OIFIG AN AIRE GNOTHAI EACHTRACHA
OFFICE OF THE MINISTER FOR FOREIGN AFFAIRS

BAILE ÁTHA CLIATH 2
DUBLIN 2

3\ December, 1990

Mr. Michael Griffin
60 Botanic Avenue
Drumcondra
Dublin 9

Dear Mr. Griffin,

On behalf of the Minister for Foreign Affairs, Mr. Gerard Collins,
T.D., I wish to refer further to your recent letter in regard to
the case of Mr. Martin Foran who is presently imprisoned in the
U.K.

The Minister has asked me to state that he is taking a close
personal interest in Mr. Foran's case and is being continuously
informed by the Irish Embassy at London about all developments
relating to it.   The Embassy has been in close contact with
Mr. Foran, his family and his legal representatives since his case
first came to the Embassy's attention in 1986.   The Embassy has
also on numerous occasions made representations to the British
authorities about various aspects of Mr. Foran's imprisonment
including treatment of his medical condition.   In addition, an
officer of the Embassy visits Mr. Foran on a regular basis.

The Minister has also asked me to convey his assurances to you that
he will continue to monitor Mr. Foran's case and ensure that
appropriate consular assistance as may be necessary is given to
him.

Yours sincerely,

John Kirwan
Private Secretary

The Irish News

Pro Fide et Patria

Telex 747170   DONEGALL STREET BELFAST   Phone 322228

Saturday, March 24, 1990
The Annunciation of Our Lord

O'Malley fury over Foran

DESMOND O'Malley, leader of the Progressive Democrats in the coalition government is not usually given to the megaphone diplomacy that so often serves as communication between Ireland and Britain. When, therefore, we find him involving himself with cold fury in the case of another Irish prisoner in an English jail, we may be sure that something stinks.

The case of Martin Foran, at present in Durham Jail, is less spectacular than that of the Birmingham Six, but it poses the same questions about police malpractices that hang heavy over that whole cynical exercise. His imprisonment represents another example of an increasing alienation of the British legal system from the idea of justice on which the British have prided themselves.

There are two elements in Martin Foran's situation. The first, and, in human terms, paramount one is that he is a sick man who has had to have major surgical treatment in order to live. The quality of any prison medical service has always been less than perfect but when that service is applied to a cancer patient within the confines of a notoriously hard prison, the whole purpose of imprisonment in itself becomes suspect.

The British tabloids rightly worked themselves into a frenzy lately over the treatment by Iraq of two persons found guilty of espionage by a military court. The case of Martin Foran would seem to merit at least some of the same feeling of public condemnation.

Clemency was asked for in Iraq and clemency should apply in Durham. Clemency or compassion or mercy — call it what you will — is not a sign of weakness but a sign of strength. It blesses those who give and those who take and is the highest symbol of that humanitarian disposition that alone differentiates the civilised from the barbarian.

Then there is the other element in this affair. Martin Foran has always protested his innocence of a charge of burglary in Birmingham. He is at present, once again, on hunger strike to draw attention to what he has always held to be another set-up by this now suspect police force.

His lawyers have appealed the original conviction. Two years have past and still the appeal is pending only. But in the meantime they have turned over a can-full of police worms that cannot be dismissed lightly.

Martin Foran was charged by the West Midlands Serious Crimes Squad which is at present under investigation by the West Yorkshire police force. On evidence of past investigation of police by police, no one here believes that anything other than a mild slap on the wrist will eventuate. However that may be, certain facts have been dredged up that add further ignominy to that now notorious department.

The defence was based upon time and place. The vital documents of that defence can no longer be found and have indeed, it is admitted, been shredded. Police regulations state definitely that all such documentation must be retained for a period of five years. The police therefore have effectively and openly broken their own regulations and, in doing so, have equally effectively undermined their credibility in the case. Martin Foran's appeal must end in the quashing of his original conviction.

Interestingly, one of the West Midlands detectives who was involved in the Foran case investigated Paddy Hill of the Birmingham Six 15 years ago.

175

'In the Public Interest.'

[A statement by prisoners.]

We, the undersigned prisoners, of mixed nationality and views. Wish to appeal to members of the public to bring pressure on the Prison Authorities, in the name of common humanity, to demand they cease their inhuman and degrading treatment of Irish prisoner Martin Foran.

Martin, a married man with children recently underwent an unsuccessful 'Colostomy' operation. In view of the fact that he recieves no medical treatment whatsoever ---- not even pain killing drugs, Martins demeanor towards his fellow prisoners can only command the highest respect.

We have witnessed the huge supprating wound that disfigures Martins frontal groin area, we have not been priviledged to witness those to the rear of his genitals. However, just seeing one, is enough to make one want to spew ---- I can only describe it as ---- "Ugh!"

I, the actual author of this unsolicited document, would not treat my dog like Martin, poor bastard, is being treated. If he does not recieve medical attention soon, I would consider him a prime candidate for gas gangrene.

It would be more merciful to take him from his cell and shoot him like a dog ---- than to leave him as he is.

With respect, and in sympathy for Martin Foran's predicament, we are, and I am ----

Bruce Childs
Graham Young.

Patrick Hackett

Optavert

Letter signed by inmates at Parkhurst

CHAPTER 22

THE END IN SIGHT

Spring Hill

Foran still held in respect the prison Governor at Parkhurst who had befriended him and had honoured all his pledges. He also kept *his* word and didn't stage any more protests. He was starting to live in hope and the years of anger were starting to ebb and he was beginning to forget the past and to settle down.

He regards his time at Spring Hill as the best of his entire prison life. He was not abused by other prisoners despite them being told he was an informer, nor was he abused by the prison staff.

Because it was an open prison, he was also allowed to spend far more time with his wife and family and, compared to what he had endured for almost 20 years, it was a blessed relief.

Foran was released from prison in August 1996.

By now he had endured two terms of imprisonment totalling a staggering 19 years and convicted for a total of 6 crimes he had not committed. His entire incarcerated life had been one of beatings and ill-treatment at the hands of prison officers and doctors. His hopes and dreams of settling down with his wife and family to a pleasant and fruitful married life had all been shattered.

In particular, he was angry that his wife and family had suffered terribly and he couldn't forgive or forget the hardship, insults and finger-pointing they had endured during that time.

His physical afflictions were now terminal from the beatings, the hunger strikes and his colostomy. He had also contracted diabetes and cancer. Collectively, they would give him a short life span, but he wasn't going to simply live out his final years feeling sorry for himself and reliving the life he had endured. He still has nightmares and wakes during the night with flash-backs of the beatings he received during his confinement.

He simply had to continue his fight for justice and clear his name and was determined to continue his protests after his release in the same way he had done while serving time.

He also wants to fight for compensation for the loss of his livelihood so he can leave his wife and family secure after he is gone.

He was therefore determined to continue his long struggle to appeal his convictions and seek the justice he so desperately fought for since his first conviction in 1974. However, he was not to know that his fight would continue for another 20 years.

Outside the Royal Courts of Justice, London, 2013

Inside the Irish Centre in Manchester

Wherever there is an opportunity to protest he is there

Manchester 2014

Manchester 2014

Until his dying breath he will go on protesting until justice is done

CHAPTER 23

APPEALS - SECOND CONVICTION

Foran's first appeal against his second conviction was dismissed in July 1986 when he had only spent a year of his second term in prison.

In 1992, four years before his release, he applied to the Home Office for a review of his case due to the unreliable evidence presented by the discredited West Midlands SCS. He was still trying to get the officers of the West Midlands Serious Crime Squad prosecuted, so he started yet another appeal.

His counsel was able to show the continually changing evidence of the police officers and the fact that the case was entirely dependent on the officers' testimony with no other supporting evidence. It was also the case that whenever supporting evidence did come to light, Foran's version of events was shown to be correct. Examples were the Custody Sheets, as it was clear these had been 'doctored'. More particularly, the original top copy of the arrest sheet could not be located. This would have proved the others produced at his trials had been changed to suit the police officer's evidence.

Foran was not going to settle for this as some of those involved were still serving officers. He therefore engaged Tyndallwoods, solicitors, to bring a complaint against the officers in order to have them prosecuted. However, the cover-up would continue as the Crown Prosecution Service decided not to prosecute. They notified the Chief Constable of the West Midlands Police of their decision and left it to him to decide if he wished to take any disciplinary action against the officers involved.

CPS

Headquarters
10 Furnival Street
London EC4A 1PE

Switchboard: 071-417 7000
Facsimile: 071-430 0154/2023
DX No: 499 City

Messrs Tyndallwoods
Solicitors
King Edward Building
4th Floor
205/213 Corporation Street
Birmingham
B4 6QB

Direct Line:

Our Reference: P/568/91

Your Reference: Chinatown?

19 MAY 1992

Dear Sir

RE: MARTIN P.FORAN

The Assistant Chief Constable of the West Yorkshire Police has
sent me a file relating to the investigation of the complaints
made by, or on behalf of, your above named client against police
officers from the West Midlands Police. The role of this office
is to review the evidence for the purposes of criminal
proceedings.

I enclose a note which gives general information about cases of
this kind.

I have reached the conclusion that the evidence is not sufficient
to justify a prosecution and I have advised the Deputy Chief
Constable of the West Midlands Police of my decision. It is now
for the Deputy Chief Constable of the West Midlands Police to
consider whether this matter discloses any purely disciplinary
offences which require action on his part and he must do this in
liaison with the Police Complaints Authority.

Yours faithfully

C J Cleugh
Head of Police Complaints Division

2 0 MAY 1992

To Foran's fury, the officers were never charged with perjury as Dame Barbara Mills, Director of Public Prosecutions at the time, decided there was insufficient evidence to prosecute any of the officers from the Squad. He was angry that even though the officers were discredited after having provided fraudulent evidence which played a key part in gaining his conviction seven years earlier, this was still not sufficient for him to win his appeal and have his conviction quashed.

Needless to say, the fact Foran was bringing these summonses against police officers did not help his relationship with the prison officers, and the beatings and mistreatment continued before he was sent to Spring Hill.

Staggeringly, just 9 days after receiving the letter from the CPS in London, Tyndallwoods received another from the Crown Prosecution Service in Birmingham informing them that there were important disclosures which were not made available to them at the time and which might be useful should they wish to make an appeal against the decision. The content of their letters follows:

Chief Crown Prosecutor
T. M. McCowran

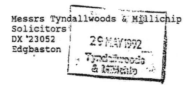

Messrs Tyndallwoods & Millichip
Solicitors
DX '23052
Edgbaston

29 MAY 1992

Tyndallwoods
& Millichip

Crown Prosecution Service

West Midlands Area Office

Dale House
31 Dale End
Birmingham
B4 7LN

Telephone 021-233-3133
Ext.
2101

Your Ref:	*Our Ref:*	*Date:*
11.nn.15821.2.foran	TMM/OYA	28/05/1992

Dear Sirs,

R -v- MARTIN PATRICK FORAN

I understand that you now represent Mr Foran who was convicted at Birmingham Crown Court on 3 May 1985 of Robbery and Conspiracy to Rob and was sentenced to 8 years imprisonment.

Mr Foran subsequently made a series of complaints against the police officers responsible for the investigation of the case against him. That investigation, supervised by the Police Complaints Authority, has, as you are probably aware, been completed and the papers were subsequently submitted to the Director of Public Prosecutions for consideration under the provisions of Part IX of the Police and Criminal Evidence Act 1984.

A detailed consideration of the papers generated by the complaint enquiry has revealed material which may be of significance to you and to Mr Foran in considering the question of a further application for leave to appeal or a possible Home Secretary's reference.

It appears to me that the enclosed copy statement of Keith Graham Barnett was not disclosed to Mr Foran or the solicitors acting for him at the time of his trial.

Additionally, when Mr Foran made his application for leave to appeal in April 1986 the Registrar of the Criminal Appeal Office wrote to the Chief Constable of the West Midlands Police concerning an allegation by Mr Foran that Detective Inspector Matthews had been suspended from duty. A copy of that letter is enclosed together with a copy of a reply to the Registrar from an Assistant Chief Constable of the West Midlands Police. The

184

information given in that letter at that time was correct but it seems to me that I should bring you up to date with what happened thereafter, namely that Detective Inspector Matthews appeared before the Chief Constable on 23 September 1986 when he was found guilty of two charges of Disobedience to Orders and two of Neglect of Duty. On three of those charges he was reduced in rank to constable and on the fourth charge he was required to resign forthwith. These matters arose following Detective Inspector Matthew's failure to attend for duty following his transfer on 12 August 1985 from detective duties to uniform duties at the Central Lock Up.

I also note that you wrote to Mr Crawford of the Police Complaints Authority on 11 January 1991 suggesting further forensic tests be carried out. Those tests were carried out by Mr Robert Anthony Hardcastle and it may be that the Police Complaints Authority have communicated the results of Mr Hardcastle's examination to you. Perhaps you would be good enough to let me know.

I should be most grateful if you would acknowledge safe receipt of this letter immediately and let me know whether there is any further assistance I can give you.

Yours faithfully,

T M McGowran
Chief Crown Prosecutor

The toing and froing would continue for years with the Chief Constable of the West Yorkshire police leading the investigation.

It was in 1992 that he would submit the results of his investigation to the Police Complaints Authority in London who then reviewed the case and, on the 10th September 1992, Foran finally received a response. As expected, they said they found no grounds whatever to suggest the officers from the Birmingham Serious Crime Squad had behaved irresponsibly or unethically.

POLIC: MPLAINTS AUTHORITY

The independent body established by Act of Parliament

to oversee public complaints against police officers
JAC

10 Great George Street
London SW1P 3AE

Telephone 071-273 6450

Mr M Foran
c\o Tyndallwoods & Millichip
Solicitors
6th Floor, Albany House
Hurst Street
BIRMINGHAM B5 4BD

Your Reference

Our Reference COM 92/139/164

Date 10 September 1992

Dear Mr Foran,

You will recall that we wrote to you on 8th May, 1991 after receiving the report of the investigation into your complaints about the conduct of officers of the West Midlands Police. The investigation was of course supervised by a Member of this Authority.

You will have seen from the Authority's interim statement that the investigation was carried out to the Authority's satisfaction.

The Authority's role now is to identify any breaches of discipline which officers of West Midlands Police may have committed in the course of their duties, to assess and where necessary recommend appropriate disciplinary action. I enclose a note which explains the independent role of the Authority in the complaints procedure and some of the factors which are taken into account before a decision is reached.

Despite the extensive enquiries which have been conducted into your complaint, nothing has emerged which supports your allegation that officers and your co-defendants conspired together to secure a conviction against you.

Your custody record has been examined, along with other official police documentation, and from the recorded actions of the officers concerned, it is clear that you are mistaken about the time of your arrest. We have seen nothing which causes us to doubt the reliability of the material documentation.

There is no dispute that some mincemeat was recovered from your vehicle following your arrest. Whilst not all the officers involved were aware of this, it was recorded on your custody sheet and was returned to your legal representative later that day.

The officers, of whom you complain, strenuously deny your allegations that they lied and fabricated evidence against you and the investigation has revealed insufficient evidence to substantiate your claims.

The Authority have noted that the Crown Prosecution Service have already informed you that they do not consider the evidence sufficient to justify criminal charges against any police officer and the Deputy Chief Constable has now told the Authority that, in his opinion, there is insufficient evidence on which to recommend any disciplinary action against the officers.

The Authority have carefully studied all the papers contained in the report of the investigation and, for the reasons given in paragraph 4 of the enclosed note, have concluded that no disciplinary action should be taken.

A copy of this letter has been forwarded to the Deputy Chief Constable.

Yours sincerely,

B A WALLIS
Member of the Authority

J. R. Stephenson

POLICE COMPLAINTS AUTHORITY   10 Great George Street, London, SW1 3AE

BACKGROUND TO THE INVESTIGATION OF YOUR COMPLAINT

1.   Your complaint has now been fully investigated. The enclosed letter, signed by a member of the Police Complaints Authority, tells you the result of this investigation and the decision as to what action, if any, is to be taken against the police officers about whom you complained.

2.   The Police Complaints Authority are an independent body. We were established by Parliament under the Police & Criminal Evidence Act 1984, and are not part of the police service. The members come from different backgrounds but none of them has served as a police officer neither has any member been employed in a civilian capacity within the police service.

3.   Our purpose is to see that a complaint made about the conduct of a serving police officer by a member of the public is dealt with thoroughly and objectively. In some cases the Crown Prosecution Service will have considered whether the evidence gathered during the investigation of your complaint is sufficient to justify criminal charges against the police officer. In these circumstances you will have already been advised of the Crown Prosecution Service's decision. If the Crown Prosecution Service decide not to prosecute the officer, the Authority have the final decision as to whether the police officer should be charged with a breach of the discipline regulations if it is not already the intention of the force to do so. For lesser offences, a police officer may be admonished, warned or simply given advice by one of his superior officers. Admonishments or warnings are normally recorded in a discipline register.

4.   Before the Authority can recommend or direct disciplinary charges we must be satisfied that the evidence is such that there is a genuine prospect of proving the charge to the same standard of proof as in a criminal court, namely *beyond reasonable doubt*. Parliament has decided that this is the standard of proof which shall apply to police discipline charges. In a large number of the cases with which we deal there is a conflict of evidence which makes it difficult to be sure where the truth lies. In many instances the evidence is contradictory between the complainant and the police officer, or officers, concerned. Without independent or other corroborative evidence the required standard of proof may not be reached. In such cases you may feel that you are being disbelieved but the decision not to recommend disciplinary charges is no reflection either on your truthfulness or that of the police officer concerned.

5.   Finally, we are prohibited by law from disclosing the report or detailed information contained in the statements of witnesses. The letter which accompanies this note has been written within these constraints.

The independent body established by Act of Parliament
to oversee public complaints against police officers

Eventually he heard that the case had been referred to the Court of Appeal by the Home Secretary, and he harnessed the support of the various organisations which previously had been sympathetic to his cause: these included Justice and Liberty who wrote to the Home Secretary on his behalf.

In September 1992, while in Wellingborough prison, he was elated to receive a copy of the letter from the Home Office stating that the Home Secretary had decided to refer his second conviction to the Court of Appeal.

MEMORANDUM

H.M.P.
2 SEP 1992
WELL...

From: J Gibbs   Telephone: 01 273 3271
          Room 216
          C3 Division   FAX 071 273 2937
          Queen Anne's Gate

To: The Governor
          HM Prison   Your Ref:
          Wellingborough
                                     Our Ref:
                                     PDP/F0523/2/4
                                     Date:
                                     24 September 1992

MARTIN FORAN: C51796

In the light of representations made to him, the Home Secretary has decided to refer Foran's convictions for robbery and conspiracy to rob to the Court of Appeal under section 17(1)(a) of the Criminal Appeal Act 1968.

In accordance with the provisions of the Act, the case will now be treated as an appeal to the Court by Foran.

Foran's representatives have been notified of the Home Secretary's decision.

R. Bromfield

pp.   J GIBBS

However, his elation soon vanished, once again, on hearing the news months later that this appeal had also failed. Furthermore, he was told that the Home Secretary would not intervene.

MEMORANDUM

From:	J Gibbs C3 Division Home Office Queen Anne's Gate LONDON	Telephone: Extension:	071-273 3000 3271

To:	The Governor HM Prison WELLINGBOROUGH	Your ref: Our ref: Date:	 PDP F0523/2/4 I5 December 1992

MARTIN FORAN: C51796

The Home Secretary has recently received representations about Mr Foran's conviction. I would be grateful if Mr Foran could be advised as follows:

> "The Home Secretary has recently received representations from the National Association of Probation Officers, Liberty and Conviction groups about your case.
>
> As you know, your case is currently pending before the Court of Appeal and so it would not be right for the Home Secretary to offer any comment on the case or to seek to intervene in any way. It is open to you to bring to the attention of the Court of Appeal any matters which you consider relevant or important to your case. You can do this through your legal representative or by writing direct to the Registrar of Criminal Appeals at the Royal Courts of Justice, Strand, London WC2A 2LL."

To his dismay his appeal was also dismissed in February 1995. It would be many years after his release that he would have the opportunity to try, yet again, for his acquittal of the crimes he knew he had not committed.

Following his release from prison he was a very sick man and he spent the first few years convalescing. It was only when he began recovering and his health had improved that he commenced reading through his files, which he had managed to retrieve while in prison. Revisiting the details of his two convictions, the failed appeals, and his medical records brought his anger to the surface again.

He had got to know several members of the Birmingham Six during his incarceration and knew they had been released in 1991 and that in 2002 they had each received around £1 million in compensation. This spurred him on as he pondered over what he had been through as an innocent man, having suffered two convictions for a total of 6 crimes he had nothing to do with. Of the other 2 charges brought he was acquitted at the trial of the first and the second was withdrawn. He could not let it rest. He was also angry at the torment his wife and family had endured for more than 20 years so, in 2010, 14 years after his release from prison, he applied to the Criminal Cases Review Commission for a review of his second case.

He engaged Olliers Solicitors and Tracy Gibbon took up his case. She instructed Elizabeth Nicholls, a barrister in Lincoln House Chambers to prepare a case to go before the Court of Criminal Appeals.

On the 5th April, 2011, Nicholls prepared a detailed case highlighting the areas of inconsistency in the evidence provided by Addison and McKenzie and that of the West Midlands SCS officers, in particular Matthews. She highlighted the fact that Matthews and his fellow officers had been directly involved in the Birmingham Six miscarriage of justice and had since been dismissed from the Force. She also stressed that the only forensic evidence obtained had shown that Foran could not have been involved in the crimes for which he was found guilty but that this evidence was suppressed from previous hearings.

The application was successful, and, on the 19th December 2012, the Criminal Cases Review Commission decided to refer it to the Court of Criminal Appeals. The final page of their review is shown.

Decision

108. The Commission has decided to refer this conviction under section 9 of the Act and this statement sets out the Commission's reasons in accordance with section 14(4) of the Act. This decision has been made by a committee consisting of three Commissioners in accordance with paragraph 6 of Schedule 1 to the Act and is signed by one of the committee on behalf of the Commission.

109. In accordance with section 14(4A) of the Criminal Appeal Act 1995 as inserted by section 315 of the Criminal Justice Act 2003, this conviction is being referred on the following grounds:

- Information, not previously considered in proceedings against Mr Foran, has come to light regarding the credibility of DI Matthews. This information, and a reassessment of other matters relating to DI Matthews that previously have been raised on Mr Foran's behalf, leads the Commission to conclude that DI Matthews' credibility is tainted; and

- Developments in case law mean that it no longer is sufficient to uphold a conviction, as was the case at Mr Foran's last appeal, that the evidence of a tainted officer is supported by an officer to whom no criticism is attached.

Signed: _____   Date: 19th December 2012

J A Goulding
C Hughes
I Nichol

The Court of Appeal Criminal Division sat on the 26th March, 2013. Elizabeth Nicholls appeared for Foran and Jonathan Laidlaw QC for the Crown before Lord Justice Leveson, Mr Justice Mitting and Mr Justice Males.

They also were asked to review the way in which Judge Malcolm Potter had conducted the trial at the Birmingham Crown Court in 1985, at which he was convicted.

They also studied the appeals which had been launched unsuccessfully in 1986 and 1995.

Having retired to make their decision, on the 16th April 2013 they found Foran's convictions for robbery and conspiracy to rob to be unsafe and ordered that they be quashed. The summary of their decision is reproduced overleaf and the full consideration of the Court of Appeal is at Appendix 6.

Needless to say Foran was delighted at this outcome after so many years fighting. However, he was annoyed that the evidence which had been put before the Court of Appeal was precisely the same evidence that had been put to the previous appeal courts and to the Home Office. No additional information had been provided whatsoever, so he kept asking himself, 'Why has it taken so long? This should have been over at my first appeal in 1986.'

Lawyer Tracy Gibbon of Olliers solicitors, son Martin and barrister Elizabeth Nicholls celebrating with Foran outside the Royal Courts of Justice, London after their victory.

IN THE COURT OF APPEAL CRIMINAL DIVISION

2 2 APR 2013

REGINA v MARTIN FORAN

Criminal Appeal Office Reference Number: 201207195 B3
Date of Birth: Not known
Indictment Number: Not known

ORDER ON THE APPEAL

THE APPELLANT having been convicted in the Crown Court at BIRMINGHAM on 3 May 1985 was sentenced on 10 May 1985 to a total of 8 years imprisonment.

THE COURT OF APPEAL CRIMINAL DIVISION on 16 April 2013 CONSIDERED the Reference by the Criminal Cases Review Commission under s.9 Criminal Appeal Act 1995

AND HAS

Allowed the appeal and quashed the convictions.

Counsel not in attendance

The Appellant was not in custody.

(for the Registrar)

Date: 16 April 2013

Criminal Appeal Office, Royal Courts of Justice
Strand, London WC2A 2LL

CHAPTER 24

APPEAL - FIRST CONVICTION

B uoyed by the success, he knew he must continue his fight to have his first conviction overturned and immediately instructed Tracy Gibbon of Olliers Solicitors to commence that appeal.

They prepared a 60 page review of his conviction highlighting the injustices he had suffered at his first trial, namely; unreliable evidence of the SCS officers, lack of forensic evidence, forged documents, and so forth. Exactly the same issues as in the second trial.

This was sent to the Criminal Cases Review Commission for them to assess whether or not the evidence warranted the case being referred to the Court of Appeal.

The review was carried out by J.A Goulding, J. England and C. Hughes, and on the 9th January 2014, they ruled that there was sufficient evidence for them to believe it was likely there had been a serious miscarriage of justice and that the case should be heard by the Court of Appeal.

Perhaps the most significant comment they made is the last item which states;

"....there is a real possibility that the Court of Appeal will overturn Mr Foran's convictions for robbery."

As in the case of his previous successful appeal, what is alarming about this referral is that the evidence brought to the CCRC on which they based their decision to refer it to the Court of Appeal is precisely the same evidence that was cited by Foran at his previous appeals, and by William Whitlock and Tom Sergeant. It is also the identical evidence that was reviewed by the Home Secretary, all of which were rejected.

A copy of the Criminal Cases Review Commission's decision, taken from the 60 page statement of the reasons his case was referred to the Court of Appeal, is shown below. The numbers indicate the number of counts (items of doubtful evidence) on which the appeal was considered.

PROTECT

Decision

235. The Commission has decided to refer this conviction under section 9 of the Act and this statement sets out the Commission's reasons in accordance with section 14(4) of the Act. This decision has been made by a committee consisting of three Commissioners in accordance with paragraph 6 of Schedule 1 to the Act and is signed by one of the committee on behalf of the Commission.

236. In accordance with section 14(4A) of the Criminal Appeal Act 1995 as inserted by section 315 of the Criminal Justice Act 2003, this conviction is being referred on the following grounds:

- Information, not previously considered in proceedings against Mr Foran, has come to light regarding the credibility of two police officers - DCI Taylor and DC Davies. This information leads the Commission to conclude that the credibility of these officers is tainted;

- Developments in case law concerning the misconduct of police officers mean that, in order to uphold a conviction, it is no longer sufficient that the evidence of tainted officers is supported by officers to whom no criticism is attached; and

- A combination of these two factors leads the Commission to conclude that there is a real possibility that the Court of Appeal will overturn Mr Foran's convictions for robbery.

Signed: Date: 9/1/14

J A Goulding
J England
C Hughes

56 of 60

Given his failing health, Foran was concerned that this Court of Appeal hearing should not drag on and immediately made representations to his MP, Lucy Powell, to try and ensure it was dealt with quickly.

Lucy Powell wrote to Chris Grayling, the Secretary of State for Justice, highlighting the injustice of the Foran case and the decision of the Criminal Case Review Commission to refer it to the Court of Appeal and asked him if he would ensure it was dealt with promptly. She received a reply from Jeremy Wright, MP, and Parliamentary Under Secretary of State for Justice letting her know it was not possible for his department to become involved in an individual case.

Lucy Powell then wrote to Foran suggesting his solicitors wrote emphasising his ill health as a reason to expedite it but this too had little effect.

Meanwhile, on examining both the submissions from the Criminal Case Review Commission and Foran's Counsel, the Crown Prosecution accepted that counts 3 & 4 were unsafe and confirmed they would not be contesting these but would be continuing on counts 5 & 6. This was confirmed in their 37 point 'Respondents Notice' dated 18th February 2014 which is reproduced at Appendix 10 In it, clause 22 reads as follows: -

"Accordingly, it is difficult to advance a reasonable argument that these convictions (3 & 4) are safe."

Olliers solicitors engaged barrister Elizabeth Nicholls, who had successfully gained Foran's first acquittal.

Elizabeth Nicholls prepared a 21 point document to serve to the Court of Appeal laying out the Grounds of Appeal for counts 5 & 6 which focused primarily on four points:

- Firstly, that the original conviction was on four counts, of which two had already been found to be unsafe on the grounds of submissions by two West Midlands Crime Squad officers who said Foran had confessed but could produce no evidence to support this. The officers had since been dismissed;

- Secondly, the identification parade and lead-up to the identification when 4 out of 5 witnesses failed to pick Foran out and the one who did had been shown a picture of Foran prior to the identification parade;
- Thirdly, the descriptions of the assailants who committed the robbery did not match that of Foran;
- Fourthly, the evidence produced by the Serious Crime Squad was from the same officers involved in the fraudulent conviction of the Birmingham Six who have been subsequently dismissed.

The full appeal document appears at Appendix 9.

The hearing was scheduled for 10.30 am on October 3rd, 2014 at the Court of Appeal in London

As the date approached, Foran and his family decided to attend and looked for transport and accommodation they could afford. They decided to take the coach from Manchester to London the day before and stay at a hostel near the Court of Appeal.

On the morning of the hearing they arrived at the Court in good time and waited for the moment when both counsels would begin to argue their case.

The presiding judges were; Lord Justice Pitchford, Mr Justice Dingemans and Mr Justice William Davis.

Counsel for the Crown Prosecution confirmed they would be contesting the conviction on counts 5 & 6 only and would not be proceeding on counts 3 & 4.

To their surprise the judges intervened to say they also wished to rule on counts 3 & 4.

Foran's counsel was concerned at this pronouncement and argued that because the Crown Prosecution were not contesting points 3 & 4 she had not prepared her client's case including these but only on counts 5 & 6.

Counsel for the prosecution were equally concerned and supported Foran's counsel saying they had no wish to proceed with counts 3 & 4.

However, the judges persisted that they wished to rule on all 4 counts.

After listening to each counsel's arguments and counter-arguments, at around midday the judges declared they would retire to make their decision within 2 weeks.

Puzzled at this turn of events, both counsels met afterwards and acknowledged the events had taken a most unusual and unorthodox turn. It had taken them both by surprise. It would be two weeks before they would discover why the judges had taken this decision.

The two weeks went slowly and Foran decided to take himself off to Ireland for another protest outside the Dáil, the Irish Parliament in Dublin.

He left his home on Tuesday, 7th October, to catch the early ferry from Liverpool. His car was stacked with thousands of leaflets ready to hand out to MPs and the public in Dublin.

When he arrived outside the parliament building the following morning there were other protests also being staged and the MPs tried to brush past them as they entered the building.

Annoyed that the people who would canvas the public for their votes at election time would now ignore large protests outside the building, Foran decided to move his protest boards in front of the gates to prevent them from entering. On being told to move by one of the MPs, he was quick to point out that they would want the same people demonstrating outside the building to vote for them in the next election. This raised a cheer from the large crowd which, by this time, had gathered round him at the entry gates.

Foran spent a week in Dublin moving his demonstration and equipment to O'Connell Street, which is the main thoroughfare in the centre of the city.

This was not the first time he had protested in Dublin as he had been there each year for the previous five years. Throughout his week-long protest he received a large amount of interest in his case which people had been following for several years.

During the week he ran out of money and could no longer afford to stay at the local hostel so he slept in his car to enable him to continue his demonstration.

He arrived back a week later on the 14th October, three days before the judgement was to be announced regarding his appeal.

So certain were he, his family and his legal team that he would not be acquitted, he began preparing for a hunger strike in London following the judgement.

On the 15th October 2014, his lawyer, Tracy Gibbon, was informed that the judgement would be announced at 9.00 am on Friday, 17th and Foran arranged to be at Olliers' offices in Manchester so he could be present with Tracy Gibbon when the formal announcement was received.

He had already prepared his car with the necessary leaflets and equipment he would be using to chain himself outside the Royal Courts of Justice in the Strand, London. He was preparing for up to four weeks without food despite knowing that starving for that long could cause his body to close down due to his diabetes.

He arose early and arrived at Olliers' offices in time for the 9.00 am announcement and an hour later it came through.

They stared at the judgement documents again and again scarcely able to believe their eyes as he had been acquitted on all counts. It then became clear why the judges had insisted upon including counts 3 & 4. They obviously wished to ensure that whatever decision they made it applied to all the counts as the same officers had been implicated in all of them. Had they left the remaining charges unheard, they would have remained inconclusive and it is my opinion that it was a clear signal from the appeal judges to the Ministry of Justice that they wished to bring the entire matter of Foran's double conviction to an end and they had concluded he was innocent of all charges.

This is the first and only recorded double miscarriage of justice to a single individual in British legal history.

Their summary quashing the conviction is reproduced here and such is the significance of their decision, their judgement is reproduced in full at Appendix 11.

recently appointed head of the Serious Crime Squad. His role would, it is submitted, have had a significant impact upon the team whom he was directing and, therefore, the truth of the evidence that the appellant made the disputed admissions on 24 October 1977 and on 3 April 1978. He was, in particular, Detective Sergeant Hancocks' senior officer. Detective Sergeant Jennings was, it is further submitted, implicated in the allegedly false evidence given at the trial of Keith Twitchell, and the taint on his credibility affects the value of his evidence that the appellant made admissions on 3 April 1978.

55.   The respondent, having considered the material available, concedes that this court could properly conclude that the verdicts upon counts 3 and 4 are unsafe. There is a sufficient taint upon the credibility of Detective Constable Davies to cast doubt upon the accuracy of his evidence. There was upon the relevant issues evidence supportive of the appellant from Prison Officer Law. There was no direct or circumstantial evidence to place the appellant at either of the robberies; therefore, there was no supporting evidence from any other source. Charles Apechis (count 3) gave a description of his attacker that bore no resemblance to the appellant and subsequently, not having been called at trial, made a statement absolving the appellant. We accept Mr Rees QC's submission that no specific findings were made against Detective Inspector Taylor and Detective Sergeant Jennings in the appeal of

Detective Sergeant Whelan and Detective

alleged confession of 24 October 1977. While we are quite findings adverse to the credibility of any officer, we cannot be sure, for the we have stated, that a verdict based upon on these alleged confessions is a verdict.

59.   Finally, there was in the case of counts 5 and 6 a positive identification of the appellant by Mr Holmes who said, when attending the identification parade, "I am not mistaken, that is the man". We are conscious of the fact that the full *Turnbull* direction was not given to the jury but we have read each of the judge's directions to the jury on the subject of identification and, in our view, the judge safely left the issue to the jury with the warning that they should look for supporting evidence. However, since we have concluded that the identification cannot be regarded as reliably supported by the evidence of confession it follows that the convictions upon counts 5 and 6 are unsafe.

60.   For these reasons the appeal is allowed and we quash the appellant's convictions upon counts 3 – 6 inclusive.

The joy and elation that consumed Foran at that point was immense. Firstly, he had been expecting and preparing for a judgement that would uphold the charges brought against him and, secondly; after forty years of fighting to have his name cleared, it was over at last.

He now had the result he always wanted. All his convictions had now been quashed and he was innocent on all charges which had been brought against him by the West Midlands Serious Crime Squad.

However, his excitement was tinged with anger when he reflected, once again, that the evidence on which they quashed his conviction was precisely the same evidence that he had provided time and again while serving his first term of imprisonment from 1978 to 1984.

Knowing that he is now confirmed as an innocent man however, doesn't bring back his 40 lost years, nor does it rectify his now terminal illness due entirely to his wrongful confinement.

His wife and children have also been badly affected by their father's absence together with the incessant police raids on their home when the children were young.

Foran has lost his entire adult life. When he should have been enjoying being a husband and father to his children, instead, he has been fighting incessantly for 40 years against false charges. In addition to Foran's own terminal illness, the family have suffered serious health and financial problems and, surely, there must now be compensation due to at least help secure what remaining years he and his wife have.

One would hope and expect that compensation would follow automatically now that the judicial system had accepted he had been wrongly imprisoned and that an interim payment would be made while the quantum was determined. However, the justice system doesn't work as simply as that as two things stand in the way.

Firstly, there is no financial assistance provided for a compensation claim and Foran was advised it would cost at least £100,000 to mount such a claim.

Secondly, the criterion for compensation now is not the same as it was at the time of the Birmingham Six due to a convenient change in the law imposed by the coalition government as recently as 2013.

These two issues would come to the fore when he decided to launch a compensation claim in May 2014 following his acquittal of his second conviction. The next chapter deals with this in more detail.

CHAPTER 25

COMPENSATION CLAIM

F oran asked his solicitors to commence an action for compensation for the 11 the years he spent in prison following his second conviction. Unfortunately, the firm he had used to quash his conviction did not deal with compensation claims so he had to find another.

Because Legal Aid is not granted for actions seeking compensation, the numerous solicitors he approached told him the cost of taking his claim would be in the region of £100,000, a figure he could never afford.

One firm of solicitors said they would act for him and would be able to secure him compensation on a no win no fee basis. However, after several months, they had not begun the application and the deadline for being able to submit the claim was looming. As a result, he had no option but to submit his own application, which he did on the 12th May, 2014.

He received an acknowledgement on the 16th May giving a timescale of around 4 months to determine whether or not his compensation claim was 'eligible'.

The question of the eligibility of his claim puzzled Foran, as he had been found innocent of the second conviction for which he had spent 11 years in prison.

Given the complexities of such an action and considering it took 10 years for the Birmingham Six to obtain their compensation using skilled legal specialists, he thought the outcome of his claim was inevitable. It stretches the bounds of credulity to think an individual could satisfactorily submit an application to the Ministry of Justice without the help and support of solicitors and barristers skilled in this field.

**Ministry
of Justice**

Rupal Patel-Suchak
Miscarriages of Justice Team
Criminal Justice Group
Ministry of Justice
8.07, 8th Floor, Red Core
102 Petty France
London SW1H 9AJ

Mr Patrick Martin Foran
Flat 8, Butler Court
Gunson Street
Manchester
M40 7WU

T 020 3334 6085
E *mojas@justice.gsi.gov.uk*

www.gov.uk

Our Ref: OPR/021/002/003/009/47

16 May 2014

Dear Mr Foran

APPLICATION FOR MISCARRIAGES OF JUSTICE

Thank you for your completed application form dated 12 May for compensation for your quashed conviction.

We shall now study the terms of the available documentation to determine whether you qualify for compensation. Our current timescales indicate that we hope to provide a substantive response within **4 months** of the date we received the application form, which was **13 May 2014**, although please be aware this timeframe is subject to change.

Please direct all future correspondence to the MOJAS email address above.

Yours sincerely

Rupal Patel-Suchak (Mrs)

As expected, this letter was followed 3 months later with a further letter rejecting his claim.

Ministry
of Justice

Hasmita Shah
Miscarriages of Justice Team
Criminal Justice Group
Ministry of Justice
8.07, 8th Floor, Red Core
102 Petty France
London SW1H 9AJ

Mr Patrick Martin Foran
Flat 8
Butler Court
Gunson Street
Manchester
M40 7WU

T 020 3334 6085
E mojas@justice.gsi.gov.uk

www.gov.uk

Our Ref: OPR/021/002/003/009/47
Your Ref:

12 August 2014

Dear Mr Foran

CLAIM FOR COMPENSATION FOR QUASHED CONVICTION
UNDER SECTION 133 OF THE CJA 1988

Further to my letter of 16 May 2014, I am now able to let you have a substantive reply to your application for compensation following the quashing of your convictions by the Court of Appeal on 16 April 2013.

The Justice Secretary has concluded that you have not suffered a miscarriage of justice for the purposes of section 133 of the Criminal Justice Act 1988 ("the 1988 Act"). Accordingly, section 133 does not oblige the Justice Secretary to pay compensation.

There is no automatic entitlement to compensation for a conviction which has been quashed. All applications for compensation are considered under the provisions of section 133 of the 1988 Act. Following the coming into force of section 175 of the Anti-Social Behaviour, Crime and Policing Act 2014, there is now a statutory definition of what will constitute a 'miscarriage of justice' for the purposes of section 133 of the 1988 Act. Compensation is payable under section 133 of the 1988 Act where a person's conviction has been reversed on the ground that a new or newly discovered fact shows beyond reasonable doubt that the person did not commit the offence, and the non-disclosure of the unknown fact was not wholly or partially attributable to the person convicted.

Section 133(5) of the Act defines 'reversed' in this context as a conviction having been quashed following an out of time appeal or following a reference to the Court of Appeal by the Criminal Cases Review Commission. Your appeal followed a referral by the CCRC and was therefore reversed for this purpose.

However, on the basis of the information available the Justice Secretary has concluded that you have not suffered a miscarriage of justice as defined by section 133 of the 1988 Act. In his view, the new evidence on the basis of which the Court of Appeal quashed your client's convictions does not show beyond reasonable doubt that your client did not commit the offences of robbery and conspiracy to rob.

INVESTOR IN PEOPLE

The Justice Secretary accepts that the fresh evidence in relation to the offence of robbery in the form of the discredited evidence of DC Matthews and the credibility of DC Preston together with the failure to disclose the forensic report might reasonably have affected the jury's decision to convict. However, whilst this rendered the conviction unsafe, the new evidence does not show beyond reasonable doubt that the applicant did not commit the offence. The Court stated that it is impossible to know what the jury would have made of the case if had been presented in an entirely different way. Having considered the judgment of the Court of Appeal, the Justice Secretary is not satisfied that your client's conviction for robbery was quashed on the ground that a new or newly discovered fact shows beyond reasonable doubt that your client did not commit the offence.

With regards to the offence of conspiracy to rob, the applicant's conviction was quashed as a result of fresh evidence of failure to disclose the forensic report and the discredited evidence of DI Matthews and DC Preston together with the limited evidence of Mr Addison. However, this does not show beyond reasonable doubt that the applicant did not commit the offence. The new evidence must be considered against the background of your client being arrested at the time and place identified by Addison as the rendezvous for a robbery. Furthermore the Court clearly stated: *we would certainly not be prepared to conclude that the appellant was innocent of the charge*. Whilst we accept that the new evidence rendered the conviction unsafe, we do not consider that it meets the test for compensation under section 133 of the 1988 Act.

In reaching these conclusions, the Justice Secretary has borne in mind the Court of Appeal's judgment in R v Ali & others [[2014] EWCA Civ 194], in which the court said (at paragraph 56) that on "*matters of credibility post-dating the conviction, although each assessment is fact-sensitive, we think it would be exceedingly rare for matters going to the credit of a witness who gave evidence at trial, to be material to an assessment by the Secretary of State of the merits of a claim under section 133*". We do not consider your client's circumstances to be one of the rare cases.

In considering the test under section 133 of the 1988 Act the Justice Secretary is mindful of the grounds on which the Court quashed your client's conviction but remains of the view that the fresh evidence does not show beyond reasonable doubt that your client did not commit the offence.

The Justice Secretary does, of course, recognise that in view of the consequences that you have suffered you will be disappointed. However I should explain that while the consequences of a conviction are factors which influence the amount of the award if an application is successful, they have no bearing on eligibility.

Finally, it is important to emphasise that nothing in this assessment is intended to undermine, qualify or cast doubt upon the decision of the Court of Appeal to quash your client's conviction. You client is presumed to be and remains innocent of the charges brought against him. His application has been rejected because his case does not in the Justice Secretary's view meet the statutory test for compensation under section 133 of the 1988 Act.

Yours sincerely

Hasmita Shah

He read the letter over and over again and there were two paragraphs which stood out.

The first stated that;

'....the basis of which the Court of Appeal quashed your conviction does not show beyond reasonable doubt that you did not commit the offences of robbery and conspiracy to rob.'

The second stated;

'..... you are presumed to be and remain innocent of the charges brought against you.'

Surely these two statements are totally contradictory and indeed they are. Had it not been for the changes made to the 1988 Act in the year preceding his claim it would not have been possible to make them.

In May 2013 the UK coalition government amended Section 133 of the Criminal Justice Act 1988 (compensation for miscarriages of justice) which previously clearly stated:

".....when a person has been convicted of a criminal offence and when subsequently his conviction has been reversed or he has been pardoned on the ground that a new or newly discovered fact shows beyond reasonable doubt that there has been a miscarriage of justice, the Secretary of State shall pay compensation for the miscarriage of justice to the person who has suffered punishment as a result of such conviction or, if he is dead, to his personal representatives,....."

The coalition's amendment included this controversial single clause in the 'Anti-Social Behaviour, Crime and Policing Bill'.

"If and only if the new or newly discovered fact shows beyond reasonable doubt that the person was innocent of the offence".

The effect of this was to change the definition of a 'miscarriage of justice' to one to be determined. In effect the victim of the alleged miscarriage of justice has to take on the roles usually undertaken by police and prosecutors and gather evidence to prove themselves innocent to the high threshold of a criminal law test, for matters which may have occurred decades earlier.

Therefore, under this new law, the fact that he was found innocent does not follow that he didn't commit the crime as far as the compensation board are concerned.

Under the circumstances it was necessary for Foran to begin the search to try and secure expert legal representation on a no win-no fee basis in order to secure full justice.

CHAPTER 26

INCONSISTENCIES WITHIN THE BRITISH JUSTICE SYSTEM

O n 10th October 2014, while putting the finishing touches to the first print of this book, I caught site of a press article printed that very day which could not have been more apposite.

Foran was wrongly accused and framed for six robberies which compounded to cause two false convictions and his imprisonment for nearly 20 years. Bearing in mind that he had continually protested his innocence, there was no evidence to prove his involvement and no one was injured and contrast that with the case of Michael Dwyer who was the subject of the newspaper article in front of me.

The previous day, on 9th October 2014, he had walked free from a court having been issued with a fourth 'last chance' to turn his life around.

Aged just 31, Dwyer had 170 previous convictions for robbery and burglary. Yes, you read it correctly and it is not a misprint, he had 170 convictions without ever having been required to step inside one of Her Majesty's institutions.

In the minds of the British people, it is this inconsistency and contradiction in sentencing which undermines the justice system more than anything else.

Britain prides itself as having one of the finest and fairest justice systems in the world. The framework for such a system might well be in place but the execution in practice is certainly not. Until the Government and legal profession get to grips with this situation and bridge the chasm which exists between the judgements and sentences meted out by different judges

Daily Mail, Friday, October 10, 2014

By Jaya Narain

A CAREER criminal who clocked up 170 convictions has walked free from court again after being handed his fourth 'last chance' to turn his life around.

Michael Dwyer, 31, had already been handed three 'last chances' by judges – two in 2004 and one in 2011 – after being convicted of dozens of burglary offences.

But after he blamed his two decades of burglary, theft and violence on a drug problem this week a judge again decided to free the serial criminal.

Recorder Tina Landale told him: 'You have been a drug addict for most of your life and it's clear you committed crime to support your drug habit.

'But maybe this time you are willing to change and I am prepared to give you one last chance. Really take the chance.

'Things are changing for you and you have got a much brighter future if you co-operate.'

Last night anti-crime campaigners condemned the judge as 'weak-minded' and said his release was an insult to his dozens of victims. Mohammed Iqbal, leader of Pendle Council, Lancashire,

'Groundhog Day justice'

where Dwyer lives, said: 'For someone to commit this level of crime over such a prolonged period of time shows what a menace he is to people. Clearly he has no regard for the law or other people.

'What is the point in people reporting crime, or the police putting in all of the hard work and bringing him to court if this crook is just going to get a slap on the wrist.

'This is Groundhog Day justice. Every time he commits a crime he is told it's his last chance, but clearly it isn't. He just keeps on getting away with it time after time.'

Dwyer, a heroin and valium addict, committed his first crime when he was just 11, and by the age of 20 had racked up over 100 convictions.

His first last chance came in July 2004, when he was in court for stealing a Hyundai coupe and almost mowing down a garage boss locking up his compound, causing £3,500 of damage before speeding off on a near 500-mile joyride.

He admitted aggravated vehicle taking, theft and other motoring offences – but was merely given a 12-month drug treatment and testing order by magistrates, who told him: 'You have a chance to sort yourself out.'

But less than six months later, in December 2004, Judge Beverley Lunt also gave him 'one last chance' when he appeared before court, where he was convicted of stealing a van and handling stolen goods.

She handed him another 12-month drug treatment and testing order. Yet in September 2007 he was hauled back in front of a judge and jailed for 90 days after he and a

cousin used a stolen taxi to try to get cash to feed their drug habits.

In April 2008 he was back in court again and jailed for 14 days for stealing lead from roofs.

Then Dwyer was arrested for burglary in February 2011 this time after breaking into a diner and

After 170 convictions, burglar gets last chance... for 4th time

Judge condemned as weak as he walks free yet again

Undeterred: Michael Dwyer was in court this week

How serial thief keeps getting away with it

LAST CHANCE 1 July 2004: Dwyer admits aggravated driving and theft after stealing a Hyundai coupe and causing £3,500 worth of damage. Magistrates tell him he is being given 'a chance to sort yourself out' and hand him a 12-month drug treatment and testing order.

LAST CHANCE 2 December 2004: He is given another 12-month drug treatment and testing order for stealing a van and handling stolen goods. Judge Beverley Lunt tells him he is being given a 'last chance' to get back on the straight and narrow.

LAST CHANCE 3 February 2011: He is arrested for burglary after breaking into a diner and stealing from the till. He is given a 12-month community order and a three-month curfew after his lawyers say he has 'had a chance to reflect on his life, with the imminent arrival of his second child'.

LAST CHANCE 4 October 2014: Dwyer is caught on his way to carry out a theft with a wrench stuffed up his sleeve and a Stanley knife in his pocket. Recorder Tina Landale says she is giving him 'one last chance' to turn his life around with a community order.

stealing £45 from the till and £75 from under the counter.

At the time he had a chance to reflect on his life, with the imminent arrival of his second child'.

Then Dwyer was arrested for burglary in February 2011 this time after breaking into a diner and a three-month nightly curfew. His

lawyers had argued he 'had a chance to reflect on his life, with the imminent arrival of his second child'.

But less than a year later, in January 2012, Dwyer was given a six-month sentence for a fling over a fight in which he smashed a window.

Unbelievably, just three months

after his release he was again before the court after he raided a pensioner's home when she was out.

This time Judge Beverley Lunt – the same judge who had freed him in 2004 – sentenced him to two years in prison, telling him: 'Nothing deters you.'

At his latest appearance before Burnley Crown Court this week, Dwyer was facing up to three years in jail after he was caught equipped for a theft with a large wrench up his sleeve and a knife in his pocket.

But he walked away with a 12-month community order with supervision and a drug rehabilitation requirement – after a probation officer and Dwyer was willing to address his behaviour.

Richard Taylor, defending, said Dwyer was on a methadone reducing programme and it was just over a year since he was last in trouble.

A spokesman for Families Against Crime said: 'This type of sentencing is no deterrent to hardened criminals and if judges can't take a tough line on law and order then who will. Judges need to be strong not weak-minded.

'This criminal appears to be untouchable and as long as that continues then he will carry on breaking the law and making people's lives a misery.'

---

for the same or similar offences, the system will continue to be undermined. More seriously, it will cause the public to lose faith in the entire legal establishment and leave itself open to criticism and ridicule by the media.

There have been countless examples of ludicrous decisions by judges which have angered the public who cannot understand why more uniformity in sentencing cannot be addressed. There is also another aspect to this which is more worrying:

When criminality is discovered within the very organisations charged with enforcing the law or delivering justice, little appears to be done as has been demonstrated in the case of Foran. Instead of its immediate exposure and rectification, a process of cover-ups begins to prevent its disclosure.

Furthermore, once revealed by the media and subsequently investigated, it is done by the very institutions under suspicion, which is akin to asking students to mark their own exam papers and it does not help allay the fears of the public.

It was Viscount Hewart, Lord Chief Justice of England from 1922 to 1940, who created the maxim; "Not only must Justice be done; it must also be seen to be done."

Regrettably, if Foran's case is anything to go by, we are still a long way short of this ideal and we have to be grateful for an investigative media which is able to expose it whenever it happens.

The treatment meted out to Foran by the police, the Courts and within the British prison system was no less than inhuman, brutal and savage and more akin to the torture experienced in far less civilised societies. Appeal after appeal was dismissed when the evidence to uphold it was clear; each court not wishing to undermine the decision of the previous one. And when the ultimate recourse was made to the Home Secretary, he relied too heavily on testimonies from the very people who were directly implicated and being accused.

POSTSCRIPT

After releasing this book, Foran received support from many sections of the community. The press and radio have requested interviews and student journalists at Middlesex University in London produced a video documentary of his experiences. He has also been asked to give talks at universities on the legal system and how it affected him.

Since his terminal illness was diagnosed, every day is precious to Foran. If he had not been so determined to prove his innocence and applied relentless pressure over a period of 40 years, his acquittals would never have happened. Even so, he had to wait 17 years after being released from prison before his second conviction was quashed and a further 18 months before the Appeal Court overturned his first conviction thereby finding him innocent of all charges.

Now, a dying man and running out of time, he is still fighting for the compensation due to him to financially secure his family when his time is up. The amendment made in 2013 to Section 133 of the Criminal Justice Act 1988 is depriving him and other innocent victims of receiving their dues. It is estimated that if all legitimate compensation claims due from the MOJ following properly constituted Appeal Court decisions were to be paid it would amount to some £70 million. You would be forgiven for making a connection between this fact and the change made to the Act.

On the 3rd November 2014 Foran began a hunger strike outside the Ministry of Justice in London and was determined to see it through. As he said to me; *"I would rather die outside the MOJ in London, than in a care home in Manchester."*

So concerned were his family about his welfare that his daughter, Helen, returned from Greece and travelled to London from Manchester to persuade him to give it up. When he refused, Helen remained with him during his vigil in order to administer his vital insulin injections and other necessary medication. They slept on the pavement for almost 2 weeks in freezing cold conditions and torrential rain with just a waterproof sheet for cover but his protest was not in vain.

Mike Penning, Member of Parliament for Hemel Hempstead and recently appointed Minister of State for Policing, Criminal Justice and Victims, visited him outside the MOJ. He had been given a copy of this book by Chris Grayling, Secretary of State for Justice and Theresa May, Home Secretary, both of whom had received a copy. Penning tried to persuade him to move his protest to outside the West Midlands Police offices in Birmingham who were the cause of his wrongful conviction and who he said had more money available. However, after so many disappointments, Foran considered this to be another case of one bureaucrat passing the buck to another with endless further delays, so he declined.

When this failed, Penning returned the following week and set up a meeting inside the MOJ with Foran and his MP for Manchester Central, Lucy Powell. Penning argued that the MOJ had no money for such claims and, in any case, it would necessitate a change in the law for them to pay it. He was, of course, referring to the amendment to Section 133 of the 1988 Act. He assured both Foran and Powell that if he pursued his case against the West Midlands Police, the MOJ would co-operate fully to help expedite matters. However, Foran could see the manipulation taking place so as far as he was concerned, the protest would continue.

It was only when his blood sugar level dropped to 3 after starving himself for 9 days and he was about to enter a coma that his daughter persuaded him to get a bus home on the 12th November. Had she not been there, his determination was such that he may well have died there and then on the steps of the MOJ.

In January 2015, Foran engaged the services of Curtis Law, a firm of solicitors experienced in litigation, and they commenced an action against the West Midland Police Force. However, after eight months of no progress, the lawyers representing the West Midlands Police reported to Curtis Law that they were concerned at having been unable to obtain any of the papers relating to Foran from the Ministry of Justice despite several requests. Bearing in mind that during his protest outside the MOJ, Penning had given Foran and his MP an assurance that if he started proceedings against the West Midlands Police, they would co-operate to provide a speedy resolution, it appeared they were now doing precisely the opposite. Once again it begs the question; why? This is an organisation which responded very speedily to Foran when confirming they would not be providing any compensation but suddenly, and without explanation, they appear to have lost his entire file. We can only postulate as to the reasons why they suddenly withdrew any co-operation thereby allowing the claim to drag on in the same way as his entire case has to date. Could it be they hoped that Foran's life expectancy preceded his on-going suit against the police for the compensation due to him?

There are further curious events that took place after his litigation started, which involved the Greater Manchester Police.

On the evening of 20th March 2015, both his daughter's (Valerie) and his own car were vandalised. Fortunately, both were captured by CCTV cameras and the offender was recorded in the act. Foran reported them to the police immediately and the culprit was identified and found to be known to both Foran and the police.

Despite being only a couple of minutes away from his daughter, Valerie's, home it took almost an hour for the police to attend despite being a woman living on her own and deaf.

They then visited Foran's care home where his car was parked in a secured car park outside the premises. After viewing the damage to Foran's car and while he was explaining to them what had happened, they then said they were detaining him and demanded to search his apartment. On enquiring why, they refused to elaborate except to say that it was for reasons of 'confidentiality' and 'on-going enquiries' and forced an entry into his apartment.

He would eventually learn that a false accusation had been made against him by the very person responsible for vandalising both his and his daughter's cars, which resulted in his daughter's car being written off. Foran believes he knows why the person concerned took the action he did as he had previous dealings with him, which will be explained in part 2 of his story to be published soon.

A video record of his arrest was made by his son together with pictures of the damage inflicted on his car. Documentary evidence of the sequence of events and the actions taken by the police are also being retained.

On his detention, the police then sought a bail condition until May preventing him from leaving the area without their permission. This was subsequently extended to the 16th July with the condition that he was to sleep every night in his flat, thus restricting his movements to within the Manchester area.

When he was told the dates of the supposed offences, he was able to provide cast iron alibis with four witnesses to prove he was nowhere near the vicinity on the days or at the times suggested. The police eventually followed up with just two of these witnesses who confirmed his whereabouts on the first date but have yet to interview the other two, one of whom is a magistrate, who could confirm he was in Birmingham on the second date. Nevertheless, they refuse to drop the charges and continued to maintain the bail conditions.

Just before appearing at the police custody centre on 16th July, he was informed that the bail conditions had been extended to 11th September but still no explanation as to why and with no charges being brought. These stringent conditions would, of course, prevent him making trips to London and elsewhere where he planned to arrange further protests.

Still with no charge in sight and just before he was due to appear in September he was informed there was no need for him to do so and he received a new bail condition ordering him to appear on the 4th November. In effect he had been under house arrest for seven months for another trumped up charge which he was easily able to disprove.

Such is the harassment which Foran has experienced over 23 years since being released from prison in 1992 that a second book is being prepared detailing all such actions and incidents.

APPENDICES

APPENDIX 1

William Whitlock MP's appeal
to Home Secretary
(from Hansard July 1982)

Search Help
HANSARD 1803–2005 → 1980s → 1982 → July 1982 → 20 July 1982 → Commons Sitting

Mr. Martin foran

HC Deb 20 July 1982 vol 28 cc373–8

Motion made, and Question proposed, That this House do now adjourn.—[Mr. Gummer.]

3.21 am

Mr. William Whitlock (Nottingham, North) While the House has been sitting, Mr. Martin Patrick Foran has entered his forty-seventh day on the roof of Her Majesty's prison, Nottingham. It is a demonstration that is intended to bring to public notice his statement of his innocence of the crimes for which he has been convicted. Many people in the Nottingham area, having learnt some details of his case, have become anxious about him and are convinced of his innocence. That deep anxiety and the fact that the prison is in my constituency has led me to raise the matter.

Foran was convicted on 21 June 1978 on four counts, involving three robberies, and was sentenced to 10 years' imprisonment on each, the sentences to run concurrently. Since then, he has consistently asserted his innocence and repeatedly staged various types of demonstration to draw attention to his case. As a result, many people, especially in the East and West Midlands have become worried about him. Many people believe that in his case there has been a miscarriage of justice of which he is the victim.

Foran is a constituent of my hon. Friend the Member for Birmingham, Ladywood (Mr. Sever), who has played a part in trying to help him. For a while, Foran was an inmate of Gartree prison in Leicestershire where he won the interest of the hon. Member for Harborough (Mr. Farr) who presented a petition to the House on his behalf in 1981.

The Bishop of Leicester has revealed that chaplains at Gartree prison have become deeply concerned about Foran's case and that some of them have become fully convinced that he was wrongly imprisoned. Other hon. Members in both Houses have taken an interest in Foran's case and have made representation to the Home Office. There have been petitions that have been signed by thousands of people. All to no avail—Foran remains in prison.

Martin Foran is no angel. He has "form"—a criminal record—but on 21 June 1978 he was not being tried for his past record. Or was he? Some people fully believe that he was framed. The main witnesses to the robberies—the people who were allegedly his victims—were not called at the trial. For some technical reason, only their statements were read out. The judge at the trial agreed that the descriptions given by the witnesses did not even remotely resemble Foran". Since then, those witnesses have said that Martin Foran was not among the persons who robbed them and that they are willing to give evidence to that effect.

No fingerprint evidence was produced at the trial and the chief constable of the West Midlands police force has said that "by genuine mistake" it was not revealed to the defence that Martin Foran's fingerprints were not found at any of the three scenes of the robberies of which he was found guilty, nor were they found on the sword that was used to cut telephone wires in one of the robberies, although other prints were found at each of the scenes.

Dealing with Foran's application for leave to appeal against both his conviction and his sentence, the Court of Appeal (Criminal Division) concluded that there were no grounds upon which Mr. Foran could reasonably expect to argue an appeal with the slightest prospect of success and his application was refused. The Court of Appeal said that his case was a confession case, not an identification case". The evidence by witnesses who were victims of the robberies that Foran was not among the robbers was therefore not thought to matter. The evidence given in court that he was at a house in Ladywood at the time of one of the robberies was thought to be of no consequence. Nor did it matter, apparently, that the absence of Foran's fingerprints at any of the scenes of the crime was not made known to the defence. Everything that would have weighed in his favour was brushed aside. As the Court of Appeal said, it was not an identification case but a confession case. Yet from the very beginning Foran has strenuously maintained that any

---

suggestion that he confessed to the crime was a complete fabrication and there is no signed confession by this man.

As I have said, there was a lack of evidence identifying Foran as participating in the robberies, but that lack of evidence was considered to be of no importance. Because that view was taken at the trial, the Court of Appeal in effect stated that identification was unnecessary and waved aside the evidence on Foran's side that had not been made available at the trial.

I find that absolutely perverse. If that kind of logic is always adopted by our legal luminaries, my previous faith in British justice must disappear. What seems to have weighed heavily with the Court of Appeal was that at the trial Foran was represented by an extremely experienced team of leading counsel and junior counsel". It seems, therefore, to have been of paramount importance that a belief in the infallibility of members of the legal profession should be upheld—no matter what the consequences for Foran, and no matter what errors of judgment the learned counsel may have made in conducting the case.

Serious doubts and considerable unease exist in the minds of many people who have taken an interest in Martin Foran's case. We owe it to ourselves as much as to Foran to investigate these doubts and to dispel that unease.

I hope that the Minister of State will be able to tell us that there is an opportunity to have further investigations and that the unease exists in his Department, too. I hope that he will be able to take steps to ensure that all the feelings about Foran are dispelled by a further investigation and by re-opening the case in some way that he has found.

3.30 am

The Minister of State, Home Office (Mr. Patrick Mayhew) I have listened with care to what the hon. Member for Nottingham, North (Mr. Whitlock) said about the case of Mr. Foran. I shall study the report of the hon. Gentleman's speech in the Official Report.

Before I deal with some of the points made I shall explain the jurisdiction that the Home Secretary has in individual cases in which it is alleged that there has been a miscarriage of justice. The duty of administering justice in individual criminal cases lies with the courts. While it is true that the Home Secretary has certain powers to intervene following a conviction, either by recommending the exercise of the Royal prerogative of mercy or by referring the case to the Court of Appeal under section 17 of the Criminal Appeal Act 1968, he must not exercise those powers in any way which tends to usurp the proper function of the courts. Therefore, in practice he can consider intervention only if significant new evidence or other material factor of substance bearing upon the reliability of the conviction comes to light which has not already been taken into consideration by the courts or which was not previously available to the defendant to be made use of in his defence.

The Home Secretary must not assess the decisions of the courts on the basis only of facts or arguments that they have themselves considered. That would be to act as though he were a further court of appeal himself. In particular, it would be wrong for the Home Secretary to intervene merely because he might have taken a different view of the facts had the original decision rested with him instead of a properly directed jury.

As the hon. Gentleman rightly said, Mr. Foran was convicted on 21 June 1978 at Birmingham Crown court of three robberies forming the subject of four counts. He was sentenced to four concurrent terms of 10 years' imprisonment. His application for an extension of time in which to appeal and for leave to appeal against his conviction and sentence was refused by a single judge on 21 May 1979 and by the full Court of Appeal on 11 March 1980.

I take the following brief description of the three robberies from the judgment of Lord Justice Donaldson, giving the judgment of the full Court of Appeal. He said: The first count arises out of an incident which occurred in the early hours of the morning of Monday 26 September 1977. A Mr. Apechis woke up to find three West Indians and a white man in his bedroom. Each was armed with a knife. He described the white man as being 18 years of age and it should be noted that the applicant was then aged 33. All four wore masks which they later pulled up. Mr. Apechis was told that he had better produce his money or it would be the worse for him, and the men departed taking £2,800 from beneath the mattress and some sovereigns, having first tied up Mr. Apechis. I now turn to the second robbery. There were three robberies in all, although they formed four counts. The second robbery occurred at half past midnight on 8 October 1977 at the home of a Mr. and Mrs. Trikain. Lord Justice Donaldson said that Mr. Trikain woke up to find a white man standing beside the bed with a bar in his hand. The intruder said that they, meaning he and others, wanted money and as long as they got it Mr. Trikain would not be hurt. Mr. Trikain then noticed that there was a coloured man on the other side of the bed. He had a bar in one hand and a torch in the other. That man ok some money from Mrs. Trikain's handbag and told the white man to keep an eye on the Trikains while he left the bedroom.

Mr. Trikain then went for the white man who departed speedily. Mr. Trikain's evidence was that both the men were young, the white man aged about 25—the accused was 33 at the relevant time—and the coloured man 18 to 20. Mrs. Trikain also agreed that the white man was about 25. The Trikains were faced with the difficulty that they could not see the white man's face and hair because he had taken the precaution of using a pullover belonging to the Trikain's daughter to put over his head. That brings me"— said Lord Justice Donaldson— to the last robbery which is the subject matter of two counts. Mr. Rice had a jeweller's shop in Sparkbrook. On 13 October 1977 a Mr. Holmes called to see him. Some time between 5.30 and 6 in the evening these two men were in the back part of the shop when two coloured men entered, followed a few seconds later by a white man who was brandishing some form of sword or cutlass which he used to cut the telephone lines. Immediately thereafter two more coloured men appeared. Mr. Rice and Mr. Holmes were ordered into the kitchen. The sword was handed over to one of the coloured men whilst the white man opened up one of the two safes. There were also two watches which Mr. Rice was repairing and they were taken and the till was emptied. While these operations were going on, Mrs. Rice arrived with her daughter, Karen. the door had been locked. Mrs. Rice knocked on it. The white man, telling Mr. Rice to keep out of sight, invited Mrs. Rice to come in. Apparently at that stage the white man decided that it would be better that all should depart. They did so in some hurry, dropping all the proceeds of the robbery other than about £30, and the sword or cutlass. Mr. Rice said that that white man was Irish, by which I take it he meant that he spoke with an Irish accent; that he had marks like moles on the sides of his face; that he was in his late twenties or early thirties; and wore a hat. Mr. Holmes who had his wrist watch and wallet taken, put the white man as being about 40 years of age and again said he had moles, specifying that they were on the right cheek. That was the summary of the facts given in the Court of Appeal. In May 1977, Mr. Foran had been arrested in connection with other matters and bailed. He jumped his bail, and a warrant was issued and he was rearrested on 24 October 1977.

Mr. Foran was then interviewed by three police officers, to one of whom, when he was alone, he is said to have admitted his part in the robbery at the jeweller's shop, which occasion he described in great detail and with considerable accuracy.

Evidence was given at the trial that Mr. Foran had confirmed this confession to two other police officers, one of whom was a detective chief inspector. On 9 November, an identification parade was held. As Mr. Foran had moles on his face, all those taking part had sticking plaster in the relevant places. Mr. Holmes positively identified Mr. Foran. Mr. Rice, however, picked out another man, as did his wife and daughter. The latter had picked out Mr. Foran from some photographs but neither the trial court nor the Appeal Court regarded that as satisfactory.

On 13 March 1978, one Errol Campbell, a West Indian, was arrested and made a statement in which he admitted to all three robberies and said that Mr. Foran was involved in each. On 3 April 1978, two police officers interviewed Mr. Foran at Leicester prison, when they read Campbell's statement to him. Their evidence was that he thereupon admitted that he had taken part in the Apechis and Trikain robberies as well as that at the jeweller's shop.

At the trial, however, Mr. Foran denied entirely that he had confessed to any of the offences at any time, said that the police had fabricated all the evidence and, indeed, said that they had beaten him up for refusing to confess.

A prison officer who had escorted Mr. Foran when he was interviewed by the police at Leicester prison, and who had seen but not heard the interview, gave evidence for the defence. His evidence was in conflict with that of the police officers on certain matters, including the attitude of Mr. Foran during that interview, and in his summing-up the trial judge was at pains to draw the attention of the jury to all the descrepancies. It was for the jury to decide which evidence it preferred.

I now return briefly to the robberies at the houses of Mr. Apechis and Mr. Trikain. Mr. Apechis described the man as being about 18 years of age, as I have mentioned. Mr. Foran was 33. Mr. and Mrs. Trikain said that the white man concerned in their robbery was about 25. That evidence was read at Mr. Foran's trial by agreement—it was not a matter of technicality, as the hon. Gentleman said, but by agreement—and the judge was again at pains in his summing-up to point out to the jury that certainly Mr. Apechis's description of the white man did not even remotely resemble Mr. Foran.

When Mr. Foran sought leave to appeal against his conviction and his sentence, he sought leave to call Mr. Apechis and Mr. Trikain to give evidence. Mr. Apechis had said in a letter before the Court of Appeal that he was sure that Mr. Foran was not present. However, the full court refused the application, principally because the case against Mr. Foran had rested not on identification, for there was none in the case of the Apechis and Trikain robberies, but upon his confession to the offences. The court commented that Mr. Apechis's description had been before the jury, which had had its attention drawn by the judge to the fact that it did not in the least resemble Mr. Foran. Similarly, the court had been reminded that Mr. Trikain had not seen the face of the white intruder. The jury was entitled, nevertheless, to accept the police evidence as to the oral confessions.

Since the trial, said Lord Justice Donaldson, it had emerged that Mr. Trikain could say that he knew Mr. Foran and that it was not he who had robbed him. The court dealt with those applications to call further evidence in the following passage. Lord Justice Donaldson said: We have given serious consideration as to whether there should be leave to appeal to enable these applications to call further evidence to be considered. We do not think there are any grounds for granting leave to call that further evidence, bearing in mind our analysis that this was a confession case and that identification or non-identification, or positive evidence that it was not the man, in the circumstances of this case would not take the matter sufficiently far beyond the state which was reached at the trial when evidence from these two men was read, to justify us giving leave for them to give evidence and reconsidering the matter. It will be clear that in the case of the two robberies to which I have just referred—the Apechis and the Trikain robberies—the case against Mr. Foran rested exclusively on the reliance to be placed on his alleged admissions at Leicester prison on 3 April. In the light of the conflict between the evidence of the police officers taking the confession and the prison officer to whom I have already referred, I have had further investigations made. These have, however, failed to reveal any further grounds for umpugning the police officers' account. It is to be remembered that the prison officer observed the interview from the adjoining room, and except for one occasion when he joined the interview at Mr. Foran's request, he did not hear the conversation between him and the police officers.

The case in respect of the offences against Mr. Rice and Mr. Holmes at the jeweller's shop is also based on Mr. Foran's alleged confessions, although in that case there is the additional factor that Mr. Holmes did positively identify him at the identification parade.

Mr. Whitlock The hon. and learned Gentleman will agree that, while one of the four people who witnessed the third robbery identified Foran, the other three identified others in the identification parade.

Mr. Mayhew That is perfectly true, but the hon. Gentleman cannot just pick on a factor and say that that is decisive to the exclusion of others.

I hope that I have dealt with the matter fairly, but a fair account of the matter has to take note of the fact that in the case of the jeweller's shop robbery there was an additional element of a positive identification on the part of Mr. Holmes.

At his trial, Mr. Foran adduced an alibi for this period—that is to say, the period relating to the jeweller's shop robbery—but, although the trial judge carefully explained to the jury that it was not for Mr. Foran to prove that alibi, the jury was evidently not led by it to doubt the prosecution's evidence as to his confession.

http://hansard.millbanksystems.com/commons/1982/jul/20/mr-martin-foran   20/03/2009

APPENDIX 2

Foran's Suicide letters

Tuosday Night
30 - 4 - 85

My loving daughter Valeri, your
daddy must go away. you
love your old daddy very
much s know. And s love
you. words wrot on paper
wont ever express the
hurt s feel from been
parted from you. Daddy is
crying, as been parted
of ill. from you hurts most
please forgiv me,
as from we been parted again.
not live

" I love you "

forgiv me,
from your
loving father
Martin

x + x x
x x
x

To his wife Valerie

"TUESDAY NIGHT"

my love,

It's TUESDAY NIGHT now for me,

I refused to give evidence in order to stop my record coming out, Julie Kevin and Gerry were very good. But love I have lost heart. the police I know will murder me because of this I know I will be found it, guilty, I just know it, guilty,

and love the judge will hit me very hard, I think 6 years, if not more,

So I have given up love, I just lost heart over the police I know

what is really destroying me, To know in my heart I never done the robbery.

But my past is against me, this is what he will sentence me on, he wont give me no chance, Val so soon after the ten year, another long sentence will destroy me,

dont think I can face another sentence. so I dont wait.

you have been to good of a wife to me, dont become a prison

(2)

window you have just had
years of what, just had sent
ask you to face that
again,

Not will I let you.
when he pass sentence on
me,

there, please please dont be
there, when you have given
your evidence, I ask
you, on what love we
have shared for each
other

please go home to
have to turn around if I
end look at the hurt in
your face then I wont
be able to hold back the
tears,

please dont let the
police see the hurt they
have caused,

I will close
my I my off in the prison
speaking. Just dont my
mind off, Just dont write
or visit.

you will ask
Ron perttor to g' won't you
a divorce, I
fight it.

what ever sentence
be me, given me will destroy
as I won't ever be

(5)

the man s was. remember love,
s will have to have that
intestine veg put at my side
some time this year,
So that
won't be nice, and no
way would s let you see
me in that state.
s would
sooner die and love to.
think of another long sentence
s think death would be
far more peacefull. s really
do,
they will tell you s
am maed or cracked up
in a few months because
no one will go to me,
when s turn my self off
my willpower, will hold out,
please remember me as s
was,
remember the happy days
we had,
they can part us, but
you have only to look at
our five children, to see five
parts of me,
we used to
joke about life after death
but if there is a way to
be you know that my spirit
is watching over you,
then s will
find a way to let you know.
val love, at a time like

this I would not w to ye over this mess

ye have had reasons to dought my love for ye re the girl called lyn s ured to speak to.

vel love, there is I one far s greater judgy then the now fee before my god,

s sware to you s have never betrayd yer love from the day we first met

this is on my childrens life.

s have never ever loved any one wi ye.

love Two things s cant fce, one" is another long sentence. the second is this veg at my side.

ye know s have no fear of death as it must be more peacefull and Trouble free then this life for s have moozed up this life with live in and out of prisons over half of my life

and NOW s have t To fce again. No love, s cant.

love should any thing happen to me please for the love ye

have for me, please respect my
wishes. have my body cremated,
please send a little bit of my
ashes to my mom
                    to be placed
near my father and my sister
Marie,

        you keep the biggest part
of my ashes, for only you
gave me the greatest joy
of a wonderfull love

                    S am
sorry that it must end
like this, But S have missed
out on the first five years of
our daughter Valeries life.

        Now S must miss out
on the last years of our
Twins life

            this is to much for
me,
        please try to forgive me,
and try to understand,

                    and never
forget, S loved you with all
my heart body and soul,
        from you
            loving husband
                martin
                    x x x
                    x x
                    a

        30 - 4 1985

228

Tuesday Night
30-4-1985

My loving Daughter Joenne, I am sorry to say you will love your old man again as the police have told far to much lies the jury won't belewe your dad, and the judge will sentence me on my past. me and you have had our little rows,

But deep down ye have always been my pet you could get any thing out of me, and ye know it,

So I want ye to be extra good to your mam she is going to need your help I haven't been much of a father to ye, ever been in and out of prison, for my past way of life I am sorry. Joenne if ye don't see me again,

think of me with love, remember the love I gave ye love that was not cross when ye smashed up your very first car, remember,

I wish I could leave ye some money but the police have even took the loan money from me, Joenne, please forgive me, and try to understand,

from your loving father
Merlin
† † † †
† † †

Tuesday Night
30 - 4 - 85

my loving Son.

I am sorry to say that you will lose your old men again. it hurts to know that Now me and you will not be able to take off to Kent. look Son when you are older, please promise me, you wont ever go into trouble, dont ever go into prison, dont ever be parted from your children when you grow up, like I have always been parted from you.

and most of all, dont let the police, over I the lies they have told about your old men as thank god, there is far more good police officers than there is bad.

and Son, please be extra good to your mom. and do as she tells you.

and when you think of your old dad, think of all the good times we had

I only wish I had some money to leave you Son. but I am broke.

just please try to understand, and forgive me. as I loved you very much

from your loving father
Martin
x x x
x x x

Tuesday Night
30 – 4 – 85.

Valerie please
post this to
Andrew.

Dear Brother,

I hope and pray
you never feel so alone as
I felt on Monday Tuesday and
shall do on Wednesday.
every time
I looked around you was not
there. Valerie could not come
into the court, because she was
a witness. you said you would
turn up on Monday. Never mind.
I can't be hurt no more now.
the police too will destroy me.
I will be found guilty.
the judge knows my past, so
he is not been fair, so I
can't win. can't face another
long sentence. Nor can I face
the thought of living with a
leg at my side.
and been parted
from Valerie and the children for
years again. No I could
not, and will not ask
Valerie to face up to that
again.
when you read this letter
my mind will be closed off.
we shall not meet in this
life again.
will you please
as my brother see to it
that should any thing happen
to me, that you help my
wife Valerie to carry on
my wishes, I want my body

231

(2

cremated. and a wee bit of
my ashes from home and places
with or dad and merrie,
so want the greatest part of my
ashes left with Valerie.
                        will you
please respect my wishes.
    good by Andrew.
                    please try to
understand, and forgive me,
        from your
            loving brother
            Martin

APPENDIX 3

Foran's detailed medical reports following his assault at HMP Liverpool.

The following examination was carried out by the Senior Medical Officer of HMP Liverpool on the 30th June 1986 immediately following the assault.

The following examination was carried out by Dr A. Khan, the Medical Officer at HMP Parkhurst the day after the assault and immediately on Foran's arrival following his transfer from HMP Liverpool.

HOSPITAL CASE PAPER (Continuation Sheet)

1986	Treatment, including Prescriptions	History and Progress of Case
June 1	Returned to Parkhurst Ex Liverpool	
1/7/86 9.40 pm	Received from HMP Liverpool. (arrived at 8.45 pm) Seen in E3 room in good light in the presence of HPO Seager and HSO Jenkins.	

Cooperative, answering to the point and gave an account of being assaulted by staff at HMP Liverpool, following a probable argument. Circumstances described by inmate.

Cooperative, civil and in a clear state of mind. Not showing any evidence of mental disorder, today.

Noticed to have several bruises all over his body. These bruises looked a few days old and some were resolving. These bruises were not accompanied by swelling but some were still tender to touch. The following bruises were noted: (L) knee (no effusion; full ROM, no obvious joint involvement.) Tender (R) shin but no bruise on (R) shin. Bruise over (L) thigh, Large bruise on (L) buttock, and (R) iliac fossa and (R) iliac crest. Several bruises on sacrum a small one on (L) shoulder and (L) upper arm. Another bruise on (L) side of chest and above (L) eye. Vision grossly normal. PERL.

No apparent eye damage. No bruises or hematomas were noted on the head. He is not distressed.

Chest - clear. CVS - PERL.

Genitals grossly NAD

PNR - grossly NAD.

Abdo. No clinical evidence of internal injury. His colostomy didn't appear traumatized. (although he complained that there was some blood.) Minimal excoriation with minimal blood & mucus.

770611/84 XLYQ512

~~apart from when he was involved in a scuffle~~

His colostomy showed no bleeding and was functional.

He has colostomy bags and manages it himself.

There doesn't appear to be any evidence of bony injuries and therefore no apparent need for Xraying him.

Cardiovascular system – grossly NAD Pulse 70/min reg. good vol

adv To remain in E (ii) rooms. Up and about.

Observe.

To be reviewed tomorrow.

3.7.86 Seen By Mr T Walsh: Age 42. Following a hunger strike (1981) developed mucous discharge +? prolapse.
1981 - Leicester Hospital bad Ivalon

Symptoms of mucus discharge persisted.

4/52 age LIF Difunctioning
- since then still has mucus discharge from within rectum and colostomy (as bad as before). Colostomy works

A few days ago said he was beaten up in Liverpool jail, not Ko'd and now feels Also he was hit in colostomy and it has bled since.

O/E Fit now.
Multiple bruises as documented:

L Temporal
L Arm
Rt side abdo
L shin
Back x 2 at waist
Rt side chest
L Buttock

No obvious bony injury.
Abdo

Min excoriation around colostomy) See
Doubled barrelled colostomy) Conslt's
Fibrosal + a bit thickened,) note for
but both views OK.) diagram
Mucus + slight blood around colostomy
but no major injury.

PR Weak and splinted
No frank blood pr.

Impression: 1. As far as alleged assault is concerned I doubt if there is any long term damage to colostom

2. He clearly has a difficult and interesting rectal problem. I think we need to

To assist the reader, I asked a doctor colleague to review Dr Khan's medical assessment, in particular his hand written notes, to understand better the terms used. This follows:

....

Page 1

1/7/86   Received from HMP Liverpool (arrived at 8.45
9.40 pm   pm). Seen in E3 room in good light in the presence
            of HPO (Hospital Prison Officer) Seager and HSO
(Hospital Senior Officer) Jenkins.

Co-operative, answering to the point and gave an account of being assaulted by staff at HMP Liverpool, following a probable argument. Circumstances described by inmate.

Is co-operative, civil and in a clear state of mind. Not showing any evidence of mental disorder today.

Noted to have several bruises all over his body. These bruises looked a few days old and some were resolving. These bruises were not accompanied by swelling but some were still tender to touch.
The following bruises were noted: (L) knee (no effusion full ROM (Range of movement)). No obvious joint involvement). Tender (L) shin but no bruises on (L) shin. Bruise over (L) thigh. Large bruise on (L) buttock. (R) Iliac fossa (concave part of the hip bone) and (R) Iliac crest (top of hip bone). Several bruises on sacrum (a triangular bone in the lower back); a small one on (L) shoulder and (L) upper arm. Another bruise on (L) side of chest and above (L) eye. Vision grossly normal. PERL (eye Pupils Equal and React to Light). No apparent eye damage. No bruises or hematomas were noted on the head. He is not distressed.

Chest – clear. CNI (Central Nervous Investigation) - PERL (eye Pupils Equal and React to Light) Cranals grossly NAD (Nothing Abnormal Detected)

PNI (Peripheral Nervous Investigation) grossly NAD (Nothing Abnormal Detected)

Abdominal – No clinical evidence of internal injury.
His colostomy didn't appear traumatised (although he complained there was some blood).
Minimal excoriation with minimal blood and mucus.

Page 2

His colostomy showed no bleeding and was functional
He has colostomy bags and manages it himself
There doesn't appear to be any evidence of lung injuries and therefore no apparent need for X-raying him.
Cardiovascular system – grossly NAD (nothing abnormal detected). Pulse 70/min, registered good volume.
Adv: To remain in E(ii) rooms overnight.
Observe. To be reviewed tomorrow.

APPENDIX 4

Recovered minutes of the interviews with Foran, Charlton and Robinson following Foran's assault

(١٧) *Doc. 44* A1.

INQUIRY INTO ALLEGATIONS MADE BY C51796 FORAN Martin Patrick

CONDUCTED BY MR W A MARTIN   GOVERNOR LEEDS PRISON

8 DECEMBER 1986

Governor: My name is Mr Martin and I am the Governor of Leeds Prison. I have been ordered to carry out a departmental enquiry into the circumstances of an incident which occurred at Liverpool on the 29 June in which you were involved and about which you made complaints.

FORAN: You are aware this has gone to the courts and solicitors are involved. In my own interests I should have a solicitor present. I have been granted legal aid.

Governor: The terms of reference which I operate on with regard to departmental enquiries are prescribed with certain rules. The procedure is I will conduct the enquiry and I have documentation, some you have been involved with which I can refer to. I would certainly want you to have the opportunity to say things to me verbally and for you to talk to me about it in a situation like this so you can say what you want to me. If you do not I will carry out an enquiry without you.

FORAN: I would have to have a solicitor present and put forward the evidence of photographs of what happened to me at Liverpool Prison.

Governor: Those photographs can be provided to me or sent to me at Leeds. The procedure under which I operate does not involve legal representation. It is departmental.

FORAN: Can I have permission to ring my solicitor, if he says yes I will carry on. I am involved in 3 legal battles with the police the solicitors involved instructed me it is now out of prison hands it has gone to the courts. I am familiar with the rules and wish to seek advice from him first.

Governor: That can be arranged. I will tell you first what will happen. I will ask you to tell me in your own words in addition to what you have written down and I would ask you one or two questions. I want your side of it and to put certain questions to you. What happened in terms of the particular procedure and sequence of events and any questions that might arise. I am quite happy for you to have a word with your solicitor. If you wish to go through with the interview we will resume.

ADJOURN

FORAN: I have spoken to the solicitor and he says that on the condition that we are supplied with a verbatim transcript of what takes place here it is alright for me to speak to you.

(18)   11

Governor:	When I have completed my enquiry I make a report to my superior the Regional Director who is a member of the Prisons Board together with all the documents. It is an internal enquiry, I can state in my report that you have asked for a copy of the record of the interview that is now going to take place and your solicitor can apply to the Home Office for a copy but it is not within my authority to give an undertaking it will be given. It is not within my terms to give agreement. It is a reasonable request to make but I would be going outside the prescribed arrangements.
FORAN:	The solicitor said as far as he was concerned there was only two answers yes or no. Your answer is no. Unless I report back to him I do not believe you are giving me a straight forward answer. Unless I can have a clear understanding that I can have a copy I do not wish to take part in the proceedings. If you wish I will go back and ask him but without his permission I cannot proceed.
Governor:	I think it would be quicker for me to check that I can give such an undertaking.

ADJOURN

Governor:	The answer is yes. You can have a copy of the transcript. I will get the Governor to call you up and give it to you.
	Before I ask you to tell me in your own words what happened at Liverpool I want to point out one or two things for my own purposes. I want to go through what happened after the incident in terms of who you complained to and what you did about it. If you give me your side. My understanding is the incident occurred on the 29 June. You left Liverpool on 1 July, 29 June was the Sunday. Can I ask you were you seen by an Assistant Governor Mr Temple on the day after, the Monday.
FORAN:	A Governor came to the cell.
Governor:	Was that the strip cell or ordinary cell?
FORAN:	In the strip cell.
Governor:	Did he give you the opportunity to write a statement about your allegations?
FORAN:	Yes.
Governor:	You wrote a statement?
FORAN:	No a slip of paper was pushed under the door. I was naked and I had no pen. I wrote a statement sometime later when I was removed from the padded cell and placed in the hospital cell.
Governor:	Do you remember was that the same day or the day after.
FORAN:	On the Monday.
Governor:	When the Assistant Governor read your statement did he read you the official warning?
FORAN:	No there was an argument over that.

(14)

Governor:	You refused to sign a copy of the warning?
FORAN:	Yes.
Governor:	After that were you seen by PMO or SMO?
FORAN:	No I was seen beforehand.
Governor:	Did the AG see you a second time and try and persuade you to sign the form?
FORAN:	No.
Governor:	Did you say anything to him that could mean you wished to withdraw your allegations?
FORAN:	No. The argument was I asked to see a solicitor or police to make allegations of assault and he said that I could not do this unless I went through the proper channels. I said I have the right to talk to my solicitor once I have seen a member of the Governor grade.
Governor:	Would you like to tell me in your own words what happened on the Sunday that caused you to make allegations?
FORAN:	I came out of my cell on the Sunday morning to go for breakfast. When I went for breakfast I was on vegan milk, I asked for the milk and one of the officers passed a remark about the milk "your not getting the milk" I thought it was best just to go back into my cell. I turned around and said "sod the milk forget it". I turned round to walk back to my cell and I was jumped on by one of the officers. Where the pantry is there are 2 doors and when he grabbed me he grabbed me from behind and pushed me up against the door and I was screaming and the bag got ripped off and doubled me up in pain. I told him I had got a colostomy. I think it was an accident. The next thing I was on the floor. I do not remember exactly what happened I was in severe pain, next thing I can remember I am being pulled to the strip cell at the end of the corridor at the back. When I got in the strip cell I said I have got a colostomy I don't want to argue with you., One Officer started kicking me badly and he jumped on my stomach and they kicked hell out of me. They came back later and the Officer came back to apologise. He said he did not know I had a colostomy.
Governor:	Was that the end of it?
FORAN:	When I came to after the hiding in the cell I was left lying in a mess. I rang the bell and asked for assistance and the tall officer with the beard came back with the mop bucket and mop and used that to mop me down. I started moaning about that I had just had an operation and I was terrified of getting infection.
Governor:	Did you do anything else, anything physical.
FORAN:	No nothing. If I had done anything physical I would have been nicked. 2 weeks after a serious operation I could hardly walk let alone do anything physical.

(20)

Governor: You speak about the officer with the beard, do you know the names of any officers?

FORAN: I don't know.

Governor: How many Officers?

FORAN: There were 4 officers involved, I only saw 2 officers hit me.

Governor: What do you remember about the 2 hitting you?

FORAN: The tall one with the beard, he is the one who flipped his lid because of my London charge. The one who was lifting my legs and kicking me he was also saying "we will teach you to take hostages"

Governor: Can you describe him?

FORAN: About 5' 8", clean faced I could not pick him out again.

Governor: You say your clothes were stripped off you, when they were ripped off what was the condition of your wound. You did say the colostomy bag was ripped off.

FORAN: I was covered in blood when they pulled the trousers off it was bleeding.

Governor: Have you got any witnesses you would like to tell me about that I might be able to trace.

FORAN: There were prisoners there but I do not know their names. The only person who saw the state of me, he came into the strip cell and stayed with me was the RC Priest.

Governor: Anybody else you can think of?

FORAN: There were a lot of prisoners about I cannot remember who.

Governor: Anything else you want to tell me about it that you would like me to take into account.

FORAN: I wondered why it had happened and up to this I had got on great in Liverpool. Naturally they were unhappy at first about what I did at Wandsworth but the whole tone of my behaviour at Wandsworth was caused by my illness. I did nothing to upset them while I was down there. Before that the officer had been very good to me. For some reason or another he just snapped on the Sunday morning he was a completely different person as if he just lost his head. When I asked to see a doctor when he eventually came down to see me he could not examine me because I was covered in blood and mucus from the open wound. I said you cannot see what is up with me he just banged the door and walked away. I started to bang on the door of the strip cell to get a doctor down there. A doctor came back and they agreed to clean me up and then examined me. He came back into the cell and had a look at me.

Governor: Did this happen in the morning or afternoon?

FORAN: Morning.

(24)

V.

Governor:	Is there anything else?
FORAN:	I was unhappy about conditions that happened after that. When I was writing my complaint I was told that if I kept my mouth shut I would be removed from the prison immediately. I was terrified and part of the conditions laid down by the Governor if I agreed to keep my mouth shut was he would get me removed from the prison. I was terrified so I agreed. When I got to Parkhurst I told the Governor and Doctor what had happened. Surely the state I was in I should not have been passed fit to leave the prison. I would like you to see the photographs. I was glad to get out but the way it was done.
Governor:	You were examined before you left the prison?
FORAN:	No sir I was not you can check with Oxford Prison, the escort had to stop at Oxford Prison and the Hospital Officer had to take me to their prison hospital on my way to Parkhurst. I had not at any time threatened anyone, all I said was "sod the milk" because I was depressed. That beating I received was completely uncalled for and the only reason it happened was because of what happened at Wandsworth. I would like to ask you to have a look at the photographs of what happened.
Governor:	Can you arrange for the photographs to be sent to me. The Governor can provide you with the address for your solicitor to send them to. I will look at these photographs as part of my enquiry.

(22)

INTERVIEW WITH HOSPITAL OFFICER CHARLTON, HM PRISON, LIVERPOOL
ON 5 DECEMBER 1986

Mr Martin explained the purpose of the interview in connection with allegations
made by C51796 FORAN

MR MARTIN:
Mr Charlton, here is a copy of the statement you made in connection with an
incident concerning Foran for you to read over and refresh your memory.
Then for the record can you state your full name an rank.

MR CHARLTON:
That is a copy of my statement.   I am Hospital Officer John Charlton.

MR MARTIN:
Do you recall the incident regarding a prisoner named Foran on 29 June 1986.

MR CHARLTON:
Yes

MR MARTIN:
At that time did you have occasion to restrain him?

MR CHARLTON:
Yes

MR MARTIN:
How did you do that?

MR CHARLTON:
Well initially he tried to assault me. He lashed out with the back of his
left hand.   I saw it coming.   I blocked it and put my hand round his
head to restrain him.   I was on my own at that time.   I got him down
to the ground and then other staff came in to help restrain him and we
used the usual control and restraints method.

MR MARTIN:
Who else was there?

MR CHARLTON:
There was Mr Frith and Mr Robinson. Mr Evans was around somewhere serving
breakfasts.   I cannot recall if he was actually involved in that.

MR MARTIN:
In your statement you mentioned that Foran threw a tray. Can you tell me
something about that?

MR CHARLTON:
He was complaining about his food, which was normal for Foran.   I tried
to calm him down. He was a vegan and was on a special diet. The food was
cheese and potato or something like that.   He was not happy with it.
I tried to calm him down and said I would sort it out with the kitchen.
But he carried on complaining and shouting about it.   He stepped back and
shouted something like "I'm not fucking having that" and flung the tray
across the landing.   I ordered him back to his room.   He was still shouting.

MR MARTIN:
So, he started to walk back but was still shouting abuse and then he lashed
out.   Did you know about his medical condition?

243

MR CHARLTON:
Yes I was working on the landing and knew about his condition.

MR MARTIN:
You mentioned control and restraints. Have you had training in control and restraints?

MR CHARLTON:
Yes I was trained in control and restraints at the school.

MR MARTIN:
Did you use only absolutely necessary force?

MR CHARLTON:
Yes I only used the minimum necessary force.

MR MARTIN:
Did you see anyone else use excessive force?

MR CHARLTON:
No, not at all sir. He was fighting and kicking his legs around and he had to be held quite firmly.

MR MARTIN:
What hold did you have on him? After other staff had arrived, and after you had held him around the neck?

MR CHARLTON:
I think I had one of his legs.

MR MARTIN:
Would I be right in describing you as a tall man with a beard?

MR CHARLTON:
Yes.

MR MARTIN:
Well that is all I want to ask you. Thank you Mr Charlton.

INTERVIEW CONCLUDED.

J. CHARLTON HO

12.

244

(24)

INTERVIEW WITH HOSPITAL SENIOR OFFICER ROBINSON, HM PRISON, LIVERPOOL
ON 15 DECEMBER 1986

A8. i

Mr Martin explained the purpose of the interview in connection with allegations
made by C51796 Foran.

MR MARTIN:
Mr Robinson you made a statement in connection with the incident regarding
Foran. Here is a copy of that statement for you to read and refresh your
memory.

MR ROBINSON:
Yes, sir, that is my statement.

MR MARTIN:
Well for the record, can you state your full name and rank?

MR ROBINSON:
Brian Robinson, Hospital Senior Officer.

MR MARTIN:
On 29 June, were you the senior hospital officer in charge?

MR ROBINSON:
Yes

MR MARTIN:
Were you involved in restraining the prisoner named Foran on 29 June 1986?

MR ROBINSON:
Yes

MR MARTIN:
Was it your decision to remove him to a strip cell?

MR ROBINSON:
Yes it was

MR MARTIN:
In what way did you personally restrain the prisoners?

MR ROBINSON:
I held both of his legs

MR MARTIN:
Did you supervise his removal to the strip cell?

MR ROBINSON:
We had to carry him down to the strip.

MR MARTIN:
Did you supervise the removal of his clothing in the strip cell?

MR ROBINSON:
Yes

MR MARTIN:
Did you take part in the removal of his clothing?

MR ROBINSON:
Yes, I removed his shoes, socks and trousers.

/1.

(26).

MR ROBINSON:
He had smeared blood all over himself.   There was blood all over his body.

MR MARTIN:
Why was that?

MR ROBINSON:
He was trying to make a lot more of it than what it was. He was bleeding from
his back passage he said but we could not look because he would not be examined.
He had done something like this in the surgical ward one Sunday when he rang
the alarm bell.   He had done a lot of verbal before but nothing physical.

MR MARTIN:
You say he was smeared with blood, but did he appear to be bleeding from any
wound?

MR ROBINSON:
No. You could tell he had smeared the blood by his hands. The palms of his
hands were covered in blood and the blood on his body was in stripes, finger
stripes where he had smeared the blood on his hands over his body.

MR MARTIN:
Were you able to take him back into ordinary location that day?

MR ROBINSON:
No he remained in the strip cell.

MR MARTIN:
Were you on the following day?

MR ROBINSON:
No I was on leave the following week. That was my only experience.

MR MARTIN:
Did you sign any forms authorising his removal?

MR ROBINSON:
No, not that day. I filled in the Occurrence Book. Actually I cannot remember
signing any forms.

MR MARTIN:
Thank you Mr Robinson. I think that is enough for my inquiry.

INTERVIEW CONCLUDED

/3.

APPENDIX 5

Barrister's note re-beatings hearing

FORAN -v- CHARLTON and THE HOME OFFICE

A D V I C E

1.   I am asked to advise generally and in respect of
evidence in this case which is set down for hearing in early
September. I saw my client in conference on 25th November
1987 and I have now seen him again in conference on 4th
August 1988 since disclosure of the Second Defendant's
documents.

2.   As regards the merits of the case, the outcome will
fall to be decided primarily on the Judge's assessment of
the oral evidence of the witnesses.   There is no doubt that
my client will start at some disadvantage in that it will be
his word, as a convicted prisoner, and those of several
prison officers. As regards the documentary evidence I have
now seen the various prison records, medical reports and the
result of an internal investigation carried out by the
Governor of Leeds Prison, the subject matter of a notice to
admit facts. These records taken with the photographs show
that my client clearly suffered some bruising, see
particularly the notes of Mr Walsh and the letter from Dr
Khan dated 11 July 1986, both of whom saw my client in
Parkhurst after his transfer thereto. Those findings
belie   the notes of the Hospital Officer who refers to the
incident and then states that there were "no injuries to the
inmate".

-2-

3.   It is also true to say that my client consistently complained about this incident from the outset to the Prison Governor, a priest Father Moran, the Board of Visitors and his M.P. It is said against him that he withdrew the complaint made to Mr Temple. He agrees that he did not state that reason was that he came to an agreement that if he was transferred to Parkhurst he would drop the complaint, so eager was he to get away from Liverpool. This is to some extent borne out by the evidence of Mr Welch who was present when the allegation was withdraw, although he says that in fact no such agreement was made by Mr Temple, although my client did suggest such a course of action. The findings of the internal inquiry are in my view irrelevant.

4.   My client's case in short is that this was a revenge attack for the hostage taking incident at Wandsworth. The documents in my view do not take the matter much further either way since the outcome will depend primarily on the Judge's view of the quality and credibility of the evidence of witnesses. In the circumstances I see no reason why this matter should not proceed to trial, although I of course recognise the difficulties that face my client in discharging the evidential burden of proof that vests upon him.

-3-

5.   As regards evidence, my client will clearly give oral
evidence of the incident and also any witnesses he is able
to call will give evidence. As I have already said, Items
1-3 of the Notice to Admit can be admitted but they are
clearly irrelevant and should not be put before the Judge
since it is the very issue that the Judge will have to
decide. As regards Item 4 I understand from my client that
he accepts that he refused to be examined by Dr Bennett.
Clearly the prison and medical notes ought to be agreed so
as to avoid the necessity of calling the makers thereof to
prove them. The inquiry should not be agreed as a document
to go into the Judge's bundle since much of it covers
evidence that ought to be given live at the trial and the
conclusions are in any event irrelevant. The photographs
and the date they were taken also ought to be agreed so as
to avoid the necessity to call the photographer.

6.   The last matter which concerns me is this. Hitherto
it has always been my opinion that the quantum of damages,
assuming that liability were proved, would comprise a sum to
compensate my client for the pain and suffering of a nasty
beating and kicking causing bruising, albeit with no long
term complications. I therefore advised when these papers
were first before me in 1987 that a medical report at that
time, some 9 months after the incident, would be otiose.

--4--

I explained this to my client in conference last year and he
accepted it. It now transpires that he was examined at St.
Marks Hospital, Kings Cross in early December 1987 with a
view to reversing the colostomy of June 1986, the colostomy
having been put in to rest his lower intestine in order to
stop excess discharge therefrom. On examination it
transpired, according to my client, that his anal sphincter
muscles no longer work which would render reversal of the
colostomy pointless. He states that the doctor who
exzamined him said that this was as a result of nerve
failure at the base of his spine which could have been
caused by kicking. I note in passing that the photographs
do show some bruising to the base of the spine.

7.   If that is the case, it may be that, assuming
liability is proved the quantum of damages will be much
greater since the result of the assault could be that my
client will have to have a permanent colostomy. The only
way to establish this is by expert medical opinion from Mr
Nicholas from St. Marks Hospital. If this is an arguable
point the case would then have to be transferred to the High
Court as damages would exceed the County Court limit. This
will clearly mean that the hearing this September will have
to be adjourned pending receipt of the medical report since
it may be that Mr Nicholas will need much more information

-5-

than he has already got and a further examination of my
client to give such an opinion. No doubt the Defendants
will not agree to such an adjournment and an application
will have to be made. It may also be that we will be
criticised for not raising this matter earlier, but for my
part I only became aware of this development recently when I
saw my client in conference. However it seems to me that
this matter must be explored and I advise that a medical
report be obtained. The question of an adjournment ought to
be raised as soon as possible and for the purposes of
information I am away from 20th August until 3rd September
1988.

MARTIN STRUTT

3 Paper Buildings
Temple E.C.4.
8th August 1988

APPENDIX 6

Letters of Support

Your Ref. _____

Our Ref. ___IJM/JS.___

All correspondence to be addressed to General Secretary.

Telephone: 745036
745036

N.E.E.T.U.
1966

National Engineering and Electrical Trade Union

CUMANN NÁISIÚNTA INNEALTHÓIREACHTA AGUS AIBHLÉISEACHTA

6 Gardiner Row, Dublin 1

Secretary,
Co-Ordinating Group on the Miscarriage of Justice,
C/O, I.C.P.O.,
57, Parnell Square,
Dublin 1.
-----------   22nd November 1990.

A Chara,

The Executive Council of the above Union received a brochure regarding the
injustices being perpetrated to Martin Foran and decided at their Executive
Council meeting to give your organisation full support of the above Union
in your efforts to secure his release from imprisonment in a British Jail.
They particularly felt that in the light of his present health his release
is justified on humanitarian grounds.

Sinne le meas,

I. J. MONELEY,
GENERAL SECRETARY (INDUSTRIAL).

Joint General Secretaries: K. M. P. McCONNELL (Financial). I. J. MONELEY (Industrial)

252

1 ⅞

C. N. T. **A. I. T.**

CONFEDERACION NACIONAL DEL TRABAJO
SINDICATO DEL METAL
FEDERACION LOCAL DE MADRID

Madrid, 21 de Abril de 1.989

Martin Foran
C51796 HMP
Parkhurst Newport

Isle of Wight PO305NXX

Gran Bretaña

Dear Comrade,

We, our mates of CNT-AIT Metal Trade from
Spain, aware of your extreme situation from DAM-IWA,
would like to show you our absolute solidarity and to
communicate we are on your side as far as you need it.

Besides writing to you, we have written
to the british embassy in Madrid and to that "Hotel"
manager condemming letters against the whole thing and
the inhuman trate that has take you to your present si
tuation.

It's not the first time, and unfortunally
not even the last one, that the Capital and its loyal
servant, the State, work that hard against those ones
who take steps towards the end of them. Therefore, we
ought to keep on consequently with our ideas and to
work hard for a world without jails and borders.

Finally, accept our best wishes for your
recovering and your expected freedom

for the trade committee
the secretary

PRISON REFORM TRUST

59 CALEDONIAN ROAD
LONDON N1 9BU

Tel: 01 - 278 9815
Fax: 01 - 833 5543

Registered Charity No. 282130

21 January 1990

Mike Shankland
137 Tullibardine Road
Sheffield
S11 7GN

Dear Mike

Thanks for your letter. I saw in the Guardian this morning that there is quite a lot about Martin Foran and the West Midlands Crime Squad - did you see it? If you didn't, do let me know and I will send you a copy. I was also standing in the queue at the health food shop local to the office when I noticed a big poster about a picket of the Home Office on February 7th for Martin Foran. I shall certainly try and make it if I can. It does seem that the campaign is actually gathering momentum and getting publicity. It's a shame the West Midlands Police have decided to shred every document over 2 years old - unbelievable!

I don't know if you are aware, but there is an enquiry into the Prison Medical Service being carried out at present. We were asked to contribute our views, but the deadline is 28 February so I think it's going to be a bit of a rush job. The most irksome thing is that the people conducting the enquiry emphasise that no-one is being asked what their opinion is of there being a separate medical service - "taken as given the need to retain a separate medical service" - which is obviously one of the most controversial issues about the prison medical service.

The gorey tales of the continuing mistreatment of Martin Foran are dreadful... I've had a good think about who else we can involve and I remembered a woman who came in to see us about a year ago. Her name is Jean Robinson and she is on the General Medical Council. She did say at the time that she might be able to help in some way, so I think you should write to her saying we gave you her name and address and see if she'll come and see Martin Foran - it's worth a try - she was a very nice woman. Her address is:

    56 Lonsdale Road
    Oxford, OX2 7EP

Let me know what her response is. Best wishes.

Diana Rushton

28th January, 1990.

Mr. Martin Foran,
No., C51796
HMP Frankland,
P.O. Box 40,
Finchdale Ave.,
Brasside,
Durham.
3YD.

Dear Martin,

Your friend Mr. George Dwyer has been in touch with me with your
conviction and consequent jail sentence.

I have a particular interest in your case as I have in the case of
the Guildford Four now released and the Birmingham Six and many
other Irish Prisoners in British jails who were wrongfully convicted
by a police force who have now being dicovered for what they are
totally discredited.

It was not the Irish people or the Irish Government or any one in
Britain that discredited this police force they discredited themselfs
with the apparent good will of the british system. I have heard much
about your case as I have about others and I would be most
anxious for you to contact me as soon as possible with a view to me
calling to see you or seeing members of your family.

Please be assured of my fullest co-operation and please let me hear
from you as soon as possible.

Very best wishes,

Yours sincerely,

Hugh

Senator Hugh Byrne,

University of Bradford Union

Richmond Road   Bradford BD7 1DP   Tel: (0274) 734135

Our Ref: CT/JS

7th July, 1988.

1 1 JUL 1988

Martin Foran,
C51796
HMP Parkhurst
Newport
ISLE OF WIGHT
PO30 5NX

Dear Martin,

You will be pleased to know that the University of Bradford Students Union recently passed policy in support of your campaign.

We are shocked and outraged at the ways in which you have been treated, and are still being treated. We have written to the Governor asking him to make sure that you receive immediate medical treatment in an external hospital, and that you are given a retrial. We have also asked for a lifting of the restriction on your mail.

We wish you well, and hope that your campaign is a success.

Yours sincerely.

C. Toft

Chris Toft
UBU PRESIDENT.

Nothing contained in this letter constitutes an order unless accompanied by an official UBU order form.

APPENDIX 7

Consideration of the Court of Appeal which quashed Foran's second conviction

IN THE COURT OF APPEAL (CRIMINAL DIVISION)

Neutral Citation Number: [2013] EWCA Crim 437

Case No: 201207195 B3

IN THE COURT OF APPEAL (CRIMINAL DIVISION)

ON APPEAL FROM BIRMINGHAM CROWN COURT

His Honour Judge Malcolm Potter

850128/30

Royal Courts of Justice

Strand, London, WC2A 2LL

Date: 16/04/2013

Before :

LORD JUSTICE LEVESON

MR JUSTICE MITTING and

MR JUSTICE MALES

- - - - - - - - - - - - - - - - - - - -

Between :

MARTIN PATRICK FORAN Appellant

- and -

THE QUEEN Respondent

- - - - - - - - - - - - - - - - - - - -

- - - - - - - - - - - - - - - - - - - -

Miss Elizabeth Nicholls (instructed by Olliers Solicitors) for the Appellant

Mr Jonathan Laidlaw QC (instructed by the Crown Prosecution Service) for the Respondent

Hearing date : 26t March 2013

- - - - - - - - - - - - - - - - - - - -

Approved Judgment

Lord Justice Leveson:

1

1. On 3 May 1985, in the Crown Court at Birmingham, before Judge Potter and a jury, this appellant was convicted of robbery and conspiracy to rob. He was sentenced to six years' and two years' imprisonment respectively, to run consecutively, thus making a total sentence of eight years. Twice since the convictions, appeals against the convictions have been unsuccessfully mounted to this court. On this, third, occasion, the Criminal Cases Review Commission has concluded that there is a real possibility that the convictions will not be upheld in the light of information not previously considered regarding the credibility of the principal police witness, Detective Inspector Paul Matthews, a member of the now notorious West Midlands Police Serious Crime Squad who interviewed the appellant, together with developments in case law since the earlier appeals concerning the position when the evidence of a tainted officer is supported by other police evidence by officers to whom no criticism is attached.

The Facts

2. The charge of robbery related to an attack at the home of the licensee of the Trident public house in Birmingham. During the early hours of 9 September 1984, he was asleep in his flat above the premises when he was woken by a youth who stood over him with a knife and shone a light in his face. Another person, who stood to the side of the bed, was wearing a balaclava and was holding what appeared to be a 2-3 foot long stave or bar. A third person was rummaging about in the room. The licensee was asked where his money was and he told the intruders where to find it. They left taking £1,700 with them. The police were summoned immediately. It was then ascertained that entry to the premises had been gained by the removal of wooden beading from two glass panels, then the removal of the glass itself.

3. It was the prosecution case that the appellant was the man wearing the balaclava, the man holding the knife was a man called Andrew McKenzie and the third man rummaging about was Paul Addison. In due course, both of these other men were to plead guilty to this offence.

4. At 11.50 am on 10 September Addison was arrested. He was interviewed by DC Preston and PC Conn. He admitted that he was involved in the robbery along with two other men, one of whom he referred to as "Martin". It was Martin, according to Addison, who had gained access to the public house by removing wooden beading around a window, using an iron bar. He continued:

"Martin had a bar and was threatening the bloke with it and Andrew had a knife and he held it to the bloke's throat. That's it. Before we did that job Martin told me about a job we were going to do today, a post office job, a £16,000 job. They were going to pick me up at 3pm today at the café and I was going to keep watch again and get £1,000."

5. Addison gave further details of a further intended robbery namely at a post office:

"Listen, Martin's got a white car, an Allegro, but I don't know if he's going to keep that or not. Anyway he's going to pick me up and me, him and Andrew are going to do the job. I'm going to keep watch and they are going in with the bars and things. Martin said he watched the place for ages and will get £16,000 easy. He said something about it being closed on Mondays. … It's over by Water Orton, that's all I know. That's everything. I was going to get £1000. Martin's done all the work on it."

2

6. He said that the men had arranged to meet at the Riviera Café in Hurst Street, Birmingham. This agreement to rob the Post Office was the subject of the charge of conspiracy to rob.

7. Acting on this intelligence, later that afternoon, DI Matthews, DC Preston, DC Jisra, DC Bartoszewicz, PC Conn, and PC Shelley waited outside the Riviera Café. The appellant arrived at 3.05 p.m., driving a white Allegro just as Addison had indicated. While still seated in his car, the appellant was approached by DI Matthews and DC Preston. After identifying himself, he was told that he was to be arrested. DI Matthews, DC Preston and PC Conn all gave evidence that the appellant was in possession of a bundle of money of which he attempted to dispose as he was getting out of his car. The officers recovered a knife, two screwdrivers, two crowbars and a crash helmet from the appellant's car.

8. The appellant was taken to Bradford Street Police station in Digbeth, Birmingham, arriving (according to the custody record) at 3.12 pm. He was interviewed under caution by DI Matthews in the presence of DC Preston, both of the West Midlands Serious Crime Squad, but with no solicitor present. According to DI Matthews and DC Preston the interview took place between 4.00 and 4.15 pm. At first the appellant denied all knowledge of the Trident robbery and of any conspiracy to rob the post office. He accused the police of taking £60 of his money.

9. According to DI Matthews and DC Preston, DI Matthews informed the appellant that Addison had been arrested and had provided a statement implicating him in the Trident robbery and the conspiracy to rob the post office in Water Orton that afternoon. The officers recorded the appellant's response as:

"I don't believe you, that's fanny!"

10. The officers then recorded that they told the appellant that they had a copy of Addison's statement which DI Matthews read out. According to the officers' witness statements and their evidence at trial the following exchange then took place:

"Foran: What can I say? It's all there, isn't it?

DI Matthews: It is correct then.

Foran: I'm not saying anything. Look, I know about it, you know I help the police. I can get the coloured lad for you.

DI Matthews: At the moment it's your part I'm interested in.

Foran: I'm not saying anything, you can't charge me on just that.

DI Matthews: We have recovered two iron bars and a knife from the car, what about those?

Foran: I've told you I'm not saying anything. I want a brief.

DI Matthews: Anybody in particular?

Foran: Yes, Ron Parker.

3

DI Matthews: Very well, if you want to see me with your solicitor, let me know.

Foran: I won't want to. You've got fuck all evidence."

11. This exchange in which the appellant first acknowledged his participation in the robbery ("What can I say? It's all there, isn't it?") and then offered to assist the police ("Look, I know about it, you know I help the police. I can get the coloured lad for you") was important evidence at the appellant's trial. The appellant has always denied making this confession, which is at the centre of this appeal.

The Trial

12. The appellant was jointly tried with Addison who pleaded guilty to the count of robbery (which he had admitted) but not guilty to the count of conspiracy to rob on the basis that he had not agreed to go along with the plan. At the trial (which proceeded over 5 days), the appellant dismissed his counsel and undertook his own defence.

13. The prosecution relied on the evidence of the police officers who were cross-examined on the basis that the exchange described by DI Matthews and DC Preston had not taken place. The appellant also took issue with the police evidence that he had been trying to get rid of money when he was arrested and challenged the times both of his arrest and his arrival at the police station. At the close of the prosecution case, the case depended on the alleged admission together with the corroborative detail of what had been recovered from the appellant's car. Addison's statement, to such extent as it had not been adopted by the appellant, was not, of course, evidence against him.

14. Dealing first with Addison's evidence in his own defence, he attempted to paint a less serious picture of his own involvement. He gave contradictory evidence as to whether the man "Martin" he had previously named was the appellant. In his evidence in chief he withdrew his allegation that Martin was the appellant and repeated this withdrawal when cross-examined by the appellant. However, under cross-examination by the prosecution, he reinstated the allegation, saying that the account he had given to police in his initial statement was correct. Having been given on oath at the trial when the appellant was present, this last evidence, although internally contradicted, was admissible against the appellant.

15. The appellant did not himself give evidence but his case was straightforward. It was that he was not at the public house at all, but had been in his car with friends at the time when the robbery took place. He had been in the company of Addison and McKenzie until approximately 2.15 am on the morning of 9 September but his car had then broken down, and the AA had been called to assist him. The car was fixed at about 2.15 am but it then broke down again, and the appellant waited at the Riviera café. He eventually returned home at 4.30 am, where his wife and a neighbour were waiting up for him. The knife was carried in the car to help to start it. He called a number of witnesses to give evidence regarding his movements on the night of the robbery.

16. The appellant's wife gave evidence that the money found on the appellant had been withdrawn from the couple's Provident Building Society account some days before his arrest: it now transpires that this money was eventually returned to her by order of the court and was

4

not held to be the proceeds of the robbery. His solicitor, Mr Daniels, gave evidence about his arrival at the police station on the day of the appellant's arrest. He maintained that he had arrived at least 30 minutes before police records suggested that he had.

17. These were the issues that the judge left to the jury and no complaint is made of his summing up, although it is relevant to point to two of the directions that he gave. The first is that the judge warned the jury that when considering the appellant's case they should approach Addison's evidence with caution, as he was a youth who was capable of changing his story and who had told lies giving deliberately contradictory evidence. He urged the jury to see whether Addison's evidence affecting the appellant was borne out by other evidence from an independent source. On the count of robbery, the only possible independent evidence was the police evidence of the appellant's confession in interview.

18. The second matter is the way the judge dealt with the appellant's interview. He emphasised that this was extremely important evidence, not only by saying so in terms, but by reading it out twice. He also referred disparagingly to the making of "the usual kind of complaint" against the police. In the light of what has since become known, that comment is, at its lowest, unfortunate. In the event, the appellant was convicted of both offences.

The Appeals

19. On 25 July 1986 this court (O'Connor LJ and Ognall J) refused a renewed application for leave to appeal against conviction and for leave to call fresh evidence. It is not apparent from the brief judgment given by Ognall J what the proposed grounds (settled by Mr Foran without legal assistance) or the fresh evidence were, but we understand that they included allegations against DI Matthews.

20. Mr Foran continued to maintain that he had been the subject of a miscarriage of justice and, some nine years later, a second appeal was mounted after the convictions had been referred to the court by the Home Secretary pursuant to section 17(1)(a) of the Criminal Appeal Act 1968. It was heard on 24 February 1995 before Russell and Pill LJJ and Turner J.

21. The Reference arose for two reasons. The first was that an investigation by the Police Complaints Authority had revealed that a forensic science report produced in September 1984 had not been provided to the prosecuting solicitor by the police, and therefore had not been disclosed to the defence, let alone adduced in evidence before the jury. The second concerned evidence which, it was said, demonstrated that DI Matthews was a discredited witness who, if the material had been placed before the jury, would not or might not have been believed.

22. Dealing with the first ground of the reference, the forensic report had concluded that the implements found in the appellant's car at the time of his arrest could not have been used to gain access to the flat above the Trident public house where the robbery had taken place. There was no question that, even by the rather different disclosure rules of the time, it should have been disclosed: the Crown did not suggest to the contrary. It was significant not least because the case advanced to the jury by the Crown was contrary to the conclusion reached by the scientist: Addison was cross examined on the basis that the tools had been used in the robbery.

23. The effect of this disclosure is significant. As Russell LJ put it when giving the judgment

5

of the court:

"It was clearly a report that should have been disclosed and Mr Treacy QC, on behalf of the Crown, realistically acknowledges that the failure to disclose the report had represented a material irregularity in the trial process. ... Accordingly as to count 1, Mr Treacy acknowledges that if the conviction is to be upheld it must be by virtue of the proviso to section 2 of the Criminal Appeal Act 1968."

24. The second reason for the Reference was the existence of fresh evidence concerning the credibility of DI Matthews. The fresh evidence in question was that (1) in 1982 DI Matthews had been convicted of driving a motor vehicle without a valid MOT certificate; (2) in 1984 his business activities had been investigated by the police authority, although no impropriety had been proved and no action had been taken; (3) there had been a suggestion in 1985 that he had embarked upon an improper association with a professional criminal, as a result of which, although no disciplinary action was taken, he was returned to uniform duties; (4) in September 1986 he had been disciplined for disobedience of orders and neglect of duty, as a result of which he was required to resign from the police force; and (5) at a trial in November 1985 of a man named Herring when DI Matthews had been the senior investigating officer, his evidence (and in particular his account of an interview with no solicitor present in which Herring had supposedly made admissions when the account of a co-defendant was put to him) had not been believed by the jury.

25. Applying the (since repealed) proviso to s. 2 of the Criminal Appeal Act that notwithstanding the material irregularity, the court considered that no miscarriage of justice had actually occurred, the appeal was dismissed. The court concluded that the evidence relating to the trial of Herring came nowhere near demonstrating that DI Matthews' evidence had been disbelieved; that the matters alleged against him amounted to "little more than muck raking in an attempt to discredit this police officer"; that there was "no material of any kind detrimental to DC Preston"; and that, despite the failure to disclose the forensic scientist's report, this would have made no

difference to the jury's verdict. It is relevant to note, however, that Russell LJ described the appellant's interview in which he had adopted Addison's statement as "an important plank in the prosecution's case", as indeed it clearly was.

26. For the purpose of the present Reference, we derive three important conclusions from this judgment. First, as counsel for the prosecution (Mr Colman Treacy QC, as he then was) acknowledged, there had been a material irregularity in the trial process due to the failure to disclose the forensic report, as a result of which the conviction on count 1 could only be saved by the application of the proviso: in other words, using the present statutory language, the onus was very much on the Crown to prove that the convictions were safe. Second, in relation to the robbery, the police evidence was acknowledged to be an important plank of the prosecution case. Third, the court concluded that the jury could have confidence in that evidence because the evidence of both DI Matthews and DC Preston was reliable, with nothing more than "muck raking" against the former and nothing detrimental at all against the latter.

Further Fresh Evidence

6

27. On 29 June 2011 the appellant sought a review of his convictions by the CCRC and, following an investigation, the CCRC concluded that there was fresh evidence giving rise to a real possibility that the court would now consider the appellant's convictions to be unsafe. It is the appellant's case that the evidence now available undermines the approach of this court on the previous appeal by demonstrating not only that the evidence of DI Matthews is indeed discredited, but that there are also (at least) serious doubts concerning the evidence of DC Preston; and that when these are combined with the acknowledged irregularity resulting from the failure to disclose the forensic report, the conviction of the appellant cannot be regarded as safe.

28. We deal first with Detective Inspector Matthews. As already indicated, he was a member of the West Midlands Police Serious Crime Squad. A substantial number of convictions arising from investigations conducted by the squad have been quashed as a result of concerns regarding the working practices adopted by officers there. Malpractice subsequently identified in the West Yorkshire Police enquiry included physical abuse of prisoners, fabrication of admissions, planting of evidence and mishandling of informants. DI Matthews has been identified in a number of cases of such malpractice and, in particular, has been associated with the fabrication of confessions.

29. The fresh evidence which the appellant seeks to introduce consists of background evidence as to the misconduct committed by the West Midlands Police Serious Crime Squad, together with evidence of DI Matthews' involvement in two cases, McIlkenny (1991) 93 Cr App R 48 (which was, of course, available at the time of the second appeal) and, more recently, O'Toole & Murphy [2006] EWCA Crim 2123. It is unnecessary to say more about the disgraceful picture painted by the general background evidence than Laws LJ said in O'Toole & Murphy itself at para. 4:

"The essence of the appeals is that since the appellants' convictions there has emerged a catalogue of corruption and misconduct in and by the West Midlands Serious Crime Squad some of whose officers were involved in the conduct of this case. Particular officers are impugned and we shall give the

detail. Apparently no less than 33 appellants have had their convictions quashed because those convictions depended on alleged confessions made to officers of the West Midlands Crime Squad. Other cases have collapsed at trial."

30. McIlkenny was the case of the "Birmingham Six". One of the accused, Hill, was interviewed by DS Bunn and (as he then was) DC Matthews. According to the police, he implicated two other accused, Murray and Sheehan. One of the issues at the defendants' unopposed appeal in 1991 was the reliability of the police evidence, although the principal issue had to do with fresh scientific evidence casting doubt on the original forensic evidence. Although the interview involving DC Matthews was not singled out for specific criticism, Lloyd LJ did describe the police evidence generally as unreliable, and as a sufficient reason for allowing the appeal:

"If we put the scientific evidence on one side, the fresh investigation carried out by the Devon and Cornwall Constabulary renders the police evidence at the trial so unreliable, that again we

7

would say that the convictions are both unsafe and unsatisfactory."

31. As we have observed, the evidence of DI Matthews' involvement in the McIlkenny case was available at the date of the previous appeal although there is no suggestion that reference was made to it. O'Toole & Murphy, however, is new. That was another CCRC reference involving a confession in interview alleged to have been fabricated by DI Matthews (at the time a detective sergeant). It raised the question whether the result of the trial might have been different if the facts relating to the West Midlands Police Serious Crime Squad in general, and some of the officers concerned in the case in particular, had been known to the defence at the time of trial. Laws LJ described the position of DI Matthews (who was one of those officers) as follows at para. 28:

"The factual points about him are crisply summarised in the CCRC statements of reasons and that account is not significantly embellished by other material. This is what the CCRC said (we leave out some unconfirmed allegations) (paragraph 51):

'In September 1986 Mr Matthews appeared before the Chief Constable and was dealt with for disobedience of orders and neglect of duty. He was required to resign from the force. There is evidence that a jury in a November 1985 case involving two defendants, Mr Herring and Mr Fitzgerald, disbelieved evidence given by DS Matthews, and as a result acquitted a defendant.

52. West Midlands Police informed the Commission that there are two entries in their formal disciplinary record in respect of Mr Matthews. The first of these was in 1982 and all references to this matter have been deleted or destroyed in accordance with their Destruction of Documents Policy. In September 1986 he appeared before the Chief Constable on charges of

disobedience to orders and neglect of duty. He was found guilty and required to resign forthwith'."

32. These were the features mentioned by Russell LJ in the first appeal although Laws LJ also referred to DI Matthews' involvement in McIlkenny. Having dealt with the position of other officers involved, he set out the applicable legal principles, in terms which we gratefully adopt:

"38. We turn to the law. What approach does the law prescribe to the use of such material as this arising in other and, as it happens, much later cases, but which, if available at the time of trial, might have had some impact on the jury's verdict? The starting point is the decision of this court in Edwards (1991) 93 Cr App R 48. The court held that there was no hard and fast rule as to what cross-examination might be allowed, or, if later events were relied on, what notional cross-examination might be contemplated.

'The objective must be to present to the jury as far as possible a fair, balanced picture of the witnesses' reliability ...' (see page 56)

39. Taking the matter shortly, the CCRC was, in our judgment, right (see the reasons in Murphy paragraph 33) in distilling from the decision in Edwards the following three categories in which the evidence of a police officer's conduct might be canvassed in another case:

(i) Convictions for a relevant criminal offence;

(ii) Disciplinary charges found proved against the officers;

(iii) Cases where the only logical explanation for a defendant's acquittal (in a different case) was that the officer's evidence must have been disbelieved.

40. In addition, however, the appellants draw attention to Zomparelli No 2, 23rd March 2000, in which Lord Bingham CJ strongly endorsed the approach in Edwards, but stressed two additional points. This is what he said:

'The first is that the judge's overall and paramount duty is to ensure the fairness of the trial. The trial process must be fair to the prosecution; the scales of justice are not balanced if heavily over-weighted in favour of the defendant. But it must be fair also to the defendant. He is entitled to a fair trial as a matter of constitutional right.

No rule of law can restrict the duty of the court to ensure a fair trial.

35. The second point we would make is this. The court in R v. Edwards was at pains to make clear that it was not seeking to lay down any hard-edged rule of law to be applied inflexibly in any case of this kind. The court recognised that the discretion of the trial judge cannot be so circumscribed as to restrict his power to do whatever justice demands in the circumstances of the individual case.'

41. Next, we should notice the decision of this court in Williams and Smith [1995] 1 Cr App R 74, to the effect that where such matters are admissible they are no less admissible on appeal merely because on the facts they involve events later in time than the events in question in the particular case. However, the length of time between the misconduct relied on and the convictions sought to be impugned can be a relevant factor in assessing the impact of a putative attack on an officer's credibility and the safety of the conviction.

42. In Deans [2004] EWCA Crim 2123 this was said by Maurice Kay LJ at paragraph 37:

'We deprecate the subsequent misconduct of the officers, particularly Detective Constable Robotham. However in the final analysis we are satisfied that the convictions were and are safe. We certainly accept that police misconduct after the events in issue and after the trial in question can render a conviction unsafe. We also accept that corruption and other reprehensible behaviour by one or more officers may infect a whole investigation notwithstanding the presence of officers against who nothing has been alleged or established. In the present case, however, we attach particular importance to the lapse of time between the events of 1988 and the trial in 1989 on the one hand and the appalling behaviour of Detective Constable Robotham, and to a lesser extent Detective Constable Davis, on the other hand. There is nothing to suggest that either of them acted otherwise than with propriety between 1988 and 1997. We consider it inappropriate to doubt convictions which occurred almost a decade before any known or alleged misbehaviour on the part of these officers.'

43. There is also authority for the proposition -- though, with great respect, we have some doubt whether it is really a point of law rather than one of good common sense -- that misconduct by police officers may be fatal to a conviction even though their tainted evidence

9

is supported by officers of whom there is no criticism whatever: see Guney [1998] 2 Cr App R 242, [1998] EWCA Crim 719. That is particularly relevant here because the Crown say that the evidence of Hornby of the interview of Murphy on 8th April 1977 was supported by that of the then DS Robinson, who eventually retired in the rank of detective chief inspector after over 32 years of service with a record of no less than 14 commendations or awards."

33. Laws LJ then concluded (at para. 44) that DI Matthews (and other officers) could properly have been cross-examined on the matters to his discredit referred to above which had emerged (including the Herring case, which here does appear to have been regarded as a case where DI Matthews' evidence was disbelieved). The 1995 decision of this court in which little or no weight was given to the Herring case does not appear to have been cited in O'Toole & Murphy but, despite this, we consider that the same conclusion as in O'Toole & Murphy must apply here, that is to say, that at the trial in the present case DI Matthews could properly have been cross examined, if those matters had been known, as to his involvement in (at least) the Herring, McIlkenny and O'Toole cases, all of which involved fabricated or allegedly fabricated confessions, sometimes in circumstances with similarities to the present case and which together suggest a disturbing pattern, against the background of his membership of the discredited West Midlands Serious Crime Squad, as well as his disciplinary record.

34. In our view such a cross-examination could not have been dismissed as mere "muck raking", at any rate without acknowledging that there was a certain amount of muck to rake. These matters might well have gone a long way towards discrediting the evidence of DI Matthews.

35. Before parting from O'Toole, there is one other detail worth mentioning. The partial admission that DI Matthews asserted that O'Toole made, when the co-defendant's statement was read to him was "What a load of fanny, didn't know there were going to be shooters". That admission (and the use of the word 'fanny' was strongly challenged. In this context, it is a matter of comment that the phrase (equally strongly challenged) attributed to the appellant when told that Addison had implicated him was "I don't believe you, that's fanny".

36. Turning to Detective Constable Preston, even if DI Matthews had been discredited, however, importance was attached by this court in 1995 to the fact that his evidence was supported by this officer, against whom nothing detrimental could be said. However, that is no longer the case. In our judgment, two matters are particularly significant.

37. The first is that it was DC Preston who took the decision not to disclose the forensic report which concluded that the tools found in the appellant's car could not have been used to gain entry at the Trident public house. When he was asked about that decision in May 1990 he sought to justify it, partly on the basis that the non-disclosure was an oversight and partly on the remarkable basis that the report "showed no useful evidence for the prosecution". The initial failure to disclose was clearly unjustified (cf. Ward [1993] 1 WLR 619) and was accepted by Mr Treacy QC to have been a

material irregularity in the trial, and the concern to which it gives rise was compounded by the fact that DC Preston was present in court when, as we have recounted, Addison was cross-examined by prosecution counsel on the basis that the tools in question had actually been

10

used to facilitate entry to the Trident public house. He had asserted that fact in chief, refuted it in answer to questions from the appellant and when cross examined by the Crown to the effect that he his retraction was a lie, said that he had made a mistake. However, despite his knowledge of the undisclosed forensic report, DC Preston did nothing to correct this line of questioning.

38. Second, DC Preston's notebook record of Addison's interview (see para. 4 above) purported to record Addison describing the commission of the Trident robbery with a "bloke" called Martin. However, it has emerged that the word which DC Preston originally wrote was "kid" and not "bloke", and that the entry was subsequently changed. The appellant, who was much older than Addison, could not sensibly have been described by Addison as a "kid" and the fact that, as now appears, Addison's initial reference was to committing the robbery with a "kid" called Martin provides some support for his evidence in chief at trial when he also used the word "kid". He was later cross-examined, again as we understand it with DC Preston present in court, on the basis that this was a change from his interview where he had used the word "bloke". Even if, as DC Preston later claimed when asked about this, the change in the notebook from "kid" to "bloke" was merely the correction of "an obvious error", this was an explanation which would have been challenged had the facts emerged at the time and might well have cast doubt on his credibility.

39. There were other matters suggested against DC Preston not the least being the discovery of a copy of the custody record which he had kept in his own records, but it is unnecessary to consider these further. The two matters described above are themselves troubling and, together, make it difficult to contend that DC Preston was an entirely untainted witness whose evidence provides independent support to the evidence of DI Matthews. It is therefore unnecessary to consider further the extent to which developments in the law have affected the position when the evidence of a tainted officer is supported by the evidence of an officer whose evidence is untainted, save to say that we agree with Laws LJ's summary in the passage cited above from O'Toole & Murphy.

40. Where then does that leave the safety of the appellant's conviction on the count of robbery? It is right to say that a cross-examination of DI Matthews and DC Preston to adduce in evidence the matters referred to above would not have been free of risk and it is plausible to contend that the Crown would have contended that it, also, was no more than 'muck raking'. The appellant would still not have been able to give evidence because (as would have been the case in any event given the allegations that were being made) it would have enabled the prosecution to put the appellant's previous convictions before the jury who would have been entitled to take them into account in considering the credibility of the allegations against the police officers. In the end it is impossible to know what the jury would have made of the case if it had been presented to them in an entirely different way. As to this we echo what Laws LJ said in O'Toole & Murphy at para. 46:

"We are, however, in no position to know what might have been the effect on the jury had the defence been armed with what is now known about these officers and used it in cross-

examination. We cannot say that that material could not reasonably have induced a doubt in the jury's mind."

11

41. In O'Toole & Murphy the case against the appellant was described as "undoubtedly formidable". Moreover, it was a case where the evidence of tainted officers was supported by that of other officers who were blameless. Nevertheless, the conviction was quashed. As we have indicated, in view of the points made above concerning DC Preston, this is not a case where there was entirely untainted supporting evidence.

42. It is clear that the conviction of the appellant for robbery depended critically on the reliability of the police evidence as to the appellant's interview. That was rightly recognised by the judge in his summing up, and by this court on appeal in 1995. Mr Jonathan Laidlaw QC for the Crown submitted that the evidence now relied on as discrediting the police evidence does not add materially to what was before this court in 1995, but we do not agree. Once the reliability of the police evidence is called into serious question, as it must be in light of the matters referred to above, we have no doubt that this conviction cannot be regarded as safe. While every case will depend on its own facts, we refer in this connection to what Laws LJ said in O'Toole & Murphy (at paras. 47 and 50):

"We are not of course -- and we desire to emphasise this -- judging the guilt or innocence of these men; far from it. We repeat, there was a formidable case against them. But in the end these convictions were obtained largely on evidence which may have been false in material respects. As it was put in Pendleton [2001] UKHL 56, the material now known about the officers, had it been available in 1978, might reasonably have affected the jury's decision to convict. ... The fact is our law has increasingly regarded the value of due process as integral to the doing of justice and the conduct of police officers is integral to due process in the administration of the criminal law."

In the context of this case, the analysis of the law now contained in decisions such as Dial & anor v. State of Trinidad and Tobago [2005] UKBC 4; [2005] 1 WLR 1660 (at paras. 31-32) and Burridge [2010] EWCA Crim 2847 (at paras. 99-101) does not affect these conclusions.

43. Turning to the conspiracy to rob, even if the evidence of the appellant's interview is left out of account, by the close of the evidence, the prosecution relied not only on Addison's evidence but on the fact that the appellant was arrested at the time and place identified by Addison as the rendezvous for a robbery, equipped with tools which it appeared were entirely consistent with those required for use in a robbery. These circumstances provided potentially powerful independent corroboration of Addison's account, such as the judge had warned the jury would be necessary if they were to accept his evidence.

44. It is necessary, however, briefly to consider the status of Addison's account as evidence against the appellant. Addison's statement in interview, adduced by the prosecution as part of the case against Addison, would not have constituted evidence against the appellant. It is only his adoption of that account when he was cross examined by the prosecution (contradicting the evidence that he had given prior to

that point in the trial) which provides any probative material and could permit the jury to regard the evidence as including not only the circumstances of his arrest (which on their own would not have been enough to sustain a conviction for conspiracy to rob) but also the account given by Addison of an agreement to meet in order to rob the Water Orton post office which was confirmed by the appellant's arrival at the agreed rendezvous equipped with items

12

of the type which Addison had described and which could have been used to carry out a robbery.

45. It could not be disputed that, on their own neither the evidence of Addison nor the circumstances of the appellant's arrest would have been a safe basis on which to convict the appellant on count 3 and it is not unimportant that no explanation has ever been offered for the appellant's appearance at the time and place that Addison had predicted. The combination, however, has greater potency and we would certainly not be prepared to conclude that the appellant was innocent of the charge. Nevertheless, bearing in mind the limited credibility that could be attached to Addison's evidence and the extent to which the evidence of the police could have been undermined, along with the admitted material irregularity in relation to disclosure, the existence of some evidence to support the allegation is not sufficient to justify a conclusion that the conviction is safe. In those circumstances, this conviction is also quashed.

Conclusion

46. In the event, for the reasons given above, we regard the appellant's convictions for robbery and conspiracy to rob to be unsafe and they are quashed.

13

APPENDIX 8

News Cuttings

LIMERICK POST, SAT.

FORAN'S PLEAS OF INNOCENCE CONTINUE

- 'MY HUNGER STRIKE WILL GO ON'

Limerickman Martin Foran is now facing his seventh consecutive Christmas behind the bars of Her Majestys Prison Frankland in Durham, England.

But this Christmas will be tougher than any before for Foran. Tougher because he is now entering his fifth week on hunger strike.

Two weeks ago, The Post contacted the prison hospital in Frankland jail and we were told that Martin was not on hunger strike.

A spokesman at the hospital said he was not refusing solid food.

But Martin and his family are adamant that the hunger strike he began on November 5th is continuing.

And it will go on, the Kileely man told us in a letter, until he sees that justice is done.

THE CASE OF MARTIN FORAN

The case of Martin Foran is a long and complex one.

He emigrated to Britain in the early 'sixties. He does not deny that, for a while, he was involved in crime but he claims he has now served fourteen years for two crimes he did not commit.

He appeared in court back in 1978 charged with robbery offences. None of the victims of the robbery were in court to identify him. One victim, Mr. Charles Apechis, testified

"I cry out but no-one hears my cry. I keep wondering why I am left to suffer for so long." Martin Foran, October 1990.

at Martin's appeal that he was innocent.

The main evidence Martin was convicted on was an "oral confession" _ a confession he denies ever making.

Foran was found guilty at the trial and sentenced to ten years in prison.

He went on hunger strike in jail, protesting his innocence. The hunger strike led to him developing serious bowel problems.

He was given an early release from prison in February 1984. He continued to claim he was innocent of the crime he had served time for. He alleges that during this period he was subject to continual police harassment.

At one stage, he was accused of a murder which had been committed while he was in prison.

In September 1984, Martin Foran was arrested again, this time charged with armed robbery.

The victim of the crime said that the robbers were young West Indians with strong Birmingham accents. Martin is middle-aged, white and has retained his strong Limerick accent.

Detective Inspector Paul Matthews of the West Midlands Serious Crime Squad claims that Foran admitted the crime to him when he was arrested. Det. Ins. Matthews was also involved in the

Birmingham Six case. He is now believed to be residing in Spain. The West Yorkshire Police, who are investigating the West Midlands squad, are keen to interview Matthews.

Martin was again found guilty and sentenced to a further term in jail.

While he was on remand in custody in the armed robbery case, his health deteriorated. He demanded medical attention but none was immediately forthcoming. To draw attention to his condition, he took a prison officer hostage.

In June 1986, he finally received medical attention when a colostomy was performed.

However, four weeks later, Foran was assaulted by four prison officers. The colostomy was ripped out. In December 1988, Foran sued the officers and he was awarded £750 compensation. An open, festering wound was left on his stomach after the attack. It has still not healed.

Martin's sentence from 1985 has now been completed. But he has to serve a further six years for taking the prison officer hostage.

Foran's health continues to worsen.

Last year he had a heart attack. He has also developed cancer in his right eye.

He was recently seen by a consultant for his stomach problem. The consultant said the original operation

was performed badly, making any further operations difficult. If another operation is performed, it may only have a 30% chance of success. It may even prove fatal for Foran.

THE CAMPAIGN

The campaign to release Martin Foran has drawn the support of many politicians including Minister Des O'Malley and other Limerick TDs.

Martin's brother, Andrew Foran, says that the family are planning to step up the campaign. This Sunday, they will be distributing leaflets outside city churches outlining Martin's case.

A successful public meeting was recently held in Dublin and more meetings are planned.

The Foran family say that Martin's morale is now very low. They have urged Limerick people to write to him at Christmas "to ease some of his pain." The address is Martin Foran C51796, HMP Frankland, Brasside, Durham, DH1 YD, England.

Meanwhile, Foran's sister Patricia says that the family hope Martin will give up his hunger strike.

"I understand why he is on the strike," she says, "but I don't think his health can stand it. I want to see my brother come out of that prison alive, not in a box."

Martin himself, now 46 years old, says he no longer fears death. Speaking a month ago, he said :

"I would sooner die than carry on in this mess. I don't fear death, it's this living hell that I fear. The spirit has just been ripped out of me."

Martin Foran, an artist's impression.

LEICESTER MERCURY, WEDNESDAY, OCTOBER 14, 1981 5

Prisoner tells Leicester Mercury:

'I escaped to prove that I am innocent'

JUST before his recapture yesterday, convicted armed robber Martin Patrick Foran told the Leicester Mercury how he escaped — and why.

Gartree prisoner Foran rang the newsroom and told how he spent 24 hours dodging from one ward to another before calmly walking out of Leicester Royal Infirmary where he had been taken with a stomach complaint.

During this time police were scouring the city for him.

Hunger strike

Foran, serving 10 years, claimed he would have been eligible for parole in January, but decided to escape "to prove my innocence."

And at the time of his arrest he was heading for Leicester. "It is my intention to stage a 14-day hunger strike on the highest building in your city," he told deputy News Editor James McPheator.

"When I have finished talking to you I will ring my MP Mr John Farr and my solicitor. I have statements to prove that I couldn't have committed the robbery for which I was jailed."

During the telephone conversation, Foran was asked numerous questions, but refused to answer some of them. He would not say where he got the clothes in which he made his escape or whether anyone had been sheltering him.

Neither would he divulge his exact location. "I am somewhere on the Nottinghamshire, Leicestershire border," he claimed.

He insisted he was determined to stage the threatened rooftop hunger strike. "I have done five hunger strikes before, you know — two of them at Gartree."

Pressed on the form of his escape he said: "I walked a dozen wards in a dressing gown dodging people. Everyone assumed I was just another patient. Then I sat in a lavatory for a few hours before walking out.

"That was on Sunday night, more than a full day after they noticed me missing."

Soon afterwards Inspector Richard Cooke of Canning Circus police station, Nottingham, accompanied by five officers, arrested Foran in Denman Street, Radford.

"He came quietly and, on the way to the station, asked me if this would mean he would lose only 30 days remission on his sentence instead of 60 days."

Foran was convicted of armed robbery on a jeweller's shop in his home city of Birmingham in 1978. Market Harborough solicitor, Mr. Roderick Bull, hopes soon to make a second appeal against Foran's conviction. An appeal to the Court of Appeal earlier this year was thrown out.

THE CASE FOR FREEING MARTIN FORAN

Dear Friends,

I HAVE been active for over two years now in the campaign to release Martin Foran, an Irish prisoner who is currently an inmate of Frankland Jail, outside Durham.

Martin is originally from Limerick but settled in the Birmingham area in the early '70s. In 1977, he was arrested by local police and charged with a series of robberies which he had taken no part in. He was sentenced to ten years imprisonment, and protested his innocence during that time. Once released in 1984 he was harassed regularly by the police who kept stopping him in the street, calling round to his house and making life difficult for him and his family. In September 1984 Martin was again charged with a robbery he had taken no part in. He is now very ill, and has had a further six years added on to his initial sentence for

attempting to take a prison warder hostage.

The current West Yorkshire Police investigation into his case is proving to be quite thorough and there seems to be new evidence which is emerging which could prove Martin's innocence on both sets of charges. The latest news is that supporters now have evidence of the systematic denial of medical treatment to Martin. A memo dated from June 1986 with a Walton Gaol title was sent anonimously to Martin's wife, Valerie. It is part of a 'Continuous Medical Report' and lists Martin's name and number, and mentions that he once took a member of staff hostage, and adds candidly 'nothing should be done to aid and comfort this individual'.

Of course it does not mention how Martin must have felt after being twice

accused of crimes he had not committed, and how he began the second sentence whilst suffering from a bowel illness. It also does not detail how Martin was moved from jail to jail, and how any appointments he had made with specialists were disrupted by this continual moving.

A press statement with a copy of the memo is being sent to sympathetic media contacts in Britain and Ireland. In Ireland, Desmond O'Malley has been very helpful. He first met Martin in Limerick when he was a lawyer. He believes that the British authorities should now release Martin.

Best wishes,

Mike Shankland

Note: An article on the Martin Foran case will appear in the next issue of the Democrat.

Irish Samaritan held in Britain

By **MICHAEL FARRELL**

A CO. LOUTH businessman, who was trying to arrange medical treatment for a seriously ill Irish prisoner, who claims to have been framed by the West Midlands police, was detained and questioned by British police in Durham at the weekend.

Mr. Seamus Mac Seain, secretary of the Louth County Association in London, read about the condition of Limerick-born prisoner, Martin Foran in *THE IRISH PRESS* recently and went to visit him in Frankland Prison in Durham last weekend.

He was so disturbed by his condition that he went straight to a hospital in Durham to see the doctor in charge of the case. He was asked to wait and then two CID officers appeared, took him into a side room and searched him.

They took him to a local police station and questioned him for another hour, asking him how he came to be involved with a "political prisoner" like Martin Foran and whether he was in the IRA.

Martin Foran has no political connections whatsoever and Mr. Mac Seain had never met him before. He explained that his involvement was purely as an Irihs businessman anxious to assist with the cost of medical treatment. He has raised his treatment with the Irish embassy in London.

Martin Foran was convicted of an armed robbery in Birmingham in 1985 on the basis of alleged statements taken by the West Midlands Serious Crimes Squad. His case is now being investigated by the West Yorkshire police, who are carrying out an inquiry into the fabrication of evidence by the squad in a number of cases.

Mr. Foran has developed an infected colostomy condition which has worsened recently and he has been refusing solid food since last Thursday

272

IRISH in Britain NEWS   November 16th 1990

Foran goes on hunger strike in Frankland

Limerick-born Martin Foran, an inmate of Frankland Prison, Co. Durham, has been on hunger strike since November 5.

Mr. Foran, who was convicted of armed robbery in Birmingham in 1985, and later had his sentence extended by six years when found guilty of falsely imprisoning a prison warder after being denied medical treatment for a colostomy wound infection, has consistently maintained his innocence.

He is refusing solid foods to highlight the fact that the West Yorkshire Police investigations into his complaints against the West Midlands' Serious Crimes Squad have been ongoing for a year without yielding a result. He was initially convicted on the evidence of alleged admissions produced by officers from the now defunct West Midlands squad.

"A couple of officers from the West Yorkshire Police visited Martin at the end of October last year. They spent several days with him, and Martin was very encouraged by the visit. Now we have been told that the squad's investigation into the West Midlands' Police could go on until next spring or even longer. The only person who has been released as a result of the West Yorkshire Police investigations so far was Hassam Khan back in February," Mike Shankland, a member of the Martin Foran Defence Campaign, told the Irish in Britain News.

Mr. Shankland was concerned that, given his deteriorating medical condition, this latest in a series of hunger strikes could affect Mr. Foran's physical well-being still further.

The Birmingham group campaigning for Mr. Foran's release has been somewhat disjointed in recent months, but, according to Mr. Shankland, is now in the process of reorganising.

"The support in Ireland for Martin's plight is very strong. We held a press conference in Dublin on October 21 and got great response from that," Mr. Shankland pointed out.

Mr. Foran's wife, Valerie, said this week that her husband was prepared to "go as far as he has to to protest his innocence."

"When I last visited him, he told me that enough was enough," she said.

No let-up by Foran

An Irish prisoner at Frankland Prison near Durham says he will continue his week-old hunger-strike in a bid to highlight his claims of wrongful conviction.

Limerickman Martin Foran has also been protesting about prison staff allegedly preventing him from getting medical treatment for a deteriorating colostomy problem. However, an appointment with a Birmingham-based specialist has been arranged for December 5 and parole has been sought for this.

The Irishman was sentenced in 1985 for a Birmingham pub robbery; he insists he could not have committed and his eight-year sentence was extended by six years in 1987 after he took a prison warder hostage.

He claims that this conviction was based on flawed evidence gathered by the now-disbanded West Midlands Serious Crime Squad, and his case is being supported by, amongst others, Des O'Malley, the Republic's Minister for Industry and Commerce. Martin Foran was at one stage a constituent of the Limerick-based TD.

Judge's link with crime squad cases

David Rose
Crime Correspondent

THE judge in a trial in which confession evidence from the West Midlands serious crime squad was challenged had earlier acted as prosecuting counsel in some of the most serious cases involving the disgraced squad, including that of the Birmingham Six.

In 1988 Mr Justice Igor Judge heard allegations at the trial of Mr Hassan Khan that his alleged confession had been fabricated.

He used his discretion, as he was entitled to do, to allow it to go before the jury — even though the Crown admitted that the confession was made in breach of the Police and Criminal Evidence Act.

As Crown counsel in the 1987 appeal by the Birmingham Six and other cases, Mr Judge had rebutted allegations that the squad fabricated evidence.

Legal sources in the West Midlands were at pains to stress last night that there was nothing improper about his conduct.

But they added: "It is not that we wish to suggest that Mr Justice Judge's conduct of the case was in any way influenced.

"But justice must not only be done, it must be seen to be done, and this may not be the case in this instance."

Ms Rita Williams, Mr Khan's common law wife and the mother of his two children, said: "There's no way I can regard what happened as justice. A few months before Hassan's trial the judge was still acting as a prosecutor. I don't think justice was done at all."

Mr Khan's case, now subject of an appeal, was heard at Birmingham Crown Court in December 1988, two months after Mr Justice Judge's appointment to the bench.

Mr Khan was convicted of an armed robbery at a Birmingham electrical store and jailed for 15 years. His appeal, which was earlier scheduled for April, will be heard next month.

Mr Khan lives in Caernarfon, North Wales, and the court heard that he went voluntarily to a police station in nearby Wrexham, where he was arrested.

He was driven at night by serious crime squad detectives

to Birmingham. An officer gave evidence that he took down Mr Khan's confession in the car, by the light of a torch hung round his neck.

The unsigned confession, according to the defence, was fabricated. Moreover, at the time of the robbery Mr Khan was recovering from the loss of two toes, although witnesses said the robber escaped by running several hundred yards.

Ms Williams said yesterday: "He couldn't possibly have done it. He was wearing a thick bandage on his foot which stopped him putting on his shoe."

The prosecution admitted that the Police and Criminal Evidence Act was breached in that Mr Khan was denied access to a solicitor for 20 hours, but Mr Justice Judge used his lawful discretion to admit the alleged confession.

Mr Judge was Crown counsel in the appeal by the six convicted of the 1974 Birmingham pub bombings in 1987.

He rejected the claim that their confessions were false and told the court: "It would have been virtually impossible to find stronger evidence that pointed to guilt except perhaps a film of the actual planting of the bombs."

He suggested the Birmingham Six would have presented even that as part of a police conspiracy.

He was prosecutor in a series of supergrass robbery and kidnapping trials in 1983, during which Mr Derek Treadaway was convicted of two armed robberies on the basis of confessions and sentenced to 15 years.

Mr Treadaway said in evidence that police had tortured him by putting a plastic bag over his head until he began to suffocate, telling him to stamp his feet when he was ready to confess. He has a civil action for assault pending.

The Lord Chancellor's department said last night there were no guidelines governing judges' sitting in cases involving police units with which they were familiar.

The Police Complaints Authority is supervising an inquiry into the serious crime squad by West Yorkshire police.

Fifty-three detectives have been transferred and two suspended, and four face criminal charges.

Mother's plea for her son's release

Report: TONY PURCELL

"PLEASE release my son. He is just as innocent as the Birmingham Six..." pleaded 78-year-old Mrs. Bridget Foran to the British Authorities last night at her home in Limerick.

Her son, Martin Foran (46), is serving an eight-year sentence in Durham Prison for a robbery which he claims he did not commit.

Mrs. Foran, who resides at O'Callaghan Avenue, Kileely, said that she was "over the moon" on hearing the news of the Birmingham Six release from prison.

"I am hoping to God and praying that their release will now open the way for many other prisoners who are innocent of their crimes and languishing in British jails", she said.

Mrs. Foran made a strong plea to the Irish Government to intensify their efforts in securing her son's immediate release from prison.

Her son's poor state of health has been a source of grave concern to the Foran family over the past few months and Government Ministers have raised the case with the British Home Secretary.

Last night, PD leader Mr. Des O'Malley, renewed his strong call to the British Authorities for Martin Foran's immediate release from prison.

"I have actively pursued Mr. Foran's case for a number of years,

■ *Mrs. Bridget Foran: "My son as innocent as the Birmingham Six."*

and I am convinced, not only that his conviction is unsafe, but on humanitarian grounds alone, he should be immediately discharged from prison and allowed to get proper medical treatment for his serious condition", stated Mr. O'Malley.

The Minister told the *Cork Examiner* that it was the same West Midlands Serious Crime Squad and some of the same individual officers who were involved in the Birmingham Six case, and who have now been exposed and completely discredited, that were

involved in Martin Foran's case.

"Purely on humanitarian grounds alone Mr. Foran should be immediately discharged from prison because he is in a bad physical condition due to an unsuccessful colostomy operation", stated Mr. O'Malley.

Meanwhile, Mr. Foran's son, Martin (25), who lives with his grandmother in Limerick, last night said "I am convinced my father is innocent and I would like the Irish Government to press the British Authorities for his early release".

I am ready to die in prison — Foran

IN 4/4/90

By HENRY McDONALD

IRISH prisoner Martin Foran has vowed that he is ready to die in jail as part of his fight for freedom.

In a letter to The Irish News yesterday, Mr Foran threatened to escalate his hunger strike by refusing to take liquids if he is moved out of the prison hospital at Frankland, Durham, into a punishment block.

Irish diplomats last night won assurances however, from prison authorities that the 47-year-old Limerick man will stay in hospital while he remains will.

In his latest letter from prison, Mr Foran says: "If it's God's will that I die so be it. My suffering will be over. If my protesting costs me my kidneys then it's a price I must pay to cry out I'm innocent."

Martin Foran started his hunger strike in protest at the alleged lack of progress in investigations by the West Yorkshire police force into his case.

He has constantly protested his innocence over a 1984 robbery conviction and a previous sentence relating to another robbery in 1978.

Mr Foran is also demanding better medical treatment inside prison. He suffers from a hernia, a stomach problem and loss of the eye.

The Irish prisoner said he "fully understood the risks" related to giving up his food and his hunger strike.

A Belfast doctor yesterday warned that Mr Foran's kidneys could cease functioning within four days of his giving up liquids.

Dr Alasdair McDonnell said: "Somebody in his condition who is already in pain and badly debilitated, I would be surprised if he got beyond four days."

"After then his kidneys start to pack in. His body starts to self poison. In his case, his cholostomy will get worse and cause further infection, which will put an even greater strain on the kidneys."

Mr Foran claims in his letter that "a dog with a broken leg would be better treated... I have been treated like an animal for almost six years."

His letter concludes: "Police have taken my freedom and prison has made my life a living hell."

Mr Foran's wife, Valerie, who visited her husband on Monday, said he has lost a considerable amount of weight.

"Martin has to give up this fast as soon as possible. I can understand his frustration with his case and his lack of medical treatment but this is not the answer," she said.

Mr Foran was arrested by officers from the now disbanded West Midlands Serious Crimes Squad.

One of the police officers involved in his arrest in 1984 former Detective Inspector Paul Matthews, also interrogated Patrick Hill, one of the Birmingham Six, in 1974.

Mr Foran claims Matthews is crucial to his case to overturn his conviction of six years ago. Matthews was discharged from the force in 1986. He is now believed to be living in Lanzarote.

Martin Foran is demanding that the West Yorkshire Police take Matthews back to Britain for questioning about his involvement in the 1984 arrest.

Last week it emerged that West Midlands officers broke their own regulations by destroying Martin Foran's custody records at the time of his arrest for a robbery at a public house in Birmingham.

The West Midlands Police guidelines state that custody records for serious crimes could be destroyed only six years after the initial arrest. In Martin Foran's case, the Birmingham police officers shredded his records two years after his arrest.

"I'll Prove My Brother's Innocence"

- FORAN CAMPAIGN HOTS UP

The brother of Limerick prisoner Martin Foran says he will prove his brother's innocence when he meets with all five local T.D.s this Saturday.

Andrew Foran told the Limerick Post this week that he was in possession of evidence that "will prove beyond a shadow of a doubt that Martin is an innocent man."

Martin Foran has just finished a hunger strike in a Durham jail where he is serving a sentence for burglaries, crimes he says he did not commit.

The five Limerick T.D.s have agreed to meet with Andrew Foran on Saturday to sift through the case.

Mr. Foran says that he has recently received documents from the West Yorkshire Police which "have definitely been tampered with" and which he feels strengthens his brother's case.

Meanwhile, Martin Foran is said to be "comfortable" in Durham prison after ending his 47-day hunger strike.

Police resist pressure for public inquiry into squad

Paul Hoyland

WEST Midlands police yesterday dismissed calls for a public inquiry into its discredited serious crime squad.

All of the squad's cases in the past three years are being investigated by the Police Complaints Authority after allegations of malpractice in obtaining confessions.

The Irish government and campaigners for the men convicted of the Birmingham pub bomb murders have called for the inquiry to examine any links between that case and the officers now under scrutiny.

The West Midlands chief constable, Mr Geoffrey Dear, announced on Monday that he had invited the assistant chief constable of West Yorkshire, Mr Donald Shaw, to conduct the inquiry under the auspices of the Police Complaints Authority.

However, there was mounting pressure in political and legal circles yesterday for an inquiry that would not involve police officers investigating other officers.

Birmingham solicitors say that some members of the squad have intimidated suspects and threatened to arrest spouses or put children into care.

The chairman of the West Midlands group of Labour MPs, Mr Peter Snape (West Bromwich East), said: "It will not, in my view, do anything to allay public disquiet to have policemen investigating other policemen. I would like to see some

sort of tribunal, headed perhaps by a distinguished QC, holding the most wide-ranging inquiry possible into the conduct of all these officers, of the squad itself and all the cases they have been involved in over the past few years."

Mr Dear said two members of the squad had been suspended and nine senior members of its CID command structure, including the head of West Midlands CID, Detective Chief Superintendent Jim Byrne, moved to non-operational administrative duties.

Thirty-nine other officers who worked in the squad between 1986-88 had been transferred to non-operational duties. Yesterday, two detectives, a superintendent and an inspector, were also transferred to administrative duties.

A spokesman for West Midlands police, Superintendent Martin Burton, insisted the public should have confidence in the PCA investigation. "Anybody who knows anything about the Police Complaints Authority supervising an investigation of this sort will know that it is the best and the most searching and most comprehensive type of investigation you can possibly have," he said.

"It's all very well for people to chuck this old chestnut into the arena again about police officers investigating police officers. There is no fudging, there is no hiding, there is nothing of that sort."

Ms Clare Short, the Labour MP for Birmingham Ladywood, who has campaigned for the release of the six men convicted of the Birmingham pub bomb-

ings, said the inquiry did not not go back far enough.

Evidence compiled by members of the squad led to the Birmingham Six being convicted in 1975. Ms Short has received 50 letters from people in prison making complaints against the squad since she announced, earlier this year, that she wanted to help to set up an independent inquiry.

"There's a sort of public admission that things were deeply wrong, that there was a real entrenched pattern of malpractice and that the serious crime squad was deciding for themselves who was guilty and then fixing them up rather than allowing our criminal justice system to perform properly," Ms Short said.

"This story goes back, involving lots and lots of people, as far as the wrongful conviction of the six men for the Birmingham pub bombings, and some of the men involved in that inquiry are still serving. So it just isn't right to say it's only the last two years.

"That means the scandal would go on and having come this far, I really hope that we can look at the whole thing once and for all."

Mr Chris Mullin, the Labour MP for Sunderland North, who has written a book on the case, also called yesterday for the case to be re-examined.

The Irish government, which has taken up the case of the Birmingham Six, yesterday called for a full report on the decision to hold an inquiry.

**Background page 2;
Serious solution, page 15**

THE GUARDIAN
Saturday August 19 1989

Records at prison 'were altered'

David Rose and Paul Hoyland

RECORDS kept by prison officers were deliberately altered in a case involving members of the now-disbanded West Midlands serious crime squad, it emerged last night.

Calls for a judicial inquiry into the squad received qualified backing yesterday from Mr Roy Hattersley, deputy leader of the Labour Party and MP for Birmingham Sparkbrook. He said it was "at least possible" that the Carl Bridgewater and Birmingham pub bombing murder cases would need to be reopened. Interrogating officers in both cases are among the squad members transferred. Mr Geoffrey Dear, the chief

constable, this week suspended two officers, transferred 53 to non-operational duties and announced a Police Complaints Authority inquiry into the squad, to be carried out by police from West Yorkshire.

The tampering with documents from Winson Green prison in Birmingham came in the case of Mr Ronald Bolden, acquitted of two armed robberies last June after spending 22 months in the prison on remand. Judge Curtis, the Recorder of Birmingham, said that some police evidence in the case — in which Mr Bolden claimed confessions and forensic evidence had been fabricated — was "totally misleading".

Mr Bolden had earlier gone on trial in October last year,

when his lawyers were served with papers falsely alleging that his solicitors, James Saunders and Co, had offered to pay another remand prisoner to make allegations about police common to both cases.

After the solicitors were forced to withdraw, the trial was abandoned. But it emerged that the police had the signing-in book from Winson Green, showing that two members of the firm had kept an appointment to see Mr Bolden and the other prisoner.

In fact, at the last moment one of the lawyers had been unable to attend. It is not known who was responsible for the alteration to the book.

There was strong pressure yesterday from Birmingham lawyers to appoint a judicial in-

quiry into the serious crime squad's activities, and further calls that the present investigation's scope be widened to include events before 1986.

Mr Stephen Jonas said he had been contacted by two clients charged by the squad and convicted before this date.

Both had claimed at their trials in 1983 and 1984 that their confessions were fabricated.

In the second case, Mr Derek Boswell, who was convicted of robbery in 1983, had asked him to reopen his case by whatever means possible.

Mr Hattersley said: "I think a judicial inquiry is something we have to examine the possibility of when we see the outcome of this inquiry."

Bolden wants cash back, page 2

Shamed CID men face new inquiry

By JAMES GOLDEN

DETECTIVES from a shamed crack team have been banned from CID work after the disappearance of crucial evidence into claims that they rigged confessions.

West Midlands Chief Constable Mr Geoffrey Dear announced his unprecedented action yesterday as he revealed that the Independent Police Complaints Authority had been called in to investigate.

He admitted the move would shake public confidence and shock the police service but he said he was determined to

uncover the truth behind the scandal. Mr Dear disbanded his controversial Serious Crimes Squad three months ago after a series of acquittals and failed prosecutions involving claims of faked evidence and confessions by the team.

The DPP is already investigating 150 allegations against his detectives including seven complaints involving 18 officers over allegedly falsified confessions.

Now all 48 officers who have ever worked for the squad since its formation in 1986 — from chief superintendent downwards — have been transferred to uniformed administrative duties.

Included are four superintendents, two chief inspectors and two inspectors.

All the hundreds of cases they investi-

gated will be reviewed. More than 70 percent resulted in guilty pleas at Crown Court. Two detectives, a sergeant and a constable have already been suspended. One sergeant has been demoted, another fined and three reprimanded.

Mr Dear said he had taken what he described as 'unprecedented' action only after discovering that documents crucial to the investigation into their activities had vanished.

'They are key documents which were vital to the prosecution and conviction of the individuals concerned. The complaints may concern the authenticity of those documents,' he said.

Mr Dear said West Yorkshire's Assistant Chief Constable has been asked to carry out a 'far reaching' investigation. Both the public and police would 'rightly demand the truth and I am determined that every step should be taken to uncover it.'

EVENING MAIL, THURSDAY, NOVEMBER 1, 1990

BC C1

Crunch meeting in Dear probe

By FERGUS SHEPPARD

POLICE authority chiefs were today deciding if former West Midlands Chief Constable Geoffrey Dear should face a disciplinary hearing.

The meeting centres around a probe into the disbanded Serious Crime Squad, and the apparent disappearance of vital evidence.

There is concern over the apparent failure of Mr Dear to secure the squad's offices between the time when the probe was announced and when the inquiry team arrived.

The police authority's Personnel Committee was considering bringing in a chief constable from an outside force to investigate the concerns.

A report from West Yorkshire Police Assistant Chief Constable Donald Shaw — called in to investigate the squad — has said Mr Dear failed to issue clear orders to seal the headquarters of the team.

Among documents missing are six complete case files, pocket books and records of squad members' movements.

The Serious Crime Squad was wound up by the then West Midlands Chief Constable amid allegations that evidence was fabricated.

However, in a statement to the police authority, Mr Dear said the Shaw report's conclusions were "damaging in me in the extreme," suggesting he was either naive or the omission was "deliberate."

O'Dea calls for British Home Office inquiry into Foran case

TIANNA FAIL backbencher and barrister Willie O'Dea yesterday called for a British Home Office inquiry into the detention of a 44-year-old Limerick man who is serving an eight-year sentence in Durham Prison for a robbery which he claims he did not commit.

Martin Foran originally from O'Callaghan Avenue, Kileely, Limerick, was yesterday described by his brother Andrew as being "very ill" in the Durham hospital.

O'Dea claimed there were certain aspects of Mr Foran's case which he found disturbing. There is

also, he said, "a suspicion that there is something wrong," in view of the "appalling record of the West Midlands police, which is under suspicion and investigation."

Deputy O'Dea said he believes there seems to be a prima-facie case for an inquiry by the British Home Office into Mr Foran's detention. He added that he would be making inquiries with the Department of Foreign Affairs about the case.

Deputy O'Dea is to study legal documents produced by Mr Foran's brother, Andrew Foran, and discuss them with a top lawyer

before contacting Foreign Affairs minister Gerry Collins.

"I'm not happy with the response he's getting from the British Home Office. There is a certain amount of stonewalling and lack of an operation. This is an urgent case because of the man's condition, and it's at ministerial level," said Deputy O'Dea.

Andrew Foran yesterday produced two statements of documents which he claimed proved his brother's innocence. The original documents were signed by Martin Foran's solicitor

Mark Phillips, in Birmingham, he said.

He further claimed that the documents used by the West Midlands police contained versions of his custody record and two versions of the record of visits and movement to prison after his arrest.

He said that his brother was arrested at 3.30 a.m. in September 10, 1985, in Birmingham. But at the time of the alleged robbery, he was more than 90 miles away with his wife and children, when his car broke down. Two men represented in the fact were witnesses to the fact

that his car had broken down, but neither had been called to give evidence.

Martin Foran's mother, Bridget, said: "I feel desperate about the case. My son should be released because he did not commit the robbery.

She claimed that two Englishmen and a Pakistani were involved in the robbery and the man who was robbed stated that Martin "you are not involved. 'You are Irish in England, you are not wanted. There is no justice for Irish people in England,' he said.

● Willie O'Dea call for inquiry.

278

PAUL FOOT reporting

DAILY MIRROR, Wednesday, June 16, 1982   PAGE 9

Why Martin Foran went through the roof

● HAVE you heard about the man who is in prison for robbery though the man he is supposed to have robbed swears he had nothing to do with it?

He spent all last week protesting his innocence on the roof at Nottingham prison.

He is Martin Foran, convicted five years ago of robbing a Mr Apechis, among others.

In March 1980, he sought leave to appeal

Mr Apechis, who got a good look at his robber, was brought to the Court of Appeal, and was shown Martin Foran.

"Is that the man who robbed you?" asked the presiding Appeal Court Judge. "No, sir, definitely

not" replied Mr Apechis.

The judges promptly refused Mr Foran leave to appeal. This was not a case of mistaken denitity, they said, because Mr Foran had not been identified in the first place!

This crass judgment infuriated Justice, an organisation which fights against wrong convictions. Mr John Farr, Tory MP for Harborough, is also convinced that Mr Foran is innocent of the Apechis robbery. On March 26, John Farr wrote to the

Home Secretary outlining what he calls "substantial new evidence". Fingerprints on a weapon used in one of the robberies are not Martin Foran's.

Nothing happened. Mr Foran escaped from Gartree Prison, tried to publicise his case in local papers, and gave himself up again. Nothing happened. Now there has been the roof protest.

What else has he got to do to convince the Home Office to re-open his case?

Ex-policeman bids for failed timeshare firm

A former West Midlands Serious Crimes Squad inspector is seeking to take over a Birmingham timeshare firm which folded last month.

Mr Paul Matthews, who was forced to resign from the force in 1986, flew from his Lanzarote home to make an offer to the receivers of Las Calas (Holidays).

Receivers say the bid, worth several million pounds, will be considered with others when the business is put up for sale.

The Acocks Green-based firm, which owes about £3 million to British banks, had previously sold 9,000 timeshare weeks for 280 flats on Lanzarote. The accountants Peat Marwick McLintock hope to sell the remaining 5,000 weeks to a holiday operator.

Mr Matthews moved into the timeshare business on the Spanish island after leaving the police.

Las Calas's parent company, Circle Holidays (International), controlled eight apartment blocks.

Mr Matthews became a director but resigned shortly before the Bank of Scotland, which is owed about £1.5 million by Las Calas, called Peat Marwick McLintock in as receivers.

C2   EVENING MAIL, THURSDAY, APRIL 12, 1990 17

Protesters chained to court doors

TWO demonstrators for the Free Martin Foran Defence Campaign handcuffed themselves to the main doors of Birmingham Crown Court today.

The doors were blocked for around half an hour with neither court staff or members of the public able to enter or leave the building.

The incident ended when police arrived with bolt cutters, releasing a man and a woman, both in their 20s, who were led to a waiting police car.

Placards

Around 20 demonstrators, bearing placards and banners, lined the court steps.

The action was organised by the group who claim that

By ROSS McCARTHY

Martin Foran, who is serving a prison sentence for robbing a pub in Birmingham, was framed by the now disbanded West Midlands Serious Crime Squad.

Martin Foran, who is in prison in Durham, has been on hunger strike for 38 days.

His wife Valerie, a mother of five, of Acacia Avenue, Kingshurst, who was at the demonstration, said: "He has lost a lot of weight but his spirits are very high. He intends to continue as long as he can even if he has to die. I hope to God that does not happen."

She continued: "He should not have been in prison in the first place."

She said her husband had been in jail for five and a half years and said: "This is to highlight what has been going on for a long time. My husband is suffering in prison. He is completely innocent."

Mrs Foran said her husband had been at home at the time of the robbery in 1984 and that there were 16 alibi witnesses.

FORAN FURY: A protester handcuffed to the Crown Court

APPENDIX 9

The Legacy of the
West Midland Serious Crime Squad

INNOCENT main page

West Midlands Serious Crime Squad

1 November 1999

**Police unit to blame
for 'dozens more injustices'**

**Miscarriages of justice emerge 10 years after
break-up of group that tortured suspects**

By Ian Burrell and Jason Bennetto

Police face calls for a full and independent inquiry as the West Midlands force prepares for revelations of at least seven new miscarriages of justice.

Lawyers last night predicted that the notorious West Midlands Serious Crime Squad, which was disbanded more than a decade ago, could be responsible for dozens of wrongful convictions that have yet to come to light. So far 30 convictions have been quashed by the Court of Appeal because of evidence that the squad fabricated evidence, tortured suspects and wrote false confessions.

The scale of the continuing scandal emerged as Keith Twitchell had his conviction for manslaughter and robbery overturned by the Court of Appeal last Tuesday.

Mr Twitchell remembers every detail of what was done to him by members of the West Midlands squad. "Somebody put this bag over my head and it was clamped tight around my mouth and eyes. I remember struggling and heaving but then I must have gone unconscious," he said.

Under those methods, described to the Court of Appeal as "a scenario of torture that beggars belief", he signed a confession that led to him serving a 12-year jail sentence for manslaughter and robbery.

Last week he became the latest victim of the squad to have his conviction overturned. Now 63, he savages the squad's officers as "lazy, incompetent and careless". He was by no means the first, or the last, victim of their actions.

In the summer of 1980 a group of ruthless armed criminals,

nicknamed the "Thursday Gang" was wreaking havoc throughout the West Midlands.

The gang had just made its biggest hit - £280,000 from a post office van in Dudley, near Birmingham - and the West Midlands Serious Crime Squad was under pressure to get some results.

The breakthrough appeared to come when one of the gang's number, Keith Morgan, agreed to become a supergrass, followed by a second member of the outfit, Richard "Mad Mac" Mackay. Based on information provided by Morgan and Mackay the squad set up a joint operation with the West Mercia police, called Operation Cat, and in Easter 1982 they carried out a series of raids that led to 29 people being charged.

Among those jailed were the brothers Donald and Ronald Brown, Patrick Gaughan and Michael Dunne.

Despite the convictions being based almost entirely on the uncorroborated evidence of Morgan, a disputed confession by Gaughan and a semi-confession by Donald Brown, the prosecutions seemed to be another successful case for the squad.

But Operation Cat started to unravel because of the conviction of another supposed member of the gang, Derek Treadaway. Treadaway's conviction was later quashed after it was revealed he was forced to sign a confession after detectives tortured him by placing plastic bags over his head.

During a successful civil action by Treadaway, who received £70,000 in damages from the police and won an Appeal Court victory, the police were severely criticised, and the supergrass handlers and their informants were discredited.

After Treadaway's case the Criminal Cases Review Commission re-examined the cases of the Brown brothers, Dunne and Gaughan and referred them to the Court of Appeal. The Browns' cases had previously been turned down by the Home Office. All four men refused to admit to the bank raids and served out their sentences. Dates for the appeal hearings have yet to be set.

The origins of the West Midlands Police Serious Crime Squad can be traced back to February 1952 when the old City of Birmingham constabulary embarked on an experiment to tackle organised crime by assembling a group of "seasoned and experienced" officers driving "wireless cars".

The Birmingham "Special Crime Squad" proved so successful that it provided the inspiration for the now

Martin Foran – The Forgotten Man

infamous West Midlands unit, which was founded in 1974.

In 1985 a series of complaints prompted an investigation by the Metropolitan Police.

The ensuing Hay report, which was never made public, criticised the squad's interviewing techniques, failure to properly use pocket books and the inordinate amount of time that officers were allowed to remain with the élite unit.

Although the report was seen by senior West Midlands officers, nothing appears to have been done to improve the practices of those serving in the squad. The complaints continued and a succession of the squad's cases were thrown out of court amid allegations of fabricated confessions.

Many of these were exposed because of the coincidental emergence of a vital new forensic technique, the Esda (Electrostatic Document Analysis) test, which revealed that officers were making up statements.

Up until 1986 members of the 25-strong squad would write out false confessions and force the suspects to sign them.

On 14 August 1989, the force's Chief Constable, Geoffrey Dear, disbanded the squad, and an investigation was set up by the independent Police Complaints Authority and conducted by West Yorkshire Police.

The PCA investigation looked at 97 complaints against the squad made between January 1986 and August 1989. Ethnic minority complaints were disproportionately high, with 35 registered by African-Caribbeans and eight by Asians.

Between March 1990 and October 1991 the inquiry passed a succession of files to the Crown Prosecution Service to consider criminal charges against some of the officers concerned. By then the Birmingham Six, convicted of the 1974 IRA pub bombings, had been freed by the Court of Appeal after an investigation in which the squad had played an important part had been shown to be flawed.

But in May 1992, Dame Barbara Mills, Director of Public Prosecutions at the time, decided that there was "insufficient evidence to prosecute" a single officer from the squad.

The PCA's final report was published in January 1993.

It revealed that officers in the squad were working "totally unrealistic" hours. Officers were abusing the overtime system, with some working 100 hours overtime a month, mostly for visits to licensed premises to "meet contacts".

The official report made no mention of the "plastic bagging" and other torture techniques referred to by the many victims of the squad whose convictions have since been quashed by the Court of Appeal.

Nor did it highlight the repeated appearance in interview notes of key "confessional" phrases such as "That bastard's really put me in it" and "You're spot on".

At the end of its £2m inquiry, the PCA recommended disciplinary charges against only seven officers. A further 10 officers would have faced charges but they had already retired, it was announced.

In the event, just four of the squad's officers - Detective Superintendent John Brown, Detective Constable Colin Abbotts, Detective Chief Inspector Bob Goodchild and Detective Constable Tony Adams - were punished for minor disciplinary offences.

Two years ago the three remaining members of the Bridgewater Four, framed by the squad in 1978, were finally set free as the Court of Appeal decided that the crucial confession had been forged.

Gareth Peirce, a lawyer who was involved in the campaign to free the Birmingham Six, said yesterday that there were still dozens of hidden miscarriages. She called for a fresh inquiry into the scale of the corruption. "I have no doubt there are dozens of people who have served time in jail but were innocent. The Serious Crime Squad were operating like the Wild West, they were out of control."

A PCA spokesman said: "We have retained all the files in the interest of justice. Everything was disclosed to the lawyers concerned. The Home Office who handled such appeals at the time were fully briefed of the technique that had been used by the squad."

Officers named in disciplinary inquiries

NO OFFICER from the West Midlands Police Serious Crime Squad has been successfully prosecuted.
DC John Perkins. Died in October 1993. Racially abused and attacked George Glen Lewis before forcing him to sign a blank confession. Framed the Bridgewater Four, boasting that his fist was a "truth drug". Perkins was involved in 17 of the 97 cases investigated by the Police Complaints Authority (PCA).

DC Graham Leake. Involved in the forged confession that led to conviction of the Bridgewater Four. Confession was described in court as a "vein of corruption and dishonesty" through the case. The convictions were quashed by the High Court in 1997. Now runs a security firm.

DC David Woodley and **DC Roger Clifford**. Accused of interfering with the course of justice by stealing interview notes in the Michael Bromell case. When charges against the pair were dropped they won libel damages from newspapers and the BBC. In 1992 Bromell won his appeal after the judge was shown documents that indicated there was "a very real possibility" the officers removed notes that could have proved his innocence.

Supt John Brown and **DC Colin Abbots**. Fined £1,500 for disciplinary offences after PCA inquiry in 1993. Brown, now retired, linked to the plastic bag technique, used in the Treadaway and Twitchell cases.

DC Tony Adams and **Det Ch Insp Bob Goodchild**. Found guilty of minor disciplinary offences after PCA investigation. Adams found to have not followed correct procedures in relation to payments to an informant.

DS Michael Hornby. Served with the squad for 16 years and was involved in the Birmingham Six and Twitchell inquiries. Retired from the force with diabetes in 1990. Has accused Chris Mullin, the MP and Birmingham Six campaigner, of pursuing a "vendetta" against the squad.

Supt George Reade, **DS Colin Morris** and **DC Terence Woodwiss**. All charged with perjury and conspiracy to pervert the course of justice in relation to their investigation of the Birmingham Six. The case against the three detectives, all now retired, collapsed when a judge ruled they could not receive a fair trial.

Insp James Price, **DC Alan Pickering** and **Tim Russell**. Named, with Supt John Brown (above) in Treadaway case over torture allegations. Decision not to bring charges against them criticised by the High Court.

See also:

George Lewis
Glen Lewis
Trevor McCalla
Keith Twitchell
Christopher Hagans/John Wilson
Valentine Cooke / Danny Lynch
Ronnie and Gerald Gall

Derek Treadaway
John Cummiskey
Robert Haughton
Trevor Campbell
Patrick Irvine
Tarlochan Singh Gill

from Hansard 16 February 1994:

West Midlands Serious Crime Squad

Mr. Mullin : To ask the Attorney-General if he will list the cases still pending before the Cour involving members of the West Midlands serious crimes squad.

Appendix 9

The Attorney-General : Currently, there are five cases before the Court of Appeal. They ar

Martin P. Foran
Roy Meads
Anthony M. Jones
Trevor McCalla
Abdul Rasheed

Mr. Mullin : To ask the Attorney-General, pursuant to his answer of 3 February, Official Re[
if he will list the cases involving members of the West Midlands serious crimes squad where

The Attorney-General : The 23 appellants whose appeals have been allowed by the Court

Defendant/Appellant	Offence
Khan Hassan	Robbery
Edwards John	Robbery
Wellington Constantine	Robbery
Cheetham Geoffrey	Conspiracy to rob
Gall Ronald T.	Assault occasioning actual bodily harm
Gall Gerard	Robbery
Lynch Daniel	Robbery
Cooke Valentine P.	Robbery
Haughton Robert	Conspiracy to cause grievous bodily ha[
Hare Delroy	Robbery
Bromell Michael T.	Unlawful wounding
Binham Gary M.	Theft
Horobin Leslie B.	Robbery
Wilcox Kevin	Robbery
Fryer Raymond	Robbery
Francis Adolphus	Robbery
Jeffers Elvis	Robbery
Lindo Paul R.	Grievous bodily harm
Hinds George A.	Theft
Smith Patrick	Robbery
Williams Seymour	Robbery
Lewis George G.	Robbery

286

APPENDIX 10

Grounds of Appeal for 1st Conviction

IN THE COURT OF APPEAL

CRIMINAL DIVISION

REGINA

V

MARTIN FORAN

GROUNDS OF APPEAL

For the attention of Tracy Gibbon

Olliers Solicitors

11 Duke Street

Manchester

M3 4NF

IN THE COURT OF APPEAL CRIMINAL DIVISION

REGINA

v

MARTIN FORAN

GROUNDS OF APPEAL

On 21st June 1978 the appellant was convicted of 4 counts of robbery before HHJ Ross QC and jury at the Crown Court sitting in Birmingham. The case has now been referred to the Court of Appeal by the Criminal Cases Review Commission and the appellant now seeks leave to appeal against these four convictions on the following grounds.

1. The evidence against the appellant on Counts 3 and 4 were 'confessions' made to two officers, namely DC Davies and DS Jennings. Both officers were in the West Midlands Crime Squad. The appellant has always maintained that he did not make these confessions.

2. The evidence against the appellant on Counts 5 and 6 was a combination of challenged confessions and identification.

3. Since the appellant's conviction, material has come to light which could be said to impugn the veracity of the officers, in particular DCI Taylor (who at the time of this case had recently been appointed as the new head of the West Midlands Serious Crime Squad) and DC Davies and DS Jennings.

4. The Crown having reviewed the case and the material available concede at paragraph 22 of their response that with regards to Counts 3 and 4: 'It is difficult to advance a reasonable argument that these convictions are safe.'

2

5.   The appellant would adopt and endorse the arguments advanced in the Crown's Response regarding Counts 3 and 4.

COUNTS 5 AND 6

6.   These counts rely upon a combination of an identification made by a civilian witness, Mr Holmes, and purported confessions made to DS Hancock and confirmed to DCI Taylor.

7.   It is submitted that the identification evidence was not substantial and any jury would have looked to the 'confession' evidence to corroborate the identification. A conviction based on the identification evidence alone is not safe.

IDENTIFICATION EVIDENCE

8.   There were 5 potential eyewitnesses. Out of these 5 witnesses only one witness, Mr Holmes, was able to pick the defendant out on an identification parade as being the man responsible. The remaining witnesses either failed to pick anyone out, or identified one of the volunteers.   Notwithstanding that all the other witnesses indicated that they had a good opportunity to see the offender, one of the eye witnesses, Karen Rice, indicated in her statement that she believed that she had seen the man responsible on a number of occasions, making this a case of recognition rather than identification. This witness was unable to identify the appellant from the identification parade.

9.   There are a number of concerns surrounding the identification process:

    i.   The 'officer in case' DC Wheelen, was present throughout the procedure. The only material now available relating to the identification parade is contained within the report of the identification parade and the final paragraph of DC Whelan's statement dated 2nd December 1977.   It is therefore difficult to recreate precisely what happened and why this officer was present. The concern must be that he would have had contact with the witnesses.

    ii.   DC Wheelen, gave evidence at the trial and confirmed that he had shown a few selected photographs to the witnesses (including Mr Rice and Karen Rice). He admitted that he had selected the photograph of the appellant

3

because he believed him to be guilty. These photographs were shown before the defendant was arrested or even identified as a suspect.

iii.   At the identification parade, Mr Foran was the only man with distinguishing moles on his face. All the participants were given thin brown paper to place on their face; however the appellant submits that this did not conceal his moles.

iv.   The appellant does not have access to Guidance to the Police on the Conduct of Identification Parades and/ or the use of photographs that may have existed in 1976, therefore is unable to identify whether any of the conduct was in breach of such guidance. The appellant would request disclosure of any national or regional guidance that existed at the time of this identification parade.

v.   Given the passage of time and paucity of material it is accepted that it is almost impossible to explore the concerns associated with this procedure. However in light of general concerns relating to the police evidence there must exist an inherent doubt regarding the conduct and validity of the parade.

CONFESSION EVIDENCE

10.   It is submitted that information has come to light that would significantly challenge the veracity of the confession evidence. DC Davies was the one officer who was connected with every aspect of the investigation of the appellant. He was responsible for the appellant's initial arrest on 3rd May 1977 and claimed that the appellant had made limited confessions to him regarding this crime. He was responsible for the appellant's arrest on 24th October 1977 and the initial interview that apparently led on to the admissions made to DC Hancock. Finally he was responsible for the supposed admission to the Apechis and Trikam robberies (Counts 3 and 4) during an interview in prison in April 1978.

11.   It is now accepted by the Crown that the convictions on counts 3 and 4 are not safe. Not least of all because the description given by the two complainants in those robberies, Mr Apechis and Mr Trikam, do not match the description of the appellant. It follows logically from this that the 'confessions' made to DCs Davies and Jennings cannot be legitimate. It is submitted that this of itself undermines the credibility of DC Davies's evidence.

4

12.   In addition to paragraph 11 there are other matters that would go to the heart of DC Davies's evidence. DC Davies was one of the officers who together with a DC Hornby interviewed Hugh Callaghan, one of the Birmingham Six. In the appeal R v McIlkenny the Court of Appeal made the following observation:

> 'If we put the scientific evidence on one side, the fresh investigation carried out by the Devon and Cornwall Constabulary renders the police evidence at trial so unreliable that again we would say that the convictions are both unsafe and unsatisfactory.'

DC Davies was not singled out for critism but he would undoubtedly fall under the umbrella of concern regarding the corrupt practises and validity of their evidence. Furthermore DC Hornby has repeatedly been identified as being associated with corrupt practises and the Crown have acknowledged that he is an officer whose evidence cannot be relied upon. The evidence now available demonstrates that DC Davies not only worked with Hornby on the Birmingham Six case but also on the case of R v Twitchell, another successful appeal relating to false confessions.

13.   It is understood that DC Davies was due to face disciplinary proceedings, the details of which no longer exist but that he retired on the grounds of ill-health and so the Force never perused their internal hearings.

14.   DCI Taylor has also featured in a number of cases whereby the convictions have been overturned due to falsified evidence. In particular the case of Twitchell. (It has already been noted that Hornby and Davies were also connected to this case.) Furthermore DCI Taylor had also been convicted of two disciplinary offences in 1982; namely Neglect of Duty and Falsehood. The appellant would be entitled to cross-examine on this material and would have impacted upon the jury's assessment of his evidence.

15.   It was the Crown's case that Mr Foran chose to admit the matters to DS Hancock and confirmed to DCI Taylor. Although there is no direct material that undermines Mr Hancock's credibility, it is submitted that his close association with DCI Taylor and DC Davies would undermine his credibility.

16.   In the course of his summing up the Learned Judge describes DCI Taylor as the 'newly appointed head of the Serious Crime Squad', which in 1978 no doubt was regarded as an impressive character testimonial. Later the Learned Judge said this

'*Once again, members of the jury, pause to consider this. You have got to decide whether Hancock is an honest witness and whether he was behaving in a way in which you would expect a responsible officer to behave. Here the police had got a serious crime on their hands. A man who has been denying it all along until now when, if Hancock is right, he decided to admit it and so Hancock took the precaution of fetching his superior officer.*'

It is impossible to underestimate the impact the information about Taylor and Davies would have had. The appellants account must have seemed implausible to a jury in 1977. However in light of the information now available about these two officers and the way they together with others conducted themselves, the appellant's assertions are no longer implausible or unlikely.

17.   It is submitted that there are other circumstances in the case that directly undermine Hancock's credibility, in particular the medical evidence. It was always the appellant's case that he was subject to physical violence. The appellant made a formal complaint via his solicitor, and a medical report was obtained. This report no longer exists. The only details we have are contained at 41 G-H and 42 A-G of the summing up. It is submitted that this evidence was/is consistent with the appellant being subject to considerable physical violence. It included wide spread bruising, which in the opinion of the author would have 'required considerable force' and also included 'linear marks which were caused by being hit or falling on a straight blunt object.' These injures are consistent with blows from a truncheon. The appellant maintained that these injuries were inflicted by a number of officers including Davies and Hancock. Davies maintained that these injuries were sustained as a result of a struggle in the car at the point of arrest. It is submitted that the Crown's explanation is no longer credible for the following reasons:

i.   The material regarding Davies and Taylor indicate that they have been associated with cases that used violence on prisoners to extract confessions.

ii.   DC Davies can no longer be regarded as a credible witness.

iii.   PC Milne was the second arresting officer. He gave evidence at the trial and did not confirm the existence of a substantial struggle that could have explained away the injuries recorded by the doctor. . His evidence is dealt with at page 23 G-H and 24 A-B. He arrived and assisted Davies place Foran in the panda car. He described the

6

292

appellant in the following manner 'the defendant did not go into the panda car as quietly as he should have done.'

iv.   If the defendant had behaved in such a violent manner that required him to be restrained to the extent of causing these injuries it is inconceivable that he would simply have been placed in the rear of the panda car accompanied only by PC Milne.

18.   It is submitted that 'Hancock's notes' exhibited at the trial are inconsistent with other evidence and again would impact upon the veracity of this officer's evidence. It was always the Crown's case that Foran refused to name the men who assisted him in the Rice robbery. Hancock records him as saying: *'Be fair that's my only hope. I'll give you them if you drop the charges.'*

In a later interview on 3rd April 1978 Davies records the appellant as saying: *'OK Johnny, fair enough but if you hadn't locked the coon up I had a 50-50 chance of getting away with it.'* and *'I've got to give it to you Johnny you've worked hard. you know I'm a bit of a con man but how did you get Campbell, did somebody put him in?'*

However according to the document produced by Hancock, Errol (Campbell) was almost the first man named by the appellant. If, as the police suggest the appellant was refusing to identify his co-defendant in order to act as leverage, it is incredible that he would name him during his conversation with DC Hancock.

19.   The Crown produced a 'note' in the course of the trial in order to support Hancock's evidence that the appellant had provided him with information. However the contents of the note purport to link the appellant to the IRA. This information would have been incredibly prejudicial to the appellant before a Birmingham jury in 1977. This evidence should never have been admitted in this form before a jury.

20.   It is submitted therefore that Hancock is not only tainted by his association with Taylor and Davies, but there are a number of independent concerns regarding his veracity.

21.   The appellant stood trial on four counts of robbery. The Crown now concedes that two of these convictions are unsafe. Inevitably, the jury considering this case would have had regard to the fact that the appellant faced 4 counts and had apparently confessed to all of those offences. It is now impossible to know

7

precisely how the conviction/confession on Counts 3 and 4 would have been used by the jury, but it would have inevitably provided support in their minds as to the correctness of the identification on and confessions to, counts 5 and 6. Therefore the fact that count 3 and 4 are now regarded as unsafe, must have an impact upon the verdicts on Count 5 and 6.

ELIZABETH NICHOLLS

Lincoln House Chambers
Tower 12
The Avenue North
Spinningfields
Manchester
M3 3BZ

2nd June 2014

8

APPENDIX 11

Crown Prosecution Response

FOR OFFICIAL USE -   CAO No.   /   /

Form **RN**

Respondents Notice and grounds of opposition to appeal against conviction or sentence *(Criminal Procedure Rules, r.68.6(5))*

ON COMPLETION PLEASE SEND THIS FORM TO THE REGISTRAR, CRIMINAL APPEAL OFFICE, ROYAL COURTS OF JUSTICE, STRAND, LONDON, WC2A 2LL

Write in BLACK INK and use BLOCK CAPITALS

The Respondent give full name

Name of Respondent   REGINA

Address   CPS APPEALS AND REVIEWS UNIT,
CROWN PROSECUTION SERVICE,
3RD FLOOR, FOSS HOUSE
1-2 PEASHOLME GREEN
YORK

Postcode   YO1 7PX   Reference   86SA2171933/TW/THS

Case Details

Name of Appellant   **MARTIN FORAN**   CAO Reference No. **201400198 B1**

The Crown Court at   **BIRMINGHAM**

Name of Judge   **HHJ ROSS QC**

Date of Conviction   **21/6/78**   Date of Sentence   **21/6/78**

Date on which appellant's notice of appeal was received by the respondent 21.1.14

Indictment No: **780013/780707-8/780909**

The Respondent is applying for: *Please tick as appropriate*

☐ Extension of time in which to give notice of opposition to appeal (give reasons below)

☐ Permission to call witness

295

Grounds of Opposition *(Criminal Procedure Rules, r68.6(6))*	1. Identify each ground of opposition on which the respondent relies, numbering them consecutively (if there is more than one), concisely outlining each argument in support and identifying the ground of appeal to which each relates. Summarise any relevant facts not already summarised in the appeal notice:

Introduction

1. The Criminal Cases Review Commission (CCRC) has decided to refer this case to the Court of Appeal on the basis that information, not previously considered in proceedings against the appellant, has come to light regarding the credibility of two police officers who gave evidence at the appellant's trial, namely DC John Davies and DCI Roy Taylor.

The safety of the convictions on Counts 3 and 4

2. It is convenient to consider these counts together because the prosecution case in respect of both allegations relied almost wholly on alleged admissions made by the appellant during the interview which took place at HMP Leicester on 3rd April 1978. In the course of his summing-up the judge observed: "What happened at this interview is absolutely crucial because it is the only evidence which connects this man with those two affairs at all". [SU, p.46C]

3. It was common ground that the interview was conducted by DC Davies and DS Jennings.

Prosecution case

4. It was the prosecution case that in the course of the interview, the officers read to the appellant a statement made by Errol Campbell in which Campbell admitted to taking part in the offences particularised in Counts 3-6 together with the appellant. The interviewing officers gave evidence that after the statement had been read, the appellant made certain remarks that clearly amounted to admissions to Counts 3 and 4. [SU, p.49B-F]

Defence case

5. In contrast, the appellant denied that he took part in either of the robberies and gave evidence to the effect that he had made no such admissions, the implication being that both of the officers had lied on oath. He agreed that the statement of Campbell had been read to him and alleged, in terms, that DS Jennings had threatened to charge his wife with an offence if he refused to make a statement admitting his part in the robberies at the jeweller's shop (Counts 5 and 6). [SU, p.62E – 64F]

6. Prison Officer David Law, the officer who escorted the appellant to and from the interview room, was called as part of the appellant's case. He was unable to help on the central issue of whether the appellant had made admissions. However, he was able to give his recollection of aspects of the interview process. [SU p.50F- 51G]

7. There were discrepancies between the account given by PC Law and the accounts given by the

interviewing officers. For example:

(a) Whereas PO Law said that he thought the appellant was reluctant to be interviewed, the officers said that at no time did he indicate that he was unwilling to see either of them.

(b) PO Law said that, as he was observing through glass partition, he saw the appellant stand up "two to four of five times" in the course of the interview whilst the officers said that he only got up once.

(c) PO Law said that he was called into the interview room because the appellant wanted him to hear him denying something (although he did not hear what was the officers were putting to the appellant at that point). In contrast, the officers maintained that PO Law did not enter the interview room at any stage.

(d) PO Law said that one of the interviewing officers left the interview room for a significant period. The officers said that neither of them did.

8.   There were also discrepancies between the evidence of PO Law and that of the appellant. For example:

(a) Whereas the appellant said that he asked PO Law to take him back to his cell on two occasions, the prison officer gave no such evidence.

(b) The appellant claimed that DS Jennings said in the presence of PO Law that he wanted to speak to the appellant without the prison officer being present and informed that the appellant that he could ask the prison officer to leave whereupon the appellant said no. There was no support for this in the evidence of PO Law who merely said that he left the interview room but gave no reason for doing so.

(c) The appellant gave evidence that he asked PO Law to leave the room after DS Jennings had told him that he wanted to speak to him alone and added that either DC Davies or the prison officer, or both, could leave. Again, there was no support for this in the evidence of PO Law.

(d) The appellant said that after the interview, when they were in the presence of PO Law, DS Jennings told him that he was going to the hospital to charge his wife. The appellant went on to say that he told DS Jennings that if he was going to the hospital, could he pass on his love to his wife and tell her not to worry. In contrast, PO Law said that after the interview, he heard the appellant say to the officers words to the effect of "Don't forget what I have told you" and went on to ask them for a favour, namely for the officers to go and see his wife.

9.   In support of his defence, the appellant could point to the fact that, in the words of the judge, the description of the white robber given by Mr. Apechis, the victim of Count 3, did "not even remotely resemble the defendant in the dock". [SU p.52H].

Main issue for jury

10. Consequently, it can be seen that the central issue for the jury to decide in determining whether the defendant participated in either of these robberies was whether they could be sure that the interviewing officers were telling the truth about the admissions made by the defendant in the course of the interview.

11. It is noted in passing that there were a number of other factual matters, over and above the contents of the interview at HMP Leicester, where there was considerable dispute between the appellant and DC Davies. For example, the appellant alleged that he received numerous bruises at the hands of DC Davies and other officers when they assaulted him during interviews at the police station following his arrest on 24th October 1973, whilst DC Davies suggested that the appellant must have received the injuries during the violent struggle that ensued when the appellant tried to resist being arrested. [SU p.22E-24C]

Fresh evidence

12. At paragraph 186 of their statement of reasons, the CCRC indicate that the credibility of DS Jennings cannot be said to have been damaged by any information that has emerged since the trial.

13. However, the same cannot be said for DC Davies. The CCRC contends that, in his case, material has emerged after the trial which damages his credibility to the extent that there is a real possibility that the Court of Appeal could quash the appellant's convictions on Counts 3 and 4.

14. The material highlighted by the CCRC can be summarised as follows:

(a) On 27th March 1991, the Court of Appeal delivered their judgment in *McIlkenny and others'* in which reasons were given for allowing the appeals against convictions of all of the appellants (the 'Birmingham Six'). In the course of their judgment, the Court of Appeal observed, "If we put the scientific evidence on one side, the fresh investigation carried out by the Devon and Cornwall Constabulary renders the police evidence at trial so unreliable, that again we would say that the convictions are both unsafe and unsatisfactory." Although it seems that DC Davies did not give evidence at the trial, the police evidence included evidence that shortly after his arrest, one of the six, Hugh Callaghan, was interviewed by DC Davies, DS Hornby and DS Bryant on 23rd November 1974. The police contended that at the outset of the interview, Callaghan indicated that he wished to confess and thereafter made a written statement under caution. The case against Callaghan rested primarily on this statement. For his part, Callaghan said that part of his statement was true, part made up for the benefit of the police and part made up by the police themselves. He did not allege police brutality save for one slap to the face.

(b) Since the decision in *McIlkenny*, there have been a series of cases which have established that

DS Hornby was deeply involved in the reprehensible activities of the West Midlands Serious Crime Squad. Many of these cases have involved disputed admissions. In *O'Toole and Murphy,*[2] the prosecution conceded that Hornby could not be relied on as a witness of truth. The CCRC observe that there appears to have been an ongoing link between DS Hornby and DC Davies at least from the time they both interviewed McIlkenny in November 1974 until April 1977, when both were involved in involved in the execution of a search warrant at the home of the appellant Murphy.

Submissions

15. The essential question is whether the convictions on Counts 3 and 4 are unsafe by virtue of the fresh evidence relating to DC Davies. This can be tested by considering whether the deployment of this material, had it been available, might reasonably have induced in the jury's mind a doubt as to the veracity of the alleged admissions.[3]

16. It seems clear from the judgment in *O'Toole and Murphy* that, had this material been available at the time of the trial, those acting on behalf of the appellant would have been entitled to cross-examine DC Davies on the Court of Appeal's observations in *McIlkenny* as to the unreliability of the police evidence, which included the disputed evidence of Callaghan's written confession. One of the officers in O'Toole's case was a DS Matthews. The Court of Appeal noted that he was one of the officers involved in *McIlkenny* and that he was concerned in the interviewing of Patrick Hill. The Court observed that while DS Matthews (like DC Davies) was not the subject of any specific criticism by the Court of Appeal in *McIlkenny,* the Court had made a general observation as to the unreliability of the police evidence. It is clear from the judgment in *O'Toole and Murphy* that the Court considered that Matthews could properly have been cross-examined on this and other matters that went to his discredit.

17. It appears that enquiries carried out by the CCRC suggest that DC Davies did not give evidence about his part in the interviewing of Callaghan. However, assuming, as seems reasonable, that DC Davies must have made a witness statement about the interview containing an account in line with the accounts given by DS Hornby and DS Bryant, then he would still be covered by the taint of unreliability.

18. The particular features of the Callaghan interview that could be argued to point to unreliability are referred to in the judgment in *McIlkenny* and include, for example, the use of two types of ink: the way the details of the interviewing officers were entered by the discredited Superintendent Reade in his schedule of interviews; and the involvement of DS Hornby.

19. It is submitted that the factors which are relevant to an assessment of the impact that this material might have had on the jury's consideration of these counts include the following:

(a) The prosecution case on Counts 3 and 4 rested primarily on the alleged admissions made during the interview at HMP Leicester

(b) This interview was carried out by two officers, DC Davies and DS Jennings, both of whom gave similar evidence about it at trial.

(c) DC Davies had, about 3½ years earlier, been involved in an interview of Hugh Callaghan, one of the Birmingham Six, which formed part of a body of prosecution evidence that the Court of Appeal described as unreliable. Callaghan alleged that part of that interview had been fabricated by police.

(d) The appellant claimed at trial that both officers had fabricated evidence that he had admitted participating in the offences in Counts 3 and 4.

(e) DC Davies played a major role in the investigation of all of the offences on the indictment. He was the only officer involved in the interviewing process relating to all six offences on the indictment, and he gave evidence in respect of other aspects of the case such as the arrest of the appellant on 24th October 1977. By way of comparison, DS Jennings's role appears to have been limited to the interview at HMP Leicester.

(f) As demonstrated above, PO Law's evidence could not help the jury as to whether the appellant made admissions. There was something for both sides in his evidence but there were significant discrepancies between the prison officer's evidence and the evidence of both interviewing officers.

(g) There were substantial differences between the description given by Mr Apechis of the white member of the gang who robbed him and the description of the appellant at the relevant time.

20. In *Guney*,[4] the Court of Appeal made reference to 'a fairly consistent approach by the Court of Appeal in cases where police officers from a particular squad or force have been proved to have misconducted themselves. If one of these officers has given incriminating evidence then the conviction has frequently been quashed whether or not that evidence appears to be supported by other officers whose credibility has not been impugned in the same way.'

21. Of course, DS Jennings supported the evidence given by DC Davies about the contents of the interview. However, given that there was little if any other evidence which supported the veracity of the alleged admissions, it is difficult reasonably to argue that had the material relating to DC Davies's credibility been deployed at trial, it would not have reasonably induced a doubt in the jury's mind in respect of Counts 3 and 4.

22. Accordingly, it is difficult to advance a reasonable argument that these convictions are safe.

The safety of the convictions on Counts 5 and 6

23. It is clearly convenient to consider Counts 5 and 6 together because the two robberies to which they relate were carried out on the same occasion by the same group of robbers at a jeweller's shop. (For convenience, these counts are sometimes referred to as one robbery.)

Prosecution case

24. There were two main aspects to the prosecution case against the appellant on these counts. The first concerned evidence of admissions made by the appellant to the police, and the second was the identification evidence given by Mr. Ian Holmes, the victim in Count 6.

25. With regard to the admissions, the prosecution case was that following his arrest on 24/10/77, the appellant was interviewed on a number of occasions in the course of which he made various admissions and statements that were consistent with guilt. The position can be summarised as follows:

    24th October 1977

    (a) The first interview began at 5.35pm on 24th October 1977. DC Davies was present with DI Curry and DS Hancocks. There were no clear admissions made in this interview. When it was put to the appellant that he matched the description of one of the robbers he replied to the effect that he knew nothing about it and it was not his style. When asked where he was at the relevant time, he said that he could not remember. [SU, p.29H-31F]

    (b) Following this first interview there was a period when the appellant was alone with DS Hancocks. The appellant did not make a clear admission to participating in the robbery but, in the course of the exchanges, he made certain remarks about which the judge remarked to the jury, "Are those the answers of a man who had nothing whatsoever to do with this crime?" [SU, 31F-34B]

    (c) The second interview began at 6.30pm. It was conducted by DC Davies and DI Curry. Again, the appellant was asked where he was at the relevant time and he replied that he did not do daytime robberies; they were not his style. [SU, p.34D-H]

    (d) At 6.55pm, there was another period when he was alone with DS Hancocks. At the end of the conversation, the appellant said to DS Hancocks that he would not say anything about the robbery until he could trust him. [SU, p.35A-C]

    (e) At 7.15pm, DS Hancocks and DCI Taylor went to see the appellant. DCI Taylor had recently been appointed as the new head of the Serious Crime Squad. DCI Taylor provided the appellant with a verbal resume of the police information concerning the robbery and the appellant indicated that he wanted to talk to DS Hancocks alone. [SU, p.35C-F]

    (f) During the third period when they were alone, the appellant said to DS Hancocks that he would reveal the identity of the four West Indians concerned in the robbery if the police would let him go. He offered to supply information about the robbery and other crimes. DS Hancocks told him that there was no question of making a bargain but the appellant then proceeded to give him information in respect of which he made a contemporaneous note. Then, the conversation returned to the robbery. The appellant admitted that he had carried it out with four West Indians but denied having the sword that was brandished during the robbery. He provided an account of the robbery but said he did not know the names of his accomplices. [SU, p.35G-39B]

(g) Following this clear admission. DS Hancocks brought DCI Taylor into the room whereupon the appellant repeated his admission to participating in the robbery and denied having the sword. The appellant went on to ask for a deal, asking that the charges be dropped if he identified the West Indians. The appellant gave an account of what occurred in the shop and when asked to make a statement, replied that he would see DS Hancocks in the morning. No such statement was ever provided. [SU, p.39C-41B]

25th October 1977

(h) In the early hours of the 25th October 1977, DS Whelan and DC Bawden attended the police station where the appellant was being held. It seems that they were not attached to the Serious Crime Squad, but were from the police station in the same locality as the robbery (Sparkhill) and were in charge of the investigation into the robbery. After a short meeting with DS Hancocks, they introduced themselves to the appellant who agreed that he had admitted responsibility for the robbery to DS Hancocks. They asked the appellant for the identities of the others involved in the robbery and the appellant replied that he could not say and he was saying no more. [SU, p.44B-F]

3d April 1978

(i) DC Davies and DS Jennings went to interview the appellant at HMP Leicester where they read to him the statement of Errol Campbell. At the end of this exercise they summarised the position by pointing out that Campbell was saying that he was involved with the appellant in the robbery of the jeweller's shop as well as two other robberies (Counts 3 and 4). The appellant replied, "Okay Johnny, fair enough, but if you hadn't have locked the Coon up, I had a 50-50 chance of getting away with it". There was no denial of the robbery at the jeweller's shop. When dealing with this aspect of the evidence, the judge described this interview as being of only marginal importance in respect of the robbery of the jeweller's shop. [SU, p.46A; p.49C-E]

3. As to the identification evidence, Mr. Holmes was the only eye-witness to pick out the appellant out at the identification parade. The three other eye-witnesses who attended the parade picked out volunteers although one of those, Karen Rice, had previously picked out the appellant when shown a number of photographs. In respect of the photograph identification by Karen Rice, the judge told the jury that it was not a piece of identification evidence on which they would want to place much weight bearing in mind that Karen Rice did not pick out the appellant on the identification parade. (It should also be noted that the in the display of photographs, the appellant was the only person with moles on his face whereas the moles on his face were covered up at the parade.) [SU, p.43C-H]

27. Leaving aside the disputed admissions, there was some support for the correctness of the identification by Mr. Holmes in that Holmes (and others) described the white male robber as having amongst other things, an Irish accent and moles on his face. The appellant possessed both of these features.

Defence case

28. The appellant gave evidence that he was elsewhere at the time of the robbery and called witnesses in support of his alibi. He asserted that he had been wrongly identified by Mr. Holmes and that the police had fabricated large parts of the evidence relating to the interviews and, in particular, the admissions and other damaging statements he was alleged to have made. He denied providing DS Hancocks with any of the information recorded in the note (save some information about his movements in Northern Ireland) and disputed Hancocks's claim to have made a note at the time. The appellant also alleged that he was seriously assaulted by DC Davies, DI Curry and DS Hancocks, and threatened by DCI Taylor during the interviews on the 24th October 1977.

Main issues for jury

29. Thus, the main issues for the jury to decide in determining whether the appellant participated in the robbery were (a) whether they were sure that Holmes had made a correct identification of the appellant and (b) whether they were sure that the appellant had made the admissions attributed to him by the police.

30. In the course of his summing-up, the judge made the following observations about how the jury should approach the identification evidence:

   (a) The case against the appellant on Counts 5 and 6 depended to a large degree upon the evidence of identification. [SU, p.10E]

   (b) It was important for the jury to look to see what other evidence there was that pointed to the identification being right or wrong; what supporting evidence was there? [SU, p.11B]

   (c) The jury were invited to consider whether Mr. Holmes was honest and accurate. They were reminded of the period between the robbery and the identification parade and the ease with which mistakes could be made. [SU, p.21B-G]

   (d) They could look to the evidence of the admissions to support the correctness of the identification [SU, p.21G - 22B].

   (e) "It is for you to decide, members of the jury, as to whether or not [the police evidence of admissions] leads you to the conclusion that the identification made by Mr. Holmes is, in fact, the correct identification." [SU, p.39B-C]

Fresh evidence

31. The fresh evidence regarding the credibility of DC Davies has been referred to above.

32. The fresh evidence relating to DCI Taylor's credibility is referred to by the Court of Appeal in *Twitchell*[5] who noted that in March 1982, DCI Taylor was found guilty of two disciplinary offences, namely neglect of duty and falsehood. The former related to inadequate recordings of payments to an informant. There were no details available in respect of the latter falsehood charge and it appears that the date on which the offences occurred is not known.

Submissions

33. The essential question is whether the convictions on Counts 5 and 6 are unsafe by virtue of the fresh evidence relating to DC Davies and DCI Taylor.

34. It has already been acknowledged that the authorities indicate that those acting on behalf of the appellant would have been entitled to cross-examine DC Davies on matters arising out of *McIlkenny* had the material been available. Equally, it is clear from the judgment of the Court of Appeal in *Twitchell* that DCI Taylor could have been cross-examined about the two disciplinary offences recorded against him had the information been available. In the context of the issues in this case, any finding of falsehood plainly has a particular resonance.

35. It is submitted that the factors which are relevant to an assessment of the impact that this material might have had on the jury's consideration of these counts include the following:

    (a) The prosecution case on Counts 5 and 6 rested primarily on the identification evidence of Mr. Holmes together with the evidence of the alleged admissions.

    (b) The fresh evidence relating to DC Davies and DCI Taylor does not directly impact on the reliability of the identification evidence. The identification of the appellant by Mr. Holmes is untainted and supported by other untainted evidence, although it has to be seen in the context of the failure of three other eye-witnesses to pick out the appellant at the identification parade.

    (c) In the light of how the judge summed the case up, it is not possible to rule out the prospect that the jury might have looked to the evidence of admissions to find support for the identification evidence of Mr. Holmes.

    (d) The period between DC Davies's involvement in the Callaghan interview and his involvement with the appellant has been noted above. The period between DCI Taylor's involvement with the appellant and his commission of the two disciplinary offences is not more than about 4½ years.

    (e) As set out above, the main evidence of admissions was given by DS Hancocks. DS Hancocks gave evidence that the first unequivocal admission was made by the appellant when they were alone together. There was also evidence of admissions given by DS Whelan and DC Bawden. The CCRC has not identified any fresh evidence going to the discredit of these three officers although, as previously stated the authorities make it plain that fresh evidence of misconduct by a police officer may be fatal to a conviction even though their tainted evidence is supported by officers of whom there is no criticism whatsoever.

(f) The only evidence that DCI Taylor gave of admissions, concerned the repetition of the admission that the appellant had allegedly made shortly before to DS Hancocks.

(g) The only evidence that DC Davies gave of the appellant making anything approaching an admission to the robbery of the jeweller's shop was in the context of the interview at HMP Leicester. This was after the appellant had allegedly made a number of earlier admissions. The judge described this interview as being of only marginal importance in this regard.

(h) DCI Taylor was the newly appointed head of the Serious Crime Squad at the relevant time and, as such, could be expected to have significant influence of his junior officers. The central role played by DC Davies in the investigation into the appellant's alleged involvement in these offences has already been highlighted. In this context, it is noted that DS Phelan and DC Bawden do not appear to have been attached to the Serious Crime Squad.

(i) One key area of dispute between DS Hancocks and the appellant was whether, during their third period alone together when the unequivocal admission was allegedly made, the appellant provided information about which DS Hancocks made a contemporaneous note. The note was produced as an exhibit in the trial although it was not detailed in the original statements of either DS Hancocks or DCI Taylor. It is an important document because although, of course, it was not independent of DS Hancocks, it is submitted that on its face, it has a quality that tends to support Hancocks' account of events rather than that of the appellant. It can be seen that the note appears to contain information relating to various matters including:

- locations connected to crime;
- named individuals concerned in crime;
- a man called Errol who is described in the note as being 5'8" with bushy hair who uses the Vine public house and frequents Small Heath; (this description fitted Errol Campbell who was not arrested in connection with this robbery until 13th March 1978);
- particular crimes;
- the claim that the appellant could recognise photographs of the West Indians in the robbery team;
- details of the appellant's movements during his recent trip to Northern Ireland in April/May 1997 together with details of various individuals and events including criminal activities.

In the course of his summing up the judge referred to the note and said, "Members of the jury, one comes back to the fact that, according to [the appellant] all these notes are the product of Hancocks' imagination. There is no other source they could have come from if they had not come from the [appellant]". [SU, p.64H]

36. Taking all of the above matters into account it is submitted that it could reasonably be argued that on the basis of the evidence relevant to Counts 5 and 6, the deployment of the fresh evidence relating to DC Davies and DCI Taylor would not have affected the decision of the trial jury to convict. The main evidence of the appellant admitting his part in the robbery came from an untainted officer who was alone with the appellant when it was allegedly made. Any suspicion that the evidence of DS Hancocks was orchestrated by DCI Taylor and/or DC Davies has to be seen in the context of the further evidence of admissions given by two further untainted officers, DS Phelan and DC Bawden who were attached to a different police unit. And although points can be made about the overall strength of the identification evidence, the fact remains that one of the victims, Mr. Holmes, made a clear identification of the appellant.

37. Accordingly it is submitted that it can reasonably be argued that the convictions on Counts 5 and 6 are safe.

2. Identify the relevant Sentencing powers of the Crown Court, if sentence is in issue:

N/A

Authorities and Documents	Identify any relevant authorities and any other document or thing that the respondent thinks the Court will need to decide the appeal: All of the relevant authorities are included in the documents enclosed with the CCRC's Statement of Reasons (see Annex C). The Court of Appeal is invited to look at the handwritten note of DS Hancocks at tab 17 of Annex C.
Certificate of Service *(Criminal Procedure Rules, r.68.6(3) & 68.6(4))*	Give details of those on whom this Notice of Opposition and any supporting documents have been served and the date and method of service: Served on Olliers Solicitors by first class post on 18th February 2014

Signature	Signed _____ Date 18th February 2014 For Respondent Details of Counsel signing on behalf of the respondent: Name Jonathan Rees QC Address 2 Hare Court Chambers DX LDE 444 Chancery Lane _____ Postcode _____ Respondent's Reference 86SA2171933
For Criminal Appeal Office Use	Date Received _____ Date Acknowledged _____

APPENDIX 12

Full Consideration of the Court of Appeal which quashed Foran's first conviction

Neutral Citation Number: [2014] EWCA Crim 2047

Case No: 201400198 B1

IN THE COURT OF APPEAL (CRIMINAL DIVISION)
ON APPEAL FROM
BIRMINGHAM CROWN COURT - HIS HONOUR JUDGE ROSS QC

Royal Courts of Justice
Strand, London, WC2A 2LL

Date: 17/10/2014

Before :

LORD JUSTICE PITCHFORD
MR JUSTICE DINGEMANS
and
MR JUSTICE WILLIAM DAVIS

- -

Between :

MARTIN PATRICK FORAN	<u>Appellant</u>
- and -	
REGINA	<u>Respondent</u>

- -
- -

Miss Elizabeth Nicholls (instructed by **Olliers - Solicitors**) for the **Appellant**
Mr J Rees QC (instructed by **Crown Prosecution Service**) for the **Respondent**

Hearing date: 3 October 2014
- -

Approved Judgment

Lord Justice Pitchford :

The CCRC Reference

1. On 12 June 1978 Martin Patrick Foran faced trial before HHJ Ross QC at Birmingham Crown Court upon an indictment charging him with six offences. In count 1 he was charged with burglary of a garage at 29 St Chad's Road, Rubery between 1 and 4 May 1977 and theft of a wallet and its contents. In the alternative, in count 2 he was charged with handling the wallet and contents. In count 3 he was charged that on 26 September 1977 he robbed Charles Apechis of £2,800 in cash and other property. In count 4 he was charged that on 8 October 1977 he robbed Natwarlal Trikain of a handbag and £35. In count 5 he was charged that on 13 October 1977 he robbed Richard Alexander Rice of a quantity of jewellery and watches, a cash box and cash. In count 6 he was charged that on 13 October 1977 he robbed Ian Lawrence Holmes of a watch, a wallet and its contents. In counts 3 - 6 Mr Foran was jointly charged with Errol Alexander Campbell. Campbell pleaded guilty to those counts and trial proceeded against Mr Foran alone.

2. During the course of the trial the judge withdrew count 1 from the jury and directed an acquittal. On 21 June 1978 the jury returned verdicts of not guilty upon count 2 and guilty upon counts 3 – 6 inclusive. Mr Foran was sentenced to 10 years imprisonment concurrent upon each count.

3. He appealed against conviction. On 11 March 1980, in a judgment a transcript of which is no longer available, the full court refused the applicant's renewed application for leave to appeal. In 1981 an effort was made to persuade the Home Secretary to refer the convictions back to the Court of Appeal. That effort was unsuccessful. In July 1982 Mr Foran conducted a roof top protest at HMP Nottingham. His case was raised in the House of Commons on 20 July 1982. The minister of state at the Home Office, Mr Patrick Mayhew QC, who had a copy of the court's judgment in his possession, reminded the House that he could not usurp the functions of the jury and the Court of Appeal. There was no new evidence that cast doubt upon the safety of the verdicts which, as Donaldson LJ had remarked in his judgment on behalf of the court, depended upon confessions by Mr Foran to the offences alleged.

4. On 7 January 2013 Mr Foran made an application to the Criminal Cases Review Commission ("the Commission" or "the CCRC") for a review of his case. On 9 January 2014 the Commission referred the convictions to this court under section 9 of the Criminal Appeal Act 1995. Henceforth we shall refer to Mr Foran as the appellant. The grounds for referral which we paraphrase are that further information has come to light that casts down upon the prosecution case proved by police officers that the appellant had confessed to the count 3 – 6 offences; accordingly, that the verdicts were unsafe.

5. On 16 April 2013 this court (Leveson LJ, Mitting and Males JJ) allowed the appellant's appeal against a quite separate conviction at Birmingham Crown Court on 3 May 1985 on the ground that police evidence was tainted (*Foran* [2013] EWCA Crim 437). However, the evidence under scrutiny in that case concerned an offence which took place in September 1984 and concerned police officers none of whom were involved in the investigation which is the subject of the present appeal.

Summary of evidence at trial

6.	On 12 April 1977 the appellant and his wife were arrested in a jeweller's shop on suspicion that they were attempting to sell stolen property. They were later released without charge. A dispute arose as to the whereabouts of the jewellery in the appellant's possession. The appellant claimed that the police had seized and not returned the jewellery. The police account was that the appellant must have discarded the jewellery after his arrest and before arriving at the police station. Shortly afterwards, acting on information provided by the appellant, the police carried out a surveillance operation in anticipation of a wages robbery. No such robbery occurred. Later, at his trial, the appellant maintained that he had given false information to the police as a hoax in retaliation for his lost jewellery. On 3 May officers attended the appellant's home looking for stolen property. They found a wallet and other documents belonging to Mr Farmer the owner of the garage the subject of count 1 in the indictment. The appellant was arrested and taken to Digbeth Police Station where he was interviewed under caution. The appellant claimed that his children had handed him the wallet the night before his arrest. The appellant was charged and released on bail to appear at Birmingham Magistrates Court on 14 June 1977. He failed to appear and a warrant for his arrest was issued. This is the background to subsequent events. In circumstances to which we shall return the appellant was arrested on 24 October 1977.

7.	In the meantime the robberies the subject of the indictment took place. As to count 3, on 26 September at 4.00 am four men, three of whom were black and of West Indian origin, and the fourth of whom was white, broke into the home of Charles Apechis carrying knives. They robbed Mr Apechis of £2,800 in cash and a quantity of half sovereigns. As to count 4, on 8 October two men, one West Indian and the other white, broke into the home of Natwarlal Trikain and his wife. They entered the couple's bedroom carrying metal bars. The black man took money out of a handbag and left the room. Taking advantage of the momentary distraction, Mr Trikain grabbed the metal bar in the white man's hand. There was a struggle; then both intruders then made their escape. As to counts 5 and 6, the loser in count 5, Richard Rice, owned a jewellers shop in Sparkbrook. Mr Holmes, the loser in count 6 visited Mr Rice shortly before closing time on 13 October. Two black men entered the shop followed by a white man brandishing a sword. He was followed by two more black men. The sword was used to sever the telephone connection to the shop while the contents of two safes were emptied into a black bin bag. Cash was also removed from the till. Mr Holmes was robbed of his wallet. Mrs Rice and her daughter, Karen, interrupted the robbery when they arrived at the front door of the shop which had by this time been locked. As a result the robbers lost their nerve and ran off leaving the bin bag behind them.

8.	On 21 October Detective Sergeant Whelan, stationed at Sparkbrook Police Station, showed Karen Price a number of photographs. She identified a photograph of the appellant as the white man at the robbery of her father's shop. The jury knew of the identification but were instructed that the only admissible evidence of identification came from Mr Holmes (see para. 9 below). On 24 October the appellant was spotted by Detective Constable Davies, a member of the West Midlands Police Serious Crime Squad, driving a car in which a woman was the front seat passenger. Knowing that the appellant was wanted by the police he called for assistance and stopped the car. He arrested the appellant and took him to Acocks Green Police Station. On 26 October while he was in custody the appellant was examined by Dr Tubb. Dr Tubb found 15 bruises on the appellant's body clustered around the front left shoulder and chest, the left upper arm, the abdomen, the right thigh and the left thigh. Their possible age was between two and four days. They were not, in Dr Tubb's opinion, the result of a mere fall because they were too widespread. Some of the marks were linear, suggesting contact with a straight, blunt object. Others were caused by contact with a larger blunt object. If the marks were caused by objects impacting on the body, the force had been considerable. The evidence of the arresting officer, Detective Constable Davies, was that the injuries must have been caused during the fight between himself and the appellant when the appellant resisted arrest. According to Detective Constable Davies punches were thrown and a violent struggle took place while the appellant was both inside and outside the car from which he was removed. Once the appellant was outside the car an officer who arrived in support saw that the appellant and Detective Constable Davies were still grappling with one another but he was unable to say what had occurred in the earlier stages. The appellant's passenger was not called to give evidence; the appellant said he could trace the witness. Detective Constable Davies suggested that the linear marks found on the appellant's body may have been caused by impact with the steering wheel of the appellant's car. There were other possibilities. The appellant's evidence was that there was no fight at the time of arrest. He maintained that later, at the police station, he was beaten up by officers frustrated that he would make no admission.

9. The prosecution had no evidence with which to identify the appellant as being a person present at the robberies the subject of counts 3 and 4. As to counts 5 and 6, there was an identification of the appellant made by Mr Holmes at an identification parade held on 9 November 1977. However, on the same day, Mr Rice picked out a volunteer, while Mrs Rice and Karen picked out a different volunteer.

10. One of the grounds of appeal to the Court of Appeal on which the appellant relied in 1980 was that Mr Apechis (count 3) had since been shown a photograph of the appellant and positively excluded him as the white man who robbed him. The appellant also sought to challenge his conviction of the robbery at Mr Rice's shop (counts 5 and 6) by relying on the prosecution's failure to disclose at trial that the sword allegedly wielded by the appellant contained a single partial fingerprint that could not have been left by him. Part of the judgment of Donaldson LJ refusing the renewed application for leave was read to the House of Commons on 20 July 1982. It contained the following passage:

> "We have given serious consideration as to whether there should have been leave to appeal to enable these applications to call further evidence to be considered. We do not think there are any grounds for granting leave to call that further evidence, bearing in mind our analysis that this was a confession case and that identification or non-identification, or positive evidence that it was not the man, in the circumstances of this case, would not take the matter sufficiently far beyond the state which was reached at the trial when evidence from these two men was read, to justify us giving leave for them to give evidence and re-considering the matters."

Thus, it is conceded by the respondent to the present appeal that the alleged confessions were central to the appellant's convictions.

11. The prosecution case was that the appellant was first interviewed at 5.35 pm on 24 October. Detective Inspector Curry, Detective Sergeant Hancocks and Detective Constable Davies were in the interview room. The appellant made no explicit denial but made no admission either. Detective Inspector Curry and Detective Constable Davies left the interview room, leaving the appellant alone with Detective Sergeant Hancocks. Detective Sergeant Hancocks gave evidence that he encouraged the appellant to respond directly to the accusation that he had participated in the robbery at Rice's shop. He suggested that the appellant must remember whether he had done the robbery or not. Detective Sergeant Hancocks, in response to the appellant's questions, told him that he would probably be asked to attend an identification parade because there were four witnesses. At 6.30 pm on 24 October the appellant was again interviewed by Detective Inspector Curry and Detective Constable Davies. He again made no admissions, saying that daylight robberies were not his style.

12. Those officers left the interview room at 6.55 pm and for a second time the appellant was left alone with Detective Sergeant Hancocks. During their conversation, according to Detective Sergeant Hancocks, the appellant said that he would say nothing about the robbery until he could trust him. He asked for time to think and the officer left the room. At 7.15 pm Detective Sergeant Hancocks returned with Detective Chief Inspector Taylor, recently appointed head of the West Midlands Police Serious Crime Squad. The officers gave evidence that they summarised their information as to the robbery at Rice Jewellers and accused the appellant of being the white man to whom the witnesses had referred. According to them the appellant said he wanted to talk alone with Detective Sergeant Hancocks because he did not know Detective Chief Inspector Taylor.

13. Detective Chief Inspector Taylor left the room. Detective Sergeant Hancocks said in evidence that the appellant started to bargain with him. He was prepared to give information about the robbery together with other crimes, including offences committed in Ireland. The officer replied that he could not make bargains but the appellant proceeded to give him information anyway. It was the defence case that Detective Sergeant Hancocks was lying. The officer's response was to produce the handwritten note there and then made to jot down the information with which the appellant provided him. Detective Sergeant Hancock's note, a copy of which we have seen, contains references to criminal associates meeting in the Vine Public House. The appellant called them "coons". They committed robberies. One of them was a man named Errol. The description given matched the appellant's co-accused Errol Campbell but the appellant did not identify Campbell as one of the robbers at Rice Jewellers. The appellant told Detective Sergeant Hancocks he would be able to recognise the robbers from photographs. He gave information about other crimes including events in Northern Ireland. The exhibit contained two A4 pages of handwriting that bear the appearance of notes spontaneously recorded and supplemented as the information emerged.

14. Detective Sergeant Hancocks said that having recorded this information he brought the appellant back to the Rice Jeweller's robbery. The appellant replied, "Well it was me and the four west Indians. What a cock-up it was". He told Detective Sergeant Hancocks how he had been recruited by the West Indians but denied that he had ever

had the sword in his hand. He claimed that it had been carried by one of the black men who entered the shop after him. He told the officers that he had got "fuck all" from the robbery because it had been "a cock-up". The appellant was asked whether he wanted to make a statement. He said that first the officer should check the information he had been given.

15. Detective Sergeant Hancocks left the room and at 8.15 pm returned with Detective Chief Inspector Taylor. In the appellant's presence Detective Sergeant Hancocks gave Detective Chief Inspector Taylor an account of what had occurred. Detective Chief Inspector Taylor asked the appellant if Detective Sergeant Hancocks' account was correct. The appellant replied that it was but he continued to insist that he had not carried the sword. He told the officers that he did not know the names of the other robbers (despite having referred to Errol earlier) but he could provide details and would do so only if the charge against him was dropped. The appellant was told that he had been identified by one of the witnesses from photographs. The officers could make no promises to him. Shortly after the interview the officers together made their notes of the appellant's account of the robberies and his admission. That account was consistent with the statements of the witnesses. The appellant told the officers "I'll give you them (i.e. the West Indians) if you drop the charges against me". Detective Chief Inspector Taylor asked the appellant if he would make a statement. He replied that he would do it "tomorrow".

16. Detective Sergeant Whelan, the officer who had shown the photographs to Karen Rice, gave evidence that at some point later that evening he had visited the appellant in custody at the police station. He had with him Detective Constable Bawden who was also stationed at Sparkbrook. Neither officer was a member of the Serious Crime Squad. Since Detective Sergeant Whelan was the officer in charge of the case in Sparkbrook he needed to see the appellant. Detective Sergeant Whelan informed the appellant that he had been told by Detective Sergeant Hancocks that he had admitted the Rice Jewellers robbery earlier that evening. According to Detective Sergeant Whelan and Detective Constable Bawden the appellant confirmed the truth of the statement. However, on the following day, 25 October, the appellant declined to make a written statement. On 22 December he was committed for trial and remanded to HMP Leicester. On 13 March 1978 Errol Campbell was arrested. He admitted his participation in the robberies charged in all four counts and in the course of his written statement implicated the appellant as the white man. The jury was informed of the statement but were directed that it was only admissible in the case of Campbell. Armed with this statement Detective Constable Davies and Detective Sergeant Jennings, both members of the Serious Crime Squad, travelled to Leicester to interview the appellant. They gave evidence that the appellant admitted his involvement and together they completed their notes of the conversation in a car outside the prison.

17. There was a dispute as to whether the appellant was willing to see the officers at all. A prison officer, Mr Law, gave evidence in the defence case. The prosecution produced a letter from the Chief Constable of the West Midlands Police to the governor of the prison confirming an arrangement for the visit. Also produced was a consent form signed by the appellant in which his rights as a prisoner in custody were set out. Mr Law gave evidence that the document was signed by the appellant either immediately outside or inside the interview room. The officers maintained that Mr Law entered the

interview room and was present when the document was signed by the appellant. Mr Law agreed that when the appellant signed the document he must have known the identity of the officers who were to interview him: the appellant was either in the room with them or could see them through the glass door. According to the officers they first asked the appellant whether he recognised the names of some West Indian men. The appellant replied that he did not. The officers informed the appellant that they had in their possession a statement from Errol Campbell who was in custody at Bardesley Green Police Station. The statement was being read aloud to the appellant when the appellant jumped up and walked to the door of the interview room saying "That's it. I have heard enough". Detective Constable Davies suggested to the appellant that it was in his own interests to listen to what Campbell had said about him. According to the officers, when informed that Campbell had implicated him in all three robberies, the appellant responded by nodding and said, "OK Johnny [Davies], fair enough but if you hadn't had locked the coon up I had a fifty-fifty chance of getting away with it". The officer asked, "Am I to take it Martin, that you are admitting your part in the other offences?" The appellant replied, "Yes, I have got to give it to you, Johnny, you've worked hard. You know I am a bit of a con man, but how did you get Campbell? Did somebody put him in?" The appellant was asked whether he wished to make a statement. He replied that he wanted to speak to his solicitor first. He asked the officers to visit his wife in hospital where she had just given birth to their child. He wanted them to tell her that he knew what he was doing.

18. In cross-examination the officers maintained that at no stage did the appellant ask that Prison Officer Law should be in the interview room. He was present when the appellant signed the consent form and then left of his own volition. Mr Law gave evidence that the appellant was reluctant to be interviewed. Through the glass partition he could see that the appellant had got to his feet on between two and five occasions. However, at no stage did the appellant terminate the interview (as he had been told he could) but, towards the end, Mr Law said that he was asked to enter the room in order to hear the appellant's denial of a proposition that was put to him. However, Mr Law could not recall what it was that the appellant was denying. Afterwards he left the room of his own volition. Mr Law recalled that as the officers were walking towards the gate while the appellant was being escorted by Mr Law back to his cell, the appellant was repeating to the officers his request for a favour which, it was apparent to him, the appellant had already made in the interview room. Mr Law could not recall what the favour was.

19. The judge reminded the jury of the appellant's evidence of this visit. The appellant said he thought he was going to be visited by his wife. We note that it would be difficult to reconcile that belief with an assertion that his wife had just given birth in hospital. The appellant said that he declined to see the officers and asked to be returned to his cell. Detective Constable Davies told him that they had his solicitor's permission to see him. He thereupon signed the consent form. The appellant said that as soon as he heard his name mentioned in Campbell's statement he stood up and asked to be returned to his cell. As we have said, that assertion was not supported by Prison Officer Law. The officer suggested that it was in the appellant's interest to listen. Detective Sergeant Jennings said that he wished to speak to the appellant alone and Detective Constable Davies left the room with Mr Law. That assertion is also inconsistent with Mr Law's evidence. The appellant claimed that Detective Sergeant Jennings told him that if he was prepared to admit the Rice Jewellers robbery he

would guarantee that his wife would not be arrested on suspicion of offences in Ireland. The appellant said that he made no admission to the officers of any offence. When informed by Jennings that he would go to hospital to charge his wife the appellant requested that he pass on his love to his wife and tell her not to worry.

20.   In his evidence the appellant denied that he was aware that he was on bail to appear at the magistrates' court in June 1977. He claimed that Detective Constable Davies had let him go on condition that if he acquired information that he was prepared to give to the police about other offences at a later stage the charge of burglary and theft of Mr Farmer's wallet (count 1) would be dropped. It was the appellant said, police bail pending further enquiries. The prosecution produced exhibit 9, the charge sheet in which, contrary to the appellant's evidence, he had been charged with the offence. The appellant denied that the reference to bail to the magistrates' court was in the copy that had been provided to him. The prosecution case was that there were up to six copies of the document. The appellant denied that the signature on the bail form was his own. However, the officer who prepared the document and obtained the appellant's signature gave evidence that had the appellant not signed his acknowledgement of bail he would not have been released from the police station.

21.   The appellant maintained that there had been no fight when he was arrested by Detective Constable Davies. At the police station he was taken to a cell by Detective Sergeant Hancocks and later retrieved by Detective Constable Davies. In the interview room were Detective Sergeant Hancocks, Detective Inspector Curry, Detective Constable Davies and a fourth, unidentified officer. The appellant said that Davies fetched some paper and told the appellant that he would now have a statement from him about the robbery. When the appellant refused Detective Constable Davies twisted his ears and said, "You are fucking Uncle John about, now make a statement". When the appellant again refused he was pulled off his chair by his hair and kicked by Detective Inspector Curry and Detective Constable Davies. The appellant said that he would prefer to talk to Curry than to him. Davies fetched a truncheon and rammed it into his stomach. Hancocks and another officer held up the appellant's legs while Curry kicked him. The appellant said that despite this beating he had never made admissions and he had not given Detective Sergeant Hancocks any information. The note made by the officer was a fabrication. The appellant accepted, however, that when Detective Sergeant Whelan visited him the Sergeant informed him that he understood the appellant had made earlier admissions to Detective Sergeant Hancocks. According to the appellant, he responded, "You have got to be joking. They beat the hell out of me."

22.   The appellant agreed that he told the police he could not recall where he was on 13 October. He said that while in custody on remand he worked backwards and recalled that he had an alibi for the time of the robbery. He had been visiting a Mrs Kyle. He recalled using a taxi because his own car was at a garage. Mrs Kyle, he agreed, had visited the appellant in prison several times. Mrs Maisey Hamilton, Mrs Kyle and Mrs Kyle's daughter gave evidence in support of the alibi. The prosecution did not dispute that the appellant had visited Mrs Kyle. They challenged that the witnesses were honest and/or accurate about the date of the visit. As to the circumstantial detail that the appellant had used a taxi because his own car was at a garage, when asked to name the garage the appellant was unable to do so and was evasive when challenged.

The summing up

23. In the course of his summing up Judge Ross QC explained to the jury that the prosecution relied on identification only in the case of the Rice Jewellers robbery in counts 5 and 6. Later, he pointed out that in relation to count 3 the victim's description of the white intruder bore no resemblance to the appellant. Although Mr Trikain and his wife (count 4) purported to give a general description of their attackers, both of them said that they had covered their faces with articles of clothing. As to Mr Holmes' identification of the appellant, (counts 5 and 6) the judge gave the jury an incomplete *Turnbull* direction. He instructed them as to the dangers of identification evidence even by perfectly honest witnesses. He pointed out the factors that the jury would need to examine in order to assess the opportunity that Mr Holmes had to make an accurate identification. They should compare his face to face identification with the description earlier given in a statement. He reminded the jury of the contrary identifications made by Mr and Mrs Rice and their daughter. The judge did not make specific reference to the court's knowledge of cases of miscarriages of justice occasioned by the identification evidence of perfectly honest witnesses. In his witness statement Mr Holmes described the white man as aged about 40 with moles on his right cheek. The appellant was aged about 30 and did have moles on both cheeks. At the identification parade all those who stood wore brown paper 'plasters' on their cheeks. Mr Holmes said that he could tell from his accent that the white man was Irish, as was the appellant. Mr Holmes had described the man as having fair hair. The appellant did not have fair hair. Mr Holmes ascribed his mistake to the fact that the man had been wearing a hat. The judge advised the jury to look for other evidence in support of the identification and informed them that the supporting evidence derived from the appellant's alleged admissions. The jury would have to resolve the dispute in the evidence as to the circumstances in which the appellant suffered his injuries and the accounts of the admissions made by the appellant to the officers.

24. The judge reminded the jury of the evidence of Police Constable Flemming, the officer in charge of the desk at Digbeth Police Station on 3 May. He did not claim to remember the appellant personally but he described the process of charge and admission to bail as routine.

25. The judge reminded the jury that the note of the first interview between Detective Constable Davies, Detective Inspector Curry and Detective Sergeant Hancocks was made jointly by the officers. He invited the jury to consider whether Detective Sergeant Hancocks was telling the truth when he said that when alone with the appellant the appellant appeared more willing to talk to him. The critical conversation occurred when Detective Sergeant Hancocks was alone with the appellant after Detective Chief Inspector Taylor's first visit with Hancocks to see the appellant at 7.15 pm. The judge reminded the jury of the relevant contents of the note Detective Sergeant Hancocks said he had made in the appellant's presence as follows (page 36):

> "Meet in the Vine Pub. Can show house in Small Heath (West Indian) with stolen gear. Col", which I suppose is there for coloured, "n.s. etc. Near Golden Hillock Road. House where robbery property goes to (can show) in Bardsley Green Road above police station – white bloke Richard Woolley. Wife knows jewellery trade and West Indian uses them. Uses his

mothers as a safe house at …" I have difficulty in reading that bit members of the jury. "She owns second hand shop at Digbeth. Ricky looks after the coons in the robberies". Then there is a series of references to different people. One was, "West Indian, Errol, 5'8" bushy hair, dresses well, uses Vine and frequents Small Heath. White girlfriend". You heard evidence from another police officer, not Hancocks, that that is a description that fits Errol Campbell a man who has been so frequently mentioned in the course of these proceedings".

The judge continued with the following comment:

"The significance really of this document which goes on later to describe various places in Ireland is this: the defendant says it was not written in his presence. He denies having given any of this information to Hancocks. Therefore, you are left to ask yourself which of the two of them is giving anything like an accurate account of this particular interview? One of the questions the Crown asks you to ask yourselves is whether it is really conceivable that Detective Sergeant Hancocks just made this document up out of thin air or whether it can only have come into existence because it is a note of what the defendant at that time was telling him. If it was, does it or does it not, in part at least, relate to Errol Campbell and, on another part, does it or does it not relate to the defendant's movements in Ireland?"

26. The judge reminded the jury that according to Detective Sergeant Hancocks the appellant gave an account of the Rice Jewellers robbery that accorded with the evidence of the witnesses. It was the appellant, Hancocks said, who described the robbery as a cock-up from which he had received no gain. The judge concluded with these words:

"Members of the jury, yours is the task to determine where the truth lies in this case. Did Detective Sergeant Hancocks make that up or is that what he was told? Not necessarily word for word as he made a note of it afterwards, but is that the substance of what he was told? If it is, is that or is it not a reasonably accurate description of what happened in Mr Rice's shop? You bear in mind his evidence about it and Mr Holmes' evidence about it and, for that matter, the evidence of Mrs Rice of how she came to the shop and upset the whole business by knocking on the door. It is for you to decide … as to whether or not that evidence leads you to the conclusion that the identification made by Mr Holmes is, in fact, the correct identification."

27. The judge summarised the evidence that Detective Chief Inspector Taylor and Detective Sergeant Hancocks returned to the appellant who repeated and expanded on the version already provided to Hancocks, while at the same time attempting to bargain his way out of the charge against himself. The judge concluded:

"Once again, are Detective Sergeant Hancocks and Detective Chief Inspector Taylor telling you the truth? Not necessarily word for word because these are not notes made as the words are spoken, they are words made shortly afterwards, but have they told you the substance of what this man was saying at that time?"

28. The judge reminded the jury of the agreed evidence that following the interview on 24 October Detective Chief Inspector Taylor went to fetch the appellant's wife so that she could visit the appellant in custody, the judge commented upon the evidence as follows:

"...at the defendant's request Detective Chief Inspector Taylor went and got Mrs Foran and brought her to the station and she was allowed to see him. Again members of the jury, it is a matter for you, but it is the defendant's version ... that in the course of these successive interviews between himself and the police officers he was beaten up because he would not confess. It is then a question for you, the officers who have just given this man a beating fetch his wife to the police station and say that she can see him within a matter of hours of the beating having taken place. It is a matter for you whether you think that is an allegation that makes sense or not."

As to the visitors, Detective Sergeant Whelan and Detective Constable Bawden, later that evening, the judge reminded the jury that the appellant did not dispute that Whelan opened the conversation by saying, "I understand from that you have admitted responsibility for that job, is that right?" The judge added no further comment but we observe that the jury may well have concluded that it was hardly likely that Whelan would have used those words to the appellant unless Hancocks had in fact told him that the appellant had made the admission. If that was the jury's view, they might also have concluded that it was improbable Detective Sergeant Hancocks would so have informed the officer in charge of the case unless the admission had been made by the appellant.

29. The judge made plain to the jury that as a matter of common sense counts 5 and 6 must stand or fall together. There was an overlap in the evidence relevant to counts 3 – 6 only in the sense that Detective Sergeant Jennings and Detective Constable Davies asserted that at HMP Leicester on 3 April 1978 the appellant made admissions to all three robberies. However, in the case of counts 3 and 4, there was no evidence independent of the police officers to associate the appellant with those offences.

The additional and fresh material

30. In the course of her submissions Ms Nicholls relied upon the statement of Charles Apechis absolving the appellant of responsibility for the count 3 burglary and upon the admission by the prosecution that by reason of an oversight the prosecution had failed to disclose the fingerprint evidence relating to the sword recovered from the scene of the robbery in counts 5 and 6. Notwithstanding the refusal of leave by the court in 1982 and the acknowledgement by the CCRC that the evidence was unlikely to assist the appellant in the present appeal, Ms Nicholls submits that these are both

factors that this court should consider when examining the safety of the verdicts. In the Commission's view, and as Ms Nicholls acknowledged, the fingerprint evidence was of marginal assistance to the appellant since the evidence revealed that the sword was handled by more than one person; it follows that at least one person handled the sword but left no recoverable finger impressions.

31. It is acknowledged on both sides that the evidence that was critical to the convictions related to the admissions allegedly made to police officers.

32. In August 1989 the West Midlands Police Serious Crime Squad was disbanded. There followed an investigation into its practices by the West Yorkshire Police under the supervision of the Police Complaints Authority. Efforts were made to trace all of those arrested by the Serious Crime Squad during the years between 1986 and 1989. There was revealed a catalogue of malpractice which included physical abuse, the generation of false confessions, the planting of evidence and the mishandling of informants. At least 33 convictions resulting from tainted evidence given by members of the squad have been quashed by this court including some convictions emanating from the work of officers who were or became members of the Serious Crime Squad as early as the mid-1970s, the most notorious of which were the convictions of the Birmingham Six (see *McIlkenny and Others* [1991] 93 Cr App R 287; see also *O'Toole and Murphy* [2006] EWCA Crim 951; *Wilcox* [2010] EWCA Crim 1732; and *Dunne and Others* [2001] EWCA Crim 169).

33. Those officers who gave evidence concerning counts 3 – 6 of the present indictment and were members of the Serious Crime Squad in 1977 and 1978 were Detective Chief Inspector Taylor, Detective Sergeant Hancocks, Detective Sergeant Jennings and Detective Constable Davies. Detective Inspector Curry, Detective Sergeant Whelan and Detective Constable Bawden were not members of the Squad.

34. Membership by police officers of the Serious Crime Squad in the mid-1970s is not an automatic gateway to successful appeals against historic convictions obtained by evidence of confession. In *John Edwards* [1991] 93 Cr App R 48, the then Lord Chief Justice, Lord Lane, gave guidance to trial judges as to the permissible limits of cross-examination of police witnesses as to credit. Giving the judgment of the court, Lord Lane said, at page 55:

> "Generally speaking, questions may be put to a witness as to any improper conduct of which he may be guilty, for the purposes of testing his credit." (Note: see now section 100 of the Criminal Justice Act 2003).

Usually, the questioner would be bound by an answer given to a question going only to credit, but where the evidence went as far as to establish bias, evidence might be called in rebuttal of any denial by the witness. Thus, evidence of systematic misconduct in the investigation of suspects or in the management of witnesses may be admissible. Lord Lane continued:

> "So far as the matters advanced by Mr Hacking [counsel for the appellant] are concerned, the police officers could certainly be cross-examined as to any relevant criminal offences or disciplinary charges found proved against them. That leaves the

following matters: should questions be permitted as to – (1) complaints by members of the public about the behaviour of the witness on other occasions not yet adjudicated upon by the Police Complaints Authority; (2) discreditable conduct by other officers in the same squad; (3) other cases in which the witness has given evidence which has resulted in acquittal of the defendant at the trial or the quashing of the conviction on appeal? This is an area where it is impossible and would be unwise to lay down hard and fast rules as to how the court should exercise its discretion. The objective must be to present the jury as far as possible with a fair, balanced picture of the witness' reliability, bearing in mind on the one hand the importance of eliciting facts which may show, if it be the case, that the police officer is not the truthful person he represents himself to be, but bearing in mind on the other hand the fact that a multiplicity of complaints may indicate no more than what was described before us as the "band-wagon" effect. We do not consider that it would have been proper to suggest to the officer in the present case that he had committed perjury of any other criminal offence by putting to him that he had been charged but not yet tried. Nor do we think that complaints to the Police Complaints Authority which have not been adjudicated on would properly be the subject to cross-examination. It would not be proper to direct questions to an officer about allegedly discreditable conduct of other officers, whether or not they happen to be serving in the same squad."

35.   Lord Lane gave consideration to the admissibility of questions concerning acquittals and other cases in which an officer had given evidence that may have been disbelieved. Having examined the authorities he said, at page 59:

> "Relevance, and therefore admissibility, is a matter of degree and has to be considered not by rule of thumb but against the background of each individual case. One of the considerations, we repeat, is the necessity of keeping the criminal process in proper bounds and avoiding the pursuit of side issues which are only of marginal relevance to the jury's decision. It will accordingly, as the judgment in *Thorne* made clear, be rare that the judge in his discretion will allow cross-examination about the activities of a witness in other cases and the outcome of those cases. The reason is that an acquittal, save in exceptional circumstances, by no means necessarily means that the jury has disbelieved the police officer who has given evidence at the defendant's submissions."

36.   The issue that arises in the present appeal is not, as in *John Edwards*, whether proper disclosure was made to the defence of the result of disciplinary proceedings to which an officer had been subject but whether, in the light of later events, it is demonstrated that the officers' evidence was unreliable and, accordingly, that the verdicts are unsafe. That would involve a consideration by the court of the particular facts of the

appeal before them, including the nature of the information available to the court as to the discredit of witnesses who gave evidence in the original trial. Ms Nicholls, in the course of her submissions disclaimed any attempt in this appeal to establish guilt by association. That which concerns this court, she accepted, is whether there is material, subsequently gathered, that taints the credit of the witness to such an extent that the safety of the verdicts is placed in doubt. That issue may be tested, and has been tested in similar appeals, by considering whether, had the material been available at the time of trial, cross examination upon it would have been permitted and, if so, whether that cross examination may have had the effect of casting doubt upon the reliability of the witness and thus the safety of the verdict. However, evidence may be tainted by subsequent events although no specific findings of corruption or perjury have been made against an officer concerned.

37.   In *Maxine Edwards* [1996] 2 Cr App R 345 the appellant had been arrested by Detective Constable Gillan and Police Constable Carroll on suspicion of being in possession of crack cocaine. At her trial she asserted that the officers were lying when they claimed that the drug was in her hands. It had been recovered from the back seat of her co-accused's car next to which she had been standing at the time of her arrest. They were also lying when they claimed she had made compromising remarks to the officers when she was being conveyed to the police station. Ms Edwards was convicted of possession of a class A drug with intent to supply, her appeal was dismissed and she was deported. Subsequently, her case was referred back to the Court of Appeal by the Home Secretary, using his powers under section 17 of the Criminal Appeal Act 1968. The arresting officers had been members of the Stoke Newington drug squad which in intervening years had been the subject of an investigation, Operation Jackpot, and severe criticism of the integrity of the squad. Several convictions that had depended upon similar evidence had been overturned on appeal, some with the agreement of the prosecution. It was argued by the respondent in the appeal of Ms Edwards, however, that, since the investigation had exposed no explicit wrongdoing by the officers who arrested her, the appeal should be dismissed. Beldam LJ, giving the judgment of the court, said at page 350:

> "Mr Aylett urged us that now enquiries had been completed and no charges had been brought, nor disciplinary action taken, involving either of the officers who gave evidence in the case of this appellant, we should take the view that there was no reason to regard her conviction as unsafe. Whilst there is much to be said for Mr Aylett's approach, the fact remains that in 1993 the degree of suspicion of the trustworthiness of the evidence of Constable Carroll, and those with whom he was working from day to day was such that the Crown considered convictions based upon that evidence could not safely be supported. Once the suspicion of perjury starts to infect the evidence and permeate cases in which the witnesses have been involved, and which are closely similar, the evidence on which such convictions are based becomes as questionable as it was in the cases in which the appeals have already been allowed."

Thus, the reach of discredit may have become institutional. Although there had been no adverse finding express or implied against Detective Constable Gillan, it was sufficient that the evidence of Constable Carroll was tainted by his discredited appearance in other cases. The appeal was allowed.

38. This was an issue again examined by the Court of Appeal in *Crook* [2003] EWCA Crim 1272 (Judge LJ, Andrew Smith J and HHJ Richard Brown). The target of the appeal was the reliability of evidence given at trial by Detective Constable Geaghan. The squad in which he served had been the subject of investigation. As a result 25 officers were charged with offences or suspended from duty. Detective Constable Geaghan was not one of them. Nonetheless it was argued that he was covered by the "general taint" of evidence of the squad's activities. Judge LJ, delivering the judgment of the court said, at paragraph 21, that taint may properly be attributed to those found guilty of misconduct and those who turned a blind eye to the misconduct of other officers of which they were aware. The same considerations did not apply to officers of whom it was not established that they either participated in misconduct or, being aware of it, said nothing. Nothing had been produced that could have been put to Detective Constable Geaghan in cross examination and his participation in the investigation was, in any event, limited. There was material that could have been put to another officer, Detective Inspector Brown, but his involvement in the investigation had also been extremely limited and he had not given evidence at the trial. In the result, the court saw no basis on which to find that the safety of the conviction was undermined.

39. Each case must be decided upon the court's assessment of its particular facts. We shall turn to examine the material on which the appellant now relies to undermine the safety of his conviction.

Detective Constable Davies

40. Detective Constable Davies was central to the investigation of the appellant although he was not present on 24 October when any alleged admission was made. He arrested the appellant for the theft of Mr Farmer's wallet. He arrested him again on 24 October 1977. He interviewed the appellant following his arrest and again after charge at HMP Leicester. Detective Constable Davies, according to the appellant, took the lead when officers adopted a threatening manner towards the appellant and assaulted him when he refused to make a statement.

41. The appellant relies upon the accepted fact that Detective Sergeant Hornby and Detective Constable Davies both served in the Serious Crime Squad, subsequently the subject of close scrutiny and criticism. It is common ground that the reliability of Detective Sergeant Hornby as a witness has been severely compromised by decisions of the court in several subsequent appeals. It is unnecessary to repeat the details here. Nonetheless, in none of those appeals has Detective Constable Davies featured either as a participant or as a witness. There are undoubtedly occasions between 1974 and 1978 when Hornby and Davies would have been working together but, with one possible exception with which we deal below, we are not persuaded that there has been any explicit or implied finding adverse to Detective Constable Davies concerning any of those occasions.

42. The appellant relies specifically upon the involvement of Detective Constable Davies with Detective Sergeant Hornby in the investigation which led to the arrest and prosecution of the Birmingham Six in November 1974. There were appeals against conviction in 1987 and 1991. In 1991 the convictions of the six men were quashed. The Court of Appeal held that two issues, considered separately, would lead to the conclusion that the convictions were unsafe. The first concerned the reliability of

chemical tests performed during the investigation for the purpose of connecting explosive material to the defendants. The second concerned the police evidence as to the making of contemporaneous notes of interview. During the appeal evidence of electrostatic document analysis (ESDA) was introduced as a means of testing the accuracy of interview records in which Richard McIlkenny reportedly made a confession. The analysis showed that the records were not contemporaneous as the interviewing officers had stated when giving their evidence at trial but were composed, at least in significant part, after the event. In 1991 the Court of Appeal found that the four officers who had contended otherwise in evidence had misled the court.

43. There also featured in the appeals in both 1987 and 1991 a document that became known as "the Reade Schedule". It had seven columns headed by Superintendent Reade respectively, "Date", "Time", "Officers", "Prisoners", "Place", "Reference", and "Knowledge of". Entries covered the period 3.15 am on 22 November to 3.15 pm on 24 November and many of them were alterations and corrections of earlier entries. When asked in 1987 what was the purpose of the document Superintendent Reade said, after giving conflicting accounts, that he could not remember. At [1991] 93 Cr App R at page 309, in his judgment given on behalf of the court, Lloyd LJ observed that it was probable that the schedule was not a running record of the interview of suspects but a record prepared shortly after the interviewing had been completed. It was argued by counsel for the appellants that the purpose of the schedule must have been to nominate, after the event, in which interview, with which officers a suspect had made admissions. At 3.05 pm on Saturday, November 23 the appellant Hugh Callaghan was interviewed. In the column headed "Officers", Superintendent Reade had written, "DS Hornby and crew". Detective Constable Davies was a member of Detective Sergeant Hornby's crew. On the last page of the schedule was written "Davies and Bryant will be OK". Other entries in the schedule caused the Court of Appeal in 1991 serious misgivings. However, in the first appeal in 1987 the court had heard Superintendent Reade give evidence and rejected the appellants' contention that the schedule was a "blueprint for perjury". In 1991 the court concluded, at page 310:

> "We need go no further than to say that on the evidence now before us, Superintendent Reade deceived the court. We do not think we should go further than that, without having heard from Superintendent Reade and the other officers alleged to be part to the conspiracy."

Lloyd LJ's reference to deceit concerned the evidence given about the interviews with Richard McIllkenny and not, as far we can discern from the judgment, those with the appellant Hugh Callaghan.

44. Detective Constable Davies did not give evidence in the trial of the Birmingham Six or in the appeals. We do not know the reason. At the time of the hearing in the present appeal it was not known whether Detective Constable Davies had made a witness statement. We have since been provided with a typed but unsigned and undated copy of Detective Constable Davies' witness statement, which appears from its pagination to have formed part of a file of evidence. He was never asked to account for the interview with Callaghan and the court in 1991 made no explicit findings in respect of it. The court's conclusions were, at page 317, as follows:

"As with Walker, the case against Callaghan rests primarily on his written statement under caution. He confessed almost at once when seen by Detective Sergeant Hornby, Detective Constable Bryant and Detective Constable Davies at 2.55 pm on Saturday November 23. As with Walker, his statement under caution is in two colours of ink. Some of Callaghan's signatures are in black ink. Some in blue. Unlike the other appellants, Callaghan does not allege police brutality other than a single slap in the face. Part of what appears in his statement is, he said, true; part he made up for the benefit of the police, and part the police made up themselves. He signed the statement under caution, implicating Hunter in the bombing of the Mulberry Bush, because he felt threatened. On the Sunday, he was seen again, he told the police that Walker was a brigadier in the IRA, Hunter a captain and the others all lieutenants. This was not a police invention, since Callaghan admitted in evidence that he had given their ranks, but said that he had picked the ranks at random, and that they were not in fact members of the IRA."

45. In his witness statement Detective Sergeant Davies said that at 2.30 pm on Saturday 23 November 1974, he went with Detective Sergeant Hornby and others to Sutton Coalfield police station where they saw Hugh Callaghan. Mr Callaghan almost immediately said that he wished to make a written statement. Hugh Callaghan, said Davies, "then threw his arms around me and sobbed on my shoulder". Shortly afterwards Detective Sergeant Hornby took down Callaghan's statement at his dictation. While the statement was taken Callaghan cried continually.

46. There is no doubt that in 1974 Detective Sergeant Hornby was the leader of a "crew" of which Detective Constable Davies was a member but we are unable to accept that by virtue alone of the entry in Superintendent Reade's schedule, the Court of Appeal can be taken as having made any finding against Detective Constable Davies, expressly or impliedly. On the other hand, at page 318 of its judgment, the court pointed out the inconsistencies between the confessions of Hugh Callaghan and John Walker. As we have seen, Callaghan accepted that in parts he told the truth while in others he lied for the benefit of the police. He claimed that some of his confession was made up by the police. This, however, was not an issue that was resolved by the court and Callaghan's allegation does not appear ever to have been put to Davies. The court had concluded that four officers, not those engaged in Callaghan's interview, had at least deceived the trial in the course of their evidence: Superintendent Reade, Detective Sergeant Morris, Detective Constable Woodwiss and Detective Constable Langford. The court concluded that in consequence the police evidence at trial was so unreliable that the convictions as a whole were unsafe and unsatisfactory.

47. In the course of argument this court expressed concern at the prospect of making adverse findings about Detective Constable Davies in the absence of such a finding by the Court of Appeal in *McIlkenny* or in any other case that his evidence had been unreliable or that his participation in an investigation had been in any way suspect. Such a finding would indeed amount to guilt by association. However, Mr Rees QC, on behalf of the respondent, drew our attention to the decision of the court in the

appellant's earlier appeal. On 3 May 1985 the appellant had been convicted of robbery and conspiracy to rob. One of the witnesses who gave evidence of an alleged confession was Detective Inspector Paul Matthews. The appellant relied on further material that had become available since his earlier appeals. First was the background evidence as to the misconduct of the West Midlands Police Serious Crime Squad. Second was Detective Inspector Matthews' involvement in the cases of *McIlkenny* (above) and *O'Toole and Murphy* [2006] EWCA Crim 2123. In the investigation of *McIlkenny* Detective Constable Matthews, as he then was, interviewed the appellant Richard Hill. He gave evidence that Hill implicated two other accused, Murray and Sheehan. Just as, in the case of Hugh Callaghan's interview, the court did not single out any officer for specific criticism but made the generic finding that the fresh investigation carried out by the Devon and Cornwall Constabulary, and in particular the ESDA evidence, rendered the police evidence and therefore the convictions unsafe. However, Detective Sergeant Matthews, as he then was, also gave evidence in the trial of *O'Toole and Murphy* whose subsequent convictions were quashed (Laws LJ, Collins and Silber JJ). It emerged in the appeal of *O'Toole and Murphy* that Matthews had in September 1986 been made the subject of an adjudication for disobedience to orders and neglect of duty. He was required to resign from the force. Furthermore, in November 1985 a jury disbelieved the evidence of the officer in the trial of Herring and Fitzgerald. These were both matters that had been raised in an earlier appeal mounted by O'Toole & Murphy. However, in the appeal of *Foran* LJ Leveson, giving the judgment of the court, pointed out (reflecting the views of Lord Lane in *John Edwards,* para. 34 above) that notwithstanding the absence of specific findings against Matthews subsequent to the earlier appeals of O'Toole & Murphy there was no hard and fast rule as to the ambit of legitimate cross-examination going to the credit of the officer. At paragraph 33 of his judgment LJ Leveson, speaking of the judgment of the court in *O'Toole and Murphy*, said:

> "33.   Laws LJ then concluded (at para 44) that DI Matthews and other officers could properly have been cross-examined on the matters to his discredit referred to above which had emerged (including the Herring case, which here does not appear to have been regarded as a case where DI Matthews evidence was disbelieved). The 1995 decision of this court in which little or no weight was given to the Herring case does not appear to have been cited in *O'Toole & Murphy*, but despite this, we consider that the same conclusion as in *O'Toole & Murphy*, must apply here, that is to say, that at the trial in the present case DI Matthews could properly have been cross-examined if those matters had been known, as to his involvement in (at least) the Herring, McIlkenny and O'Toole cases, all of which involved fabricated or allegedly fabricated confessions, sometimes in circumstances with similarities to the present case and which together suggest a disturbing pattern, against the background of his membership of the discredited West Midlands Serious Crime Squad, as well as his disciplinary record."

48.   With respect to Mr Rees's argument, we see a stark distinction to be made between the positions of Detective Inspector Matthews and Detective Constable Davies. It may

be that if there was in the present case hard or even inferential evidence of misconduct to the witness' discredit in other cases, or of his suspected participation in corrupt practices with witnesses or defendants, cross-examination as to his involvement in the interviews of Hugh Callaghan would have been permissible. In the present case, however, not only is there no evidence to Detective Constable Davies' discredit in other cases but he did not give evidence in the trial of *McIlkenny and Others*. In the absence of an adverse finding by the Court of Appeal, the basis for putative cross-examination in Mr Foran's trial would have been flimsy and inconclusive. All that exists is a suspicious entry in the Reade Schedule that, at best, is likely to have been double hearsay for which there may be a perfectly innocent explanation. Had there been evidence that, as in the case of Detective Inspector Matthews, Davies was implicated in any way in the corrupt practices of the Serious Crime Squad in the 1980s, this court would be able to take a different view. In the absence of such evidence we are un-persuaded that we should approach the position of Detective Constable Davies in the present appeal as though he were in the same position as Detective Inspector Matthews in Mr Foran's successful appeal against his 1985 conviction. We conclude that the assertions made as to Detective Constable Davies' credibility amount on examination to no more than unsubstantiated speculation within the third category of witnesses described by Judge LJ, as he then was, at paragraph 21 of his judgment in *Crook*.

Detective Chief Inspector Taylor and Detective Sergeant Jennings

49. We turn to the role of Detective Chief Inspector Taylor. Mr Taylor was an important witness since the prosecution asserted that, on two occasions, he was consulted by Detective Sergeant Hancocks and then accompanied Detective Sergeant Hancocks to interview the appellant. He confirmed Detective Sergeant Hancocks' evidence that during the last interview between them on 24 October the appellant was admitting the robbery at Rice Jewellers. Detective Sergeant Jennings interviewed the appellant with Detective Constable Davies at HMP Leicester on 3 April 1978.

50. The material on which the appellant relies concerns the police investigation into Keith Twitchell's alleged participation in a robbery and manslaughter that took place on 13 November 1980, three years after the investigation in the present case. After Mr Twitchell's unsuccessful appeal against conviction in 1983, the CCRC referred the matter back to the court in 1998. In *Twitchell* [2000] 1 Cr App R 373 (Rose LJ, Vice President, Jowitt and Hooper JJ), the appeal was allowed and his convictions were quashed. Keith Twitchell was arrested at 11.55 am on the morning of the robbery in which the victim was shot dead. A stolen Ford Escort had been used to facilitate the robbery of a Securicor van. The police evidence was that recovered from the defendant's girlfriend's home was his cloth cap on which was found, on examination by a forensic scientist, a single fibre that matched the carpet in the stolen Ford Escort. A stolen Daimler was also used in the robbery to facilitate escape. The police gave evidence that Twitchell was seen in the car after the robbery, that tools from the stolen Daimler were found in Twitchell's motorcar and that toys and a tool box from the Daimler had been found in Twitchell's lock-up garage. The appellant's case was that these items had been planted by the police. However, the Court of Appeal proceeded on its assessment that the case against the defendant rested primarily on admissions allegedly made in interview.

51. The defendant was interviewed on 14 November. At first he said he was at home at the time of the robbery. The officers gave evidence that, when they produced the statements of his two co-accused, the defendant began to make admissions. Those officers included Detective Sergeant Hornby, Detective Sergeant Jennings and Detective Constable Brown. Twitchell's account was that he had made no such admissions. He was stripped so that his clothes could be forensically examined. He was effectively naked. He was told that the officers wanted a statement. When he refused to make a statement the officers screamed at him. He was handcuffed to a chair and a plastic bag was placed over his head. In consequence and in fear he signed a statement written by the officers and, the following day, signed a second statement. He also admitted a robbery in Sheffield of which he was later acquitted in a separate trial. Mr Twitchell did not implicate Detective Sergeant Jennings personally in the physical assault upon him but he was present, he said, during at least part of the fabricated interview when pressure was being placed upon him to make a confession.

52. Detective Chief Inspector Taylor gave evidence that he was present during the first interview and he could therefore confirm that no assault had been committed by his officers on the defendant. Mr Twitchell's evidence was that Taylor was not present. Detective Sergeant Brown later became Chief Superintendent. Some years later, in a civil action for damages brought by another convicted but unrelated defendant, Mr Treadaway, against the Chief Constable of the West Midlands Police, Mackinnon J made an explicit finding to a high degree of probability that Mr Treadaway had been assaulted by five officers of the Serious Crime Squad including Detective Sergeant Brown in circumstances not dissimilar to those alleged by Mr Twitchell. As a result Mr Treadaway's conviction was quashed.

53. In the appeal of *Twitchell* the prosecution conceded that evidence of the findings against Detective Sergeant Brown in *Treadaway* were admissible as also were two disciplinary findings of March 1982 against Detective Chief Inspector Taylor, one for neglect of duty concerning payments to an informant and another for falsehood, the nature of which was unspecified. Other material going to credit was available in respect of other officers (but not Jennings). The respondent conceded that had this material been available to counsel to cross-examine the officers at trial the effect upon the jury's consideration of the evidence of confession was likely to have been "devastating". Accordingly, the Court of Appeal allowed Mr Twitchell's appeal against conviction. It is argued by Ms Nicholls that this material would have been admissible in the cross-examination of Detective Chief Inspector Taylor and Detective Sergeant Jennings. Mr Rees QC responded that there had been no explicit finding in *Twitchell* against either man. The Court of Appeal had allowed the appeal not because the allegations made by the appellant against Taylor and Jennings were established (Rose LJ, Vice President, stated at page 385 that the court made no findings against any individual officers) but because the material available would have been used to effect in cross examination before the jury.

Discussion and conclusion

54. It is accepted by the Commission that there is no direct evidence of malpractice against Detective Constable Davies, Detective Sergeant Hancocks, Detective Constable Bawden and Detective Sergeant Whelan, all of whom gave pivotal evidence in the trial of the appellant in 1978. However, it is submitted that there was implied in the judgment of the Court of Appeal in *McIlkenny* in 1991 a finding that

the investigating team, including Detective Constable Davies, was corrupt or, if not corrupt, at least tainted to a degree that puts the credibility of Detective Constable Davies' evidence on oath in serious doubt. We have already expressed our reasons for rejecting this argument. While we accept that the taint of institutional corruption may affect the credit of an individual witness against whom no specific finding has been made, we note that this was an investigation in 1977 and that on no occasion since has Detective Constable Davies been implicated in corrupt practice. It is argued that the subsequent disciplinary findings against Detective Chief Inspector Taylor are important because, had they preceded the appellant's trial, they would have provided ammunition for cross-examination as to credit. He was also tainted subsequently by his involvement in the trial of *Twitchell* and thus susceptible to accusations of corruption in his dealings with suspects. In 1977 Detective Chief Inspector Taylor was the recently appointed head of the Serious Crime Squad. His leadership role would, it is submitted, have had a significant impact upon the team whom he was directing and, therefore, the truth of the evidence that the appellant made the disputed admissions on 24 October 1977 and on 3 April 1978. He was, in particular, Detective Sergeant Hancocks' senior officer. Detective Sergeant Jennings was, it is further submitted, implicated in the allegedly false evidence given at the trial of Keith Twitchell, and the taint on his credibility affects the value of his evidence that the appellant made admissions on 3 April 1978.

55.   The respondent, having considered the material available, concedes that this court could properly conclude that the verdicts upon counts 3 and 4 are unsafe. There is a sufficient taint upon the credibility of Detective Constable Davies to cast doubt upon the accuracy of his evidence. There was upon the relevant issues evidence supportive of the appellant from Prison Officer Law. There was no direct or circumstantial evidence to place the appellant at either of the robberies; therefore, there was no supporting evidence from any other source. Charles Apechis (count 3) gave a description of his attacker that bore no resemblance to the appellant and subsequently, not having been called at trial, made a statement absolving the appellant. We accept Mr Rees QC's submission that no specific findings were made against Detective Chief Inspector Taylor and Detective Sergeant Jennings in the appeal of *Twitchell*. The ground upon which the court allowed the appeal was that had the material been available for cross-examination the effect would have been devastating. We have posed the question: why would cross-examination have been devastating? In our judgment, the material available for cross-examination of Detective Chief Inspector Taylor and Detective Sergeant Brown in *Twitchell* was so damaging to the credibility of those officers that there was serious doubt whether the jury would have been prepared to accept them as witnesses of truth. That being the case, Detective Sergeant Jennings' own evidence would have suffered the same taint since he was supporting the thrust of their evidence. We consider that, in the absence of any other admissible evidence implicating the appellant in the robberies charged in counts 3 and 4, any legitimate attack upon the credit of either Detective Constable Davies or Detective Sergeant Jennings would affect the safety of the verdicts upon those counts. The fact that we have found that there was nothing in the background or later events to cast doubt on the honesty of Detective Constable Davies does not determine the question whether the verdicts on these counts were unsafe. We recognise that our reasoning differs from that of the respondent. In our judgment, it is enough that there is material on which Detective Sergeant Jennings could legitimately have been cross-examined to effect. We have no way of knowing how that would have affected the jury's decision

upon the reliability of the confession allegedly made at HMP Leicester on 3 April 1978 but we are clear that the challenge would have cast renewed light on its reliability. We are persuaded that we cannot be sure that the verdicts on those counts are safe. We consider a further route to the same conclusion in the following paragraphs.

56.   We turn to counts 5 and 6. While, some three to four years later, Detective Chief Inspector Taylor was accused and convicted of disciplinary offences which went to his honesty and therefore affected the fairness of the trial of Mr Twitchell in 1982, there is no evidence of malpractice by him before the investigation of Mr Twitchell's case in November 1980, fully three years after the investigation in the appellant's case. However, the appeals of *OToole. Murphy and Wilcox* all concerned the investigation of robbery by the Serious Crime Squad in 1977 and in *Twitchell* the allegation was that Detective Chief Inspector Taylor had falsely placed himself in an interview in order to give dishonest support to the evidence of other officers.

57.   Detective Sergeant Hancocks, admittedly an untainted witness, was able to produce a document at trial that has the hallmarks of contemporaneity and was consistent with the evidence of the progression of the critical interview leading, as he said, to the appellant's admissions. It was inconsistent with the appellant's complete denial that he had given any information to the officer about robberies or Ireland. In our judgment, this document must have been central to the jury's consideration of counts 5 and 6. On the other hand, the legitimate point was made by Ms Nicholls in argument that no contemporaneous note of admissions from the appellant to the Rice Jewellery robbery was made by Mr Hancocks even though, according to the officer, he immediately went on to make them. Furthermore, it did not follow that because the jury accepted the handwritten note as genuine they were bound to accept the critical evidence of admissions. There was open to the jury the conclusion that the appellant did attempt to strike a bargain by giving information about others but may not have made any admission of his own guilt. The evidence of Detective Sergeant Whelan and Detective Constable Bawden, also untainted witnesses who did not serve in the Serious Crime Squad, provided, as we have said, significant support for Detective Sergeant Hancocks' evidence, since Whelan was hardly going to ask for confirmation from the appellant that he had made admissions unless Hancocks had told him that he had. That, however, does not resolve the question whether the admissions had in fact been made to Detective Sergeant Hancocks before Detective Sergeant Whelan arrived at the police station. If by reason of an attack on the credibility of Detective Chief Inspector Taylor the jury had doubts about the truthfulness of the evidence of Detective Sergeant Hancocks it seems to us that a ripple effect would inevitably follow.

58.   The question we have to resolve is whether the specific material available for cross examination of Detective Chief Inspector Taylor and the general taint upon the leadership of the Serious Crime Squad in 1977 is sufficient to place the confession evidence in doubt. We consider that cross examination of Detective Chief Inspector Taylor would have had some impact upon the issue facing the jury. That fact was bound to place the evidence of officers of the Serious Crime Squad under pressure, particularly the evidence of Detective Sergeant Hancocks and Detective Constable Davies. Although we readily accept that it is not possible to assess with any certainty what the outcome would have been, we are clear that the jury would not have

approached the evidence in categories each one hermetically sealed from the next. Cross-examination of the head of the Serious Crime Squad as to the honesty and reliability of the investigation may well have had the effect of causing the jury to examine with increased scepticism the issue as to how the injuries to the appellant had been caused. It may also have had an effect on the jury's assessment of the truth and accuracy of the appellant's alibi evidence. Once the jury were faced by this means with a further challenge to the accuracy and truthfulness of Detective Constable Davies' evidence, there would have been a further ripple effect on their examination of his evidence in support of the confession allegedly made on 3 April 1978, and the evidence of Detective Sergeant Whelan and Detective Constable Bawden supporting the alleged confession of 24 October 1977. While we are quite unable to make findings adverse to the credibility of any officer, we cannot be sure, for the reasons we have stated, that a verdict based upon on these alleged confessions is a safe verdict.

59. Finally, there was in the case of counts 5 and 6 a positive identification of the appellant by Mr Holmes who said, when attending the identification parade, "I am not mistaken, that is the man". We are conscious of the fact that the full *Turnbull* direction was not given to the jury but we have read each of the judge's directions to the jury on the subject of identification and, in our view, the judge safely left the issue to the jury with the warning that they should look for supporting evidence. However, since we have concluded that the identification cannot be regarded as reliably supported by the evidence of confession it follows that the convictions upon counts 5 and 6 are unsafe.

60. For these reasons the appeal is allowed and we quash the appellant's convictions upon counts 3 – 6 inclusive.